From
SILENT DESPERATION
to QUIET STRENGTH

Deborah Jayne

GROUND TRUTH PRESS
NASHUA, NEW HAMPSHIRE

From Silent Desperation to Quiet Strength

Journal entries were left in their original form.

Published by GROUND TRUTH PRESS
　　　　P. O. Box 7313
　　　　Nashua, NH 03060-7313

Copy Editor: Bonnie Lyn Smith

Cover Design: Bonnie Lyn Smith

Cover Photo Credits:

　　Eagle and sky: iStock.com/Andreas Nesslinger
　　Branches: iStock.com/Andi Edwards
　　Cage: iStock.com/francescoch

First printing 2022
Printed in the United States of America

Trade paperback ISBN-13: 978-1-7359307-9-4
Trade paperback ISBN-10: 1-7359307-9-2

Dedication

I dedicate this labor of love to my three amazing daughters who have been my deepest source of earthly joy and courage as well as my motivation to press in and persevere despite the seen and unseen forces against me. My gratefulness for their immediate, unwavering, and loving support throughout the many changes in all of our lives is beyond measure. Always my daughters and now, too, my dearest friends...

...I love you more!

***It is God who works in you to will
and to act in order to fulfill His good purpose.***
(Phil. 2:13 NIV)

I cannot dedicate this work to my Father God because, in my eyes, it is already His book; I have only been His ready scribe, guided and inspired by the Holy Spirit. I gave Him free rein to use my life story as He willed for His purposes and for His honor and glory. Our compassionate Lord Jesus gathered all of the broken pieces of my shattered life and torn-apart dreams strewn over 25 years of heartache and lovingly began to create a unique mosaic with the fabric, fragments, experiences, and unspoken words of my life. It may not be beautiful and will never be perfect, but it is inlaid upon a rock-solid foundation that cannot be shaken or destroyed again by any earthly force, as it is held together by an eternal love and weight of glory.

May the words of this book touch many lives and be the key that unlocks the cages of those imprisoned by some form of abuse or bondage, setting free the multitude of captives who have been waiting in silent desperation to be rescued!

By grace I have been saved...twice.
You are my God, my Lord, my Savior, and my Knight!

***"So you also, when you have done all that you were commanded, say,
'We are unworthy servants; we have only done what was our duty.'"***
(Luke 17:10)

"Where the serpent has bit you the most you have the greatest destiny."

—Leif Hetland,
Seeing Through Heaven's Eyes:
A World View That Will Transform Your Life

Table of Contents

INTRODUCTION

**And my tongue will talk of Your righteous help all the day long,
for they have been put to shame and disappointed
who sought to do me hurt.**
(Ps. 71:24)

I HAVE ALWAYS had a passion for writing ever since I was a young girl. I especially loved to use words that rhymed; it became a sort of game. I love words and their power of expression. In my youth I enjoyed creating homemade cards, wrote plays that were acted out by the neighborhood kids for parents and friends, and developed a passion for reading and writing poetry. I was, and still am, an avid reader and would pass countless hours lost in the pages of mystery books.

Unbeknownst to me at the time, challenging my mind to process obscure clues shroud in a world of mystery, secrets, deception, hidden agendas, and manipulative behaviors would train me in ways I had never imagined I would need. As it turns out, it proved invaluable in preserving my sanity in the madness I would find myself living in—a million miles away from the innocence of a trusting girl. Many years later, as my faith grew and deepened, so would my ability to trust in the discernment of the Holy Spirit to lead me in all truth and to not solely rely on my own ability to reason and understand.

> **Trust in the LORD with all your heart, and do not lean on your own understanding. In all your ways acknowledge Him, and He will make straight your paths. Be not wise in your own eyes....** (Prov. 3:5-7)

What I want to leave you with here is that *nothing* that becomes a part of our life, our experiences, or our story is ever wasted; all things have a place and purpose if we allow God to use them for good.

And we know that for those who love God all things work together for good, for those who are called according to His purpose. (Rom. 8:28)

As I became a young adult, Victorian-era romance novels became my favorite choice. The ladies were depicted as refined and beautiful while donned in their elaborate gowns, which, at the time, I imagined would be just wonderful. I have long relinquished that thought, as there is no one who loves their blue jeans more than I do...and a corset? I don't think so! The gentlemen of the day carried an air of distinction and authority as they roamed their mansions and estates. Of course, the most exciting male character was portrayed as a handsome and debonair scoundrel who always ended up being the most chivalrous as the story unfolded—strong and gallant, like the ideal knight who lived by a strict code of honor and courage. He would always rescue the damsel in distress and ride off with her on his powerful stallion. They would fall in love and live happily-ever-after!

At the age of 25, I thought I had married my very own "knight in shining armor." I met this tall, handsome military man while we were both assigned to the same Army Reserve Headquarters Training Unit. Because I was dating another gentleman at the time, we became only friends. But I always felt as if he "noticed" or "saw" me and that he had a desire to "know" me when I was in his presence. Not understanding that these deep desires to be *seen, heard,* and *known* were my vulnerable places even back then, I was easily drawn into the snare of his narcissism, which was *camouflaged* in kindness and an easygoing manner. As it turns out, I also have many of the character traits that are very desirable to a narcissist, which made me a target on two levels. Not too long after the breakup of my former relationship, we began dating (always a bad decision, but what did I know?), and the rest, as they say, is history.

Introduction

I would berate myself many years later for falling prey to such a man—for my foolishness and lack of insight. But the Lord would reveal to me, when the time was right, that my desire to be seen, heard, known, and loved was not unique to a weak minority. Rather, they are universal longings in every human heart—yearnings placed there by God who intended them to be fulfilled. This began my quest to discover more about these yearnings: how and why they originated and are so important to our overall sense of well-being. I wanted to understand what happens when these crucial elements are not fulfilled as well as the wonderful results when they are.

In this book we'll look at some people of ancient times, as preserved in the Bible, who also lived in a form of silent desperation such as myself and many others. We will examine how their cries for help were answered and their needs were satisfied. We will also look into the heart and mind of an individual with Narcissistic Personality Disorder (NPD) in its various degrees, survival techniques when caught in their snare, and various paths to freedom. I'll speak into what character traits are commonly looked for in prospective victims, who are "bought" more like a new car or household appliance, rather than cared for as a beloved spouse or other relationship formed in deception. You are indeed a *victim of abuse* in a relationship with a narcissist even if you bear no outward bruises, scars, or broken bones. Although the wounds inflicted by an individual with NPD are usually invisible to the untrained eye as the manipulative emotional and mental abuse suffered is commonly perpetrated "behind closed doors," it is no less painful—and, in fact, can be in many ways worse—than the visible manifestations of abuse.

The purpose of this book is to shed light upon, grant understanding of, offer coping mechanisms within, point out roads to healing amidst, and instill hope into a growing problem that is plaguing our marriages, families, workplaces, churches, communities, nation, and world. I have found that knowledge is power! The Bible says, **"My people are destroyed for lack of knowledge"** (Hosea 4:6). I hope these pages answer some of your questions of how and why many people become victims of those who have become *lovers of self.*

I write this book without any advanced degrees in psychology nor for monetary fees.

I am not a professional counselor, although I have had sessions with a few counselors who were experienced in understanding and addressing this form of mental illness. The content of this book is largely based upon my 25 years of experience being married to a narcissist and what I have learned during my own personal and painful journey while living within the same walls as someone with this increasingly common and destructive exaltation of self. I share here an interesting excerpt that I read taken from a speech delivered on February 15, 2017, at a Hillsdale College Leadership Seminar in Phoenix, Arizona, by Herbert E. Meyer. I feel it applies to anyone who has long-term experience in a particular situation in which they have earnestly sought wisdom and understanding as I have regarding NPD.

> You cannot say something insightful, or even something intelligent, on a subject or issue about which you don't know anything. Analysts must be among the world's most knowledgeable individuals in their fields of expertise. And they must have that one elusive and unquantifiable skill that so often brings success in every venture: the ability to spot a pattern with the fewest possible facts—the ability to look at what's known and combine this with their own knowledge, experience, and good judgment, to come up with a new idea or insight.[1]

He spoke about a man named Bill Casey who did just this "by sitting quietly in his office; reading, writing, and—thinking."

This had become the pattern of my own life when I was immersed in my most desperate situations in which I needed clarity, insights, wisdom, and the ability to see the unseen with little tangible evidence (although evidence does surface over time when you know

---

[1] Herbert E. Meyer, *Hillsdale College Leadership Seminar* (Phoenix, AZ: February 15, 2017).

what to look for). It was in these quiet places while reading, writing, pondering, thinking, and praying that the patterns began to take on form and illuminate my mind's eye. While centered in this state of being still and attentive, I was able to clearly hear God's voice speak truth into my heart. I would write this in one of my many journals on September 5, 2015:

> *From years of living with [someone with] a Narcissistic Personality Disorder and receiving Your insights, I can pick up the scent of a narcissist like a hound dog.*

Trust in your instincts and God-given intuition (woman's intuition is a real gift!) when you perceive a pattern or cycle of behavior that is causing dysfunction instead of harmony. Think upon it, test it, and then wait patiently to discern its source. The excellent professional information I have accumulated from a few sources on this subject, as well as knowledge gleaned from my own personal experiences with counseling, have broadened my understanding of—and confirmed my diagnosis of—the oppressive silent abuse I (and many others) have experienced living with this anomaly.

Some of my most helpful, comforting, empowering, and healing sources (apart from the Word of God) have come from talking personally with (or reading firsthand accounts of) women who themselves have been married to or in a relationship with a narcissist and/or someone with another form of addictive and dysfunctional behavior. When you live in a place of silent desperation—trapped in the endless cycle of bizarre, erratic, irrational, dark, deceptive, destructive, and manipulative behaviors that are almost impossible to explain to another because of the hidden and nonsensical nature of it all—you feel so isolated in your pain. It is like stumbling upon a refreshing oasis in the middle of a desert wasteland to talk with someone who *finally understands you* and knows what you are living amidst! This is true in any case or circumstance in which someone is being oppressed, abused, neglected, or enslaved, or is feeling isolated, misunderstood, and unloved. Through my personal story, my eyes have been opened and my heart enlarged to see the universal human need of *all* people to be seen, heard, known, and loved in a world that is becoming increasingly insensitive to and lacking love for anyone but self.

I write this book with a heart of deep gratitude for the multitude of blessings that have been bestowed upon my life from the hand of God. But please know that these words also spring forth from a place of silent desperation that almost consumed me. On countless occasions an unwelcomed dark cloud blew over what could have been sunny days of peace, joy, contentment, and love. In the midst of my beautiful garden of blessings, there lay hidden briars, the thorns of which would slowly tear me apart from the inside out as I walked gingerly through 25 years of what would become my private hell alongside a narcissist. It is my hope and prayer, whether you are a believer or nonbeliever in the Christian faith, that if you find yourself suffering from some form of abuse or injustice in which God never intended, you are led to a place of enlightenment, empowerment, peace, comfort, healing, hope, joy, courage, freedom, and quiet strength!

> **The LORD is the everlasting God,**
> **the Creator of the ends of the earth.**
> **He will not grow tired or weary,**
> **and His understanding no one can fathom.**
> **He gives strength to the weary**
> **and increases the power of the weak.**
> **Even youths grow tired and weary,**
> **and young men stumble and fall;**
> **but those who hope in the LORD will renew their strength.**
> **They will soar on wings like eagles;**
> **they shall run and not grow weary,**
> **they will walk and not be faint.**
> (Isa. 40:28-31 NIV)

1
Silent Desperation

For it is not an enemy who taunts me—then I could bear it;
it is not an adversary who deals insolently with me—
then I could hide from him.
But it is you, a man, my equal,
my companion, my familiar friend.
(Ps. 55:12-13)

M Y LIFE BECAME a living hell: a prison sentence; not behind
visible bars but set in place by a gold ring and a vow. A
nightmare I couldn't escape upon waking. A silent place of pain
because it was invisible to the outside world, but a daily reality to my
lonely heart and confused mind. I was visible but never seen. I spoke
but was never heard. I was present but was never known. An
inescapable cycle of bizarre behaviors, lies (without shame), evolving
patterns, empty promises, and fake identities. It was an insanity that
kept me walking on the edge of despair into years of numbness,
emptiness, near hopelessness, and incredible loneliness. The darkness
of it all almost swallowed my life—body, soul, mind, and spirit.

Any attempt at below-the-surface communication became
meaningless words, an ocean of deceit, inexcusable excuses, promises
void of fulfillment, twisted manipulations, and an endless stream of
nothingness until all words trickled to a halt and ran dry. I, out of a
means of survival, began to live—not by what was seen or heard—
but by what *wasn't*. I lived by intuition, my senses heightened to that
of a person who is blind or deaf. Even with that, I was still often
sideswiped when I stumbled upon countless "bombs" that would rip
apart the last shreds of wishful thinking, thoughts of basic human
decency, and my happily-ever-after dream. The accumulation of these

dark manifestations sent me into such emotional turmoil that I lived like a soldier in a war zone, aware that my husband-turned-enemy was near and waiting for the next opportunity to assault me and my fragmented identity, fragile nerves, and broken heart. It got so that just being in his presence would trigger such inner stress and adrenaline rushes that I realized I was suffering symptoms of Post-Traumatic Stress Disorder (PTSD). Trying to cope with the truth of that which was *surreal* yet very real, while also processing the slow revelation of my unraveling secret life, became a constant challenge.

To keep our family intact, secure, and strong until I could finally find my way toward an answer to the madness, I had to "stay the course" and "play the game" despite the ever-changing rules. I truly felt that one day I could flip on the right switch and my husband would be enlightened to his destructive ways and dark behaviors. I believed that victorious restoration would be had; for with God all things are possible (Matthew 19:36), and I could do all things through Christ who would strengthen me until that triumphant day (Philippians 4:13)! I waited almost 25 years for that day, which never came. It would be almost 20 years before the Lord would reveal what truth lay behind the masks that had left me in silent desperation. And although my husband didn't change, my circumstances didn't change, and my loneliness and anguish didn't change, *I* changed. As my spouse almost completely broke this jar of clay into tiny pieces, I became barely recognizable to who I once was. But in God's perfect timing, He gathered up all of my broken pieces and gently remolded me, placed me into the Refiner's fire, and then brought me forth—stronger, purer, and ready for new life in Him alone. It was in this place of breaking and surrender that He exchanged my silent desperation for quiet inner strength, and I will joyfully never be the same again!

This is a personal story of my experience living within the silent abuse and bondage called Narcissistic Personality Disorder (NPD), and how I not only survived but now thrive because my Lord saved me from the ruins. It is a testimony of how even in the depth

2

of our dark despair and unmet yearnings of the heart, God sees us, hears our cries, knows everything about our plight, and has compassion for us. He is tirelessly eradicating the evils of this fallen world and exchanging them for good, to bring something beautiful out of the ashes! May this book be a powerful source of hope, knowledge, truth, courage, justice, peace, healing, and freedom.

As for you, you meant evil against me, but God meant it for good.
(Gen. 50:20)

**He gives beauty for ashes,
gladness for mourning,
and hope for despair**
(Isa. 61:3)

Dear Lord,

This life often seems to me an intricately woven web and I, the sad and sorry insect that got caught up in it. I have struggled against the confines of it, feeling trapped but remembering the blessed moments of freedom and longing to fly again. My struggle against its threads only serve to bind me more. I would feel victorious when I thought I had made some gain, only to find I was no better off than I was before. Things looked so bleak as each attempt to escape left me exhausted, drained, and discouraged. My enemy looms ever near, taunting me to just give up the fight. Despite the dismal circumstances, just one more try—one more angle—seemed worth the effort to keep pressing on toward freedom and peace. As the enemy grew impatient and I felt him draw near, I finally surrendered myself to my fate. I lay still in my confinement and waited.

It was in that quiet time of surrender and complete submission that I felt the threads that gripped me so tightly begin to loosen. At first I thought I was dreaming or that I had died; and I had. I had died to self and was made alive again in Christ. The bonds that had held me captive now felt like arms of protection and love. The soft breeze of new life swung me gently on the wings of God's grace and mercy. I finally realized that my Lord was with me all along; He was with me through each struggle, battle, fear, and temptation. And that it was in my weakness that You alone were strong and more than sufficient for me. As you breathed new life into my renewed spirit, I was once more free to fly above the confines of this earthly body and broken heart. I realized with absolute certainty that it was in my complete brokenness that I was made completely whole. I lay in the silken web quietly knowing my enemy who laid the trap is ever near and watching, but also very aware that my Savior is even nearer and will set me free at just the right time.

JOURNAL ENTRY — April 8, 2013

What draws the narcissist to you like a moth to a flame are the very things they will come to despise and hate in you as the closer they get to the light that intrigued them becomes the very source that illuminates their weaknesses, insecurities, self-loathing, and hidden secrets.

JOURNAL ENTRY — November 27, 2016

Ah, the narcissist love/hate relationship! "I love what you do for me because I need you, but I love to make you feel unloved and unwanted because I hate myself because I need you. Therefore, I have to hate either you or myself...and I choose to hate you and love me!"

You Want...Life With a Narcissist
By Deborah Jayne

You want me to smile,
but you give me no joy.

You want me to hug you,
but you make me feel unsafe.

You want me to hold your hand,
but you stay at arm's length.

You want me to kiss you,
but you share no intimacy.

You want me to laugh,
but you always make me cry.

You want me to share,
but you give so sparingly.

You want me to trust,
but you always tell lies.

You want me to open up,
but you are so closed.

You want me to talk,
but you remain silent.

You want me to be transparent,
but you stay hidden.

You want to hear my thoughts,
but you never listen.

You want my whole heart,
but share none of your own.

2
The Classic Characteristics of a Person With Narcissistic Personality Disorder (My Education of the Dark Side)

A SYMPTOM OR group of symptoms are labeled as a disease or disorder because they exhibit certain distinguishable qualities that set them apart from other diseases or illnesses. When a person is diagnosed with cancer, although it may manifest in different parts of the body and take on many forms, there are specific qualities and characteristics of the disease that categorize it as a form of cancer. A person diagnosed with Attention Deficit Disorder (ADD) is given that diagnosis because they manifest enough of the commonly known attributes. Likewise, although there are differing degrees and manifestations of Narcissistic Personality Disorder (NPD), certain recurring and distinguishing character traits become apparent. To be honest, the depth of my initial understanding of a narcissist was that they were vain (having an excessively high regard for one's self, looks, etc.; conceited) and seemed to enjoy looking at themselves in the mirror. I have learned through personal experience that this is certainly true. However, the depth of the disorder in its totality is a different "animal" altogether, and I was completely unaware for many years that it was this mental illness that was growing like an insidious disease and overshadowing every aspect of my life, marriage, and family.

As I stated in the Introduction, a narcissist "shops" very carefully for their victim. Most of them become almost completely codependent on their "object," so they must choose wisely who will become their desired "host." I know that the words "object," "host," and "supply" sound like terrible terms to describe a spouse or significant other in a relationship, but they unfortunately—yet very accurately—reflect how a narcissist views their mate. After many years in my marriage, I actually used the word "object" in describing to my husband how he made me feel *before* I ever had knowledge of what I was dealing with. Male narcissists choose a mate that matches their ideal of a "trophy" wife or girlfriend (and prospective mother, if a family is part of the "plan"): a woman they consider impressive in physical appearance, intelligence, character, how others view her, etc. This is a very personal evaluation stemming from the mind and needs of the narcissist, not a stroke to my own ego! A female narcissist will go "shopping" for similar attributes in a partner.

By our one-year anniversary, not only was I already being confronted with what seemed like irresponsible and irrational behavior—which I had been hopeful was just a maturity issue that would work itself out over time—but I was also pregnant with our first child. By the time I was expecting our second daughter three years later, his cold indifference was manifesting itself with more frequency and in hurtful ways behind closed doors. I was still highly determined and positive that the more frequent turbulence was something that time, patience, love, and communication would eventually smooth out, making right all that was starting to go wrong. I would use these incentives to keep my hope alive, and our beautiful family together, for almost two decades before the Holy Spirit would reveal the *truth* to my spirit during a desperate time of prayer: "Your husband is a narcissist"...spoken as clearly and simply as that. This knowledge initiated my lessons into a truth I desperately needed to know while it simultaneously validated a dark world that I had wished didn't exist.

I was praying this Scripture when the Spirit spoke to me:

Make me to know Your ways, O LORD;
teach me Your paths.
Lead me in *the truth* and *teach me*...."
(Ps. 25:4–5, emphasis mine)

I will fill in more of the gaps of how this abusive and manipulative disorder plays itself out in very specific ways, habits, behavior patterns, repetitive cycles, etc., with remarkably very little variance. As I wrote earlier, there are degrees within every disorder, but the classic characteristics are within a recognizable range for those who have experienced a significant amount of time in a relationship with a narcissist, especially when one knows what to look for. Truthfully, it is quite uncommon for a person to stay in a marriage or relationship with a narcissist for 25 years, as the union formed in its early stage is long dead, and the victim is usually deeply frustrated and/or shattered. There are often many years of counseling, therapy, and healing that follow the trail of tears and pain once the victim is released from their entanglement to a narcissist: either by fleeing, force, or rescue. By God's grace and with my fighter spirit that was determined that our marriage "would not fail," I was able to endure the dysfunctional environment long enough to experience (and even anticipate) firsthand the bizarre behavior patterns in all their dark forms.

The personal stories I have heard, as well as those I have read about since my enlightenment, are eerily similar despite a person's race, background, education level, vocation, etc. The heart and mind of a narcissist are the key determining factors. I believe that there are very specific components that play into the development of this mindset, which I will touch on in subsequent chapters. For now, though, I want to lay out a list of classic character traits commonly associated with Narcissistic Personality Disorder. I know this list is lengthy, but I believe that including as many of the characteristics that are medically documented (and I have experienced personally) can be empowering to people in a relationship with a narcissist. Victims are often perplexed about what they *know* is the reality of their lives, yet they have no printed words to validate what feels like insanity. (Note: Since narcissism is on a continuum, some people will have more traits than others; these are not all-inclusive.)

The characteristics of a narcissist[2] are as follows:

* Self-centered; their needs are paramount, supreme, higher than any other
* No remorse for mistakes or misdeeds
* Unreliable and undependable
* Does not care about the consequences of their actions
* Projects faults onto others—high blaming behavior; it's never their fault
* Little to no conscience
* Insensitive to the needs and feelings of others
* Puts on a good front (persona) to impress and exploit others
* Low stress tolerance; easy to anger and rage
* Manipulates others in order to meet their own needs
* Rationalizes easily; twists conversations for their own gain but at the other person's expense; if trapped, they keep talking, clam up, change the subject, or get angry
* Pathological lying
* Have a tremendous need to control situations, conversations, other people
* No real values; mostly situational
* Often perceived as caring and understanding, and uses this to manipulate
* Uses sex to control
* Does not share ideas, feelings, or emotions
* Conversation controller; must have the first and last word
* Lives a secret life: hides money, friends, activities
* Likes annoying others and to create chaos and disruption for no reason
* Moody: switches from "nice guy" to angry without much provocation
* Repeatedly fails to honor financial obligations or think about financial issues
* Seldom expresses appreciation unless using it as a manipulation tool
* Grandiose; convinced they know more than others do and are correct in all they do
* Lacks ability to see how they come across to others

[2] Adapted from: Ann Bradley, "Narcissistic Abuse," *Narcissistic Abuse* (blog), October 7, 2011, https://narcissisticabuse.com/characteristics-of-the-narcissist/.

* Defensive when confronted about their behavior; never their fault
* Can become emotional and tearful; this is about show and frustration rather than true sorrow
* Breaks a person's spirit to keep them dependent
* Uses threats and intimidation to keep others close to them
* Sabotages partner; wants them to be "happy" only through them and have few outside acquaintances
* Highly contradictory
* Very convincing; must convince people to side with them
* Hides their real self; always "on," performing for others
* Kind only when they are getting what they want from you
* Has to be right, has to win, has to look good
* Announces and states rather than discusses; tells rather than asks
* Does not discuss openly; has a hidden agenda
* Controls the money of others but spends freely on self
* Unilateral condition of: "I am okay and justified so I don't need to hear your position, opinions, or ideas"
* Does not listen and does not care; always feels misunderstood
* Talks about their surface "feelings" and irritations, not acknowledging their partner's
* Not interested in problem-solving (counseling) as they see themselves with no problems
* Very good at reading people so they can manipulate them
* Apparent absence of empathy as well as emotional maturity
* May be charming and humble in public; acts as innocent victim to gain sympathy
* Puts people down behind their backs
* Promises things they have no intention of giving
* Easily bored; changes their source of "supply" (mates, friends, coworkers)
* You feel miserable with this person; they drain you; anyone who has been in love with a narcissist will testify that the experience left them lifeless

Whew! I know. After the Holy Spirit revealed to me that I was dealing with a narcissist, I was anxious to discover what that really meant and finally shed some light on something that had overshadowed my life for so long. I knew that everything I was experiencing for over 20 years was *real* (although when you live within the bizarre for long enough, you begin to question your own sanity!);

yet, this information only served to affirm what my heart, mind, and intuition had been screaming for years. It had a name; this real, yet elusive, phenomenon that plagued our marriage, our family, and my entire life had a name!

At the same time, though, I was filled with a gnawing fear that I couldn't quite voice. I knew in my spirit that something that had invaded every crevice of my being wasn't going to be a good thing. The above list was the first thing that popped up on my screen when I googled for information. My hands were shaking, my mouth was dry, I felt hot and cold at the same time, and tears slid down my face as line after line spoke directly into my silent insanity. The force behind the dark veil was without a doubt Narcissistic Personality Disorder. Somehow, it would have been easier to know that my spouse didn't realize what he was doing. But the truth is that narcissists know *exactly* what they are doing, which I slowly and sadly became aware of over the years. The hell they create for their "object(s)" is a conscious choice and a delight for their narcissistic ego.

My reality was now confirmed. When I reached the end of the list, I sat numb, not knowing if I should feel relieved or fall into deeper despair. The solution, course of action, remedy, and counsel most often given to victims of such abuse was a resounding "Get out...it is a match made in hell!" Narcissists do not change for they have no desire to change; they are unable or unwilling to acknowledge anything wrong within themselves. Any problems are external. They see themselves as autonomous. This attitude makes the whole idea of marriage as a union between two people quite ridiculous in the true heart and mind of a narcissist. It was vastly different from the mindset that I, as a Christian woman had, which was deeply committed to the vow I had made "until death do us part" (even if made under false pretenses on my husband's part).

At this point in time, I entered into a new dimension of spiritual conflict that would rage between us—and within my own soul—for many years to come. In the present moment, though, I cried out to God and asked, "Why did You wait so long to tell me?" As I sat in the quiet office staring at the computer screen, I heard His simple, yet gentle and compassionate answer: "You weren't ready to hear it yet." I bowed my head in silent surrender and gratefulness, acknowledging that He was right. If I had known all those years ago what I knew in this very moment, I would have left. I wouldn't have been able to persevere in ignorant hope if I had known the truth in my yet-untamed spirit. But I also knew in that defining moment *all* I would have missed and lost had I not stayed and let the strength, hope, and love of Jesus Christ carry me through and deepen my faith for such a time as this. What now?

> My inward parts are in turmoil and never still; days of affliction come to meet me.
> I go about darkened, but not by the sun; I stand in the assembly and cry for help.
> ...the pain that gnaws me takes no rest. (Job 30:27-28, 17)

> But He knows the way that I take; when He has tried me, I shall come out as gold. My foot shall hold fast to His steps; I have kept His way and have not turned aside. For He will complete what He appoints for me, and many such things are in His mind. (Job 23:10-11, 14)

Additional, and Often Subtle, Characteristics of NPD: The Man Behind the Mask

"When we see nothing more to life than the satisfaction
of our own appetites and ego, it is vanity."
–Robert Ango, a Priest

JOURNAL ENTRY – July 2013

I love to teach as much as I love to learn, but this is one education I wish I could ignore or pass over. But knowledge is power, knowledge equals responsibility, knowledge spurs action.

I have come to believe that knowledge is power. I knew that I could cope much better with the pain, strife, and dysfunction in my marriage and home when I had an understanding of its root. This is why I felt it important to furnish and fortify victims of a person with NPD with as much knowledge that I could supply based on research and personal experience.

I began to journal in 2000, but I started serious journal writing at the beginning of 2011. As the communication between my husband and I dwindled steadily over the years down to a mere trickle—my fears, anxieties, stress and pain levels, and silent desperation kept increasing until the floodwaters threatened to completely overtake and drown me. As I was forced into silence by a man who wouldn't see me, hear me, desire to know me, nor love me, writing my words was my only real outlet for all that was in turmoil within me.

As I started writing this book in early 2017, I read through the stacks of diaries chronicling my life. The joys and wonderful blessings that added beauty, color, and light to my days are intricately woven within the dark fabric of years spent living in a state of rejection, abandonment, loneliness, suffering, and often despair. When I wrote my unspoken words, it was like recording symptoms of an unknown disease for years and writing every detail of how it was affecting my life. Not knowing the proper term for the source of the pain that I suffered, I only knew it was slowly killing me. I realize now that, before I ever googled or read a single article of information on Narcissistic Personality Disorder, I had been documenting the characteristics, behavior patterns, and subsequent devastation of its effects on the victim(s) as I breathed in its toxic fumes daily for over two decades.

Because narcissists very rarely seek counseling or help for what clinically falls under a psychopathic mental illness,[3] much of the subject matter is gleaned from studies and information gathered from

---

[3]Another very closely related disorder is Antisocial Personality Disorder, and oftentimes these two disorders overlap to the point where one is barely distinguishable from the other; my spouse mirrored many of the characteristics of Antisocial Personality Disorder as well.

the victims and professionals counseling and treating them. This is usually a spouse or someone closely related to the abuser. It may sound incredulous, but there is not a single piece of information that I have heard or read that I have not also personally experienced in one form or another after 25 years in its snare. Trust me…I do not say that with any sort of pride but only deep sadness for our family, myself, and even my (now) ex-spouse who is himself a victim of his own darkness! That I can corroborate with current professional information on this prevalent disorder gives credence to its findings.

As I dared to look into this mental illness further (a hurting victim can only digest so much negative and disturbing information at one time), I felt the compilation of the following insights helped to more thoroughly fill in many holes that still remained—the missing pieces that made the warped jigsaw puzzle complete. They are as follows:[4]

* Anyone with a giving personality and desire to help others *attracts* narcissists—you give, they take. It is an utterly confusing dynamic, not the least because it is so surreal.

* One of the keys to *sanity* is understanding that, when it comes to love, narcissists come from a completely different place. Narcissistic love is more superficial. It is not love that connects you from core to core, nor is it soul-based. It is a love based on functionality.

* The ability to see other people at a deeper level requires the ability to see ourselves at a deeper level. It is impossible to love someone who will not let themselves be seen or known by you, as they can't even see their own "self" in truth and reality.

* Narcissists treat others like "appliances" or "objects"; that is as far as their own level of awareness of themselves can go. They are unavailable to us because—in a deeper way—they are unavailable to themselves.

* We cannot have a truly loving relationship with a narcissist no matter how hard *we try*; there is nothing to deeply connect to. All we can

---

[4] This list was adapted from the following article as well as from handouts given to me that did not include citations: Caroline van Kimmenade, "Narcissistic Love versus Unconditional Love," The Happy Sensitive, December 13, 2012, https://thehappysensitive.com/narcissistic-love-versus-unconditional-love/.

really do is *love a "dream"* we have of them. (This reality was crushing to my heart and answered so many questions.) They have made themselves completely unavailable to unconditional love.

* Bad boundaries: Narcissists do not recognize boundaries; others exist to meet their needs or might as well not exist at all.

* In public they act charming and polite, pretending to be the perfect husband (wife, parent, etc.). In private, they are withdrawn and unavailable, showing little regard for the well-being of others unless they want something. (This was a *hugely* perplexing issue and the source of much conflict in our marriage. I am a very social person and often planned or we attended many social gatherings; the night-and-day nature of my husband's performance was not only extremely hurtful but also maddening! This aspect of the disorder would later cause many to not believe me because of what they had witnessed in public settings. I knew that this would be an issue I would have to face once the Lord pulled me out of its snare.)

* If confronted regarding their behavior, narcissists remain indignant and above any questions about said behavior.

* They believe they deserve things they haven't worked for and regularly benefit from others' honest, hard work.

* Narcissists "love" their spouse (significant other) *as long as they continue to reliably provide them with what they need.* Narcissists are looking for meaning to fill up their emptiness; they need people. They seek relationships to cater to their needs, stroke their ego, and control and use at their disposal. Once the person no longer satisfies their needs, the narcissist discards them. (This explained my husband's lack of emotion or care when I left him. Even though by that time I was so well-versed in his "game" that I fully expected the cold, unemotional reaction, I will not lie and say that it didn't hurt!)

* Narcissists look at themselves in the mirror but only see themselves and what they want—nothing else. They feel nothing. Even if they are not good-looking, in the mirror they see themselves as good-looking. Their minds always lie to them as they lie to fool others around them. They want everyone to see them as perfect; they do not see faults in themselves.

* Narcissists "look outward" for a view that will reflect them as wonderful, similar to codependency. Rather than having good self-esteem, they lack it and feel empty. They must gain their pseudo (counterfeit) self-esteem from external sources such as a spouse, children, lovers, extended family, etc. Everyone is reduced to an object, and these objects are known as "supplies" that *a narcissist feeds on and ultimately drains!*

16

* Narcissists are vulnerable to shame (rather than guilt), using people without considering the cost of doing so. They offer flattery toward those who affirm and admire them. (This wears off as the game wears down until they eventually completely ignore you.)

* Narcissists exaggerate their achievements.

* Except for their *fantasies* of perfection and their envy of others who have what they lack (a love/hate relationship develops within this realm), they are empty inside. They have no real self to bring into a relationship but desperately need someone to help maintain their emotional equilibrium. The ideal person is someone willing to become an extension of them and their fragile ego—someone who will serve as an object of admiration, contempt, and often equal amounts of both. The sign over the door ought to read: "Abandon self, all ye who enter here."

* Narcissists use sex as a substitute for love and intimacy. Some of them work at becoming good at pleasing their partner. They spend time learning the techniques that they use because the better they get at "pleasing" you, the more narcissistic "supplies" they are likely to secure—and the more powerful they feel. This is part of how they win control over the "object"!

* Narcissists don't want intimacy that reveals their faults and insecurities, but they are keen to show that they are capable of living a "normal life" and having "normal relationships" (this depends on the person). Their own self-image requires that other people also see *their love object* in an idealized way. Often, the male narcissist selects a trophy wife, and the female narcissist selects a trophy husband or significant other.

* The narcissist "loves" their children because they are a part of their self-image as a *successful* husband (wife) and father (mother).

* Despite the many flaws and mediocrity (inferiority) of their "object," narcissists need to convince themselves that those around them are worthy to be their sources of supply.

* One of the most frightening elements of a person with NPD is that the individual has a *definite consciousness* of their actions, yet *without guilt, conviction, or care*. That they are completely detached from both themselves and their victims is unsettling beyond words, dangerous, and profoundly sad.

**Vindicate me, O God, and defend my cause...
from the deceitful and unjust man deliver me!
Send out Your light and Your truth; and let them lead me...**
(Ps. 43:1)

17

In all honesty, I didn't intend to divulge so much clinical information on NPD. However, as the Holy Spirit was leading the writing process, I felt I was to include more in-depth insights for reasons beyond my initial understanding. As I stated earlier, I believe that knowledge is power and, in this case, can be a life (and sanity) saver! The more thorough understanding you have about NPD, it begins to open up your ability to see the invisible yet instinctively felt nature of the beast. When you are equipped with an arsenal of pertinent information, it helps you to stay focused and calm when the onslaught comes so that you can keep from getting pulled into the tide of emotions such as frustration, fear, anxiety, anger, confusion, etc.

As I had to learn *the hard way* through years of his baiting that repeatedly caught me in a trap, it gives me hope and peace to know that my "training" can now be put to good use in helping other victims cope with their own personal struggles until they gain more clarity through professional help (or, as for myself, from the Lord) on how to proceed in a healthy and safe way. I know without a shadow of a doubt that if I had not been armed with the knowledge and wisdom I needed to endure, be prepared for, counter, and even begin to ignore the almost constant attacks, I would have succumbed to the calculated objective of my destruction. Because I finally understood the tactics of the game, I was empowered to wait patiently with ever-increasing grace until such time as the Spirit would begin to reveal—and then prepare—the way for my departure.

A wise man is strong, and a man of knowledge increases power.
(Prov. 24:5 NASB)

The Makings of a Narcissist

As in water face reflects face, so the heart of a man reflects the man.
(Prov. 27:19)

It is not fully known what causes NPD, yet more and more determining factors are becoming associated with this particular mental illness, as well as several others, which fall under the definition

18

and characteristics of a psychopath. Scientific study of the brain, however, reveals that individuals with NPD have less gray matter in the left anterior insula: the part of the brain related to empathy, emotional regulation, compassion, and cognitive functioning. Genetics and psychobiology also come into play—the connection between the brain, behavior, and thinking. Narcissism is most often an adult diagnosis, after significant patterns of behavior are established, usually beginning in adolescence.

> **Narcissism[5]**
> The word comes from a Greek myth in which a handsome young man named Narcissus sees his own reflection in a pool of water and falls in love with it.

Adversity in childhood puts a person at risk for future personality disorders. Long-term stress during a time when the mind and developing personality are supposed to be *receiving nurturing* can actually affect brain development. *Healthy attachment* is crucial in these years. According to Dr. Steve Bressert, Ph.D.,[6]

> Most professionals subscribe to a biopsychosocial model of causation—that is, the causes are likely due to biological and genetic factors, social factors (such as how a person interacts in their early development with their family and friends and other children), and psychological factors (the individual's personality and temperament, shaped by their environment and learned coping skills to deal with stress). This suggests that no single factor is responsible—rather, it is the complex and likely intertwined nature of all three factors that are important.

The following factors, though, appear to be key during the developmental phase of childhood:[7]

---

[5] All boxed definitions throughout this book are from: Michael Agnes, *Webster's New World Dictionary,* 4th ed. (Cleveland, OH: Wiley Publishing, Inc., 2003).

[6] Steve Bressert, "Narcissistic Personality Disorder," (2019). Psych Central. (Psych central, February 27, 2019), https://psychcentral.com/disorders/narcissistic-personality-disorder.

[7] Christina Gregory and Krista Soriano, "Tell Me All I Need to Know About Narcissistic Personality Disorder," Psycom.net, accessed December 19, 2021, https://www.psycom.net/personality-disorders/narcissistic/. Updated October 25, 2021.

* Being born with an oversensitive temperament
* Learning manipulative behaviors from parents and peers
* Receiving excessive praise from parents and others over one's looks and abilities
* Inconsistent parental caregiving; unreliable or unpredictable care
* Being overindulged by parents and/or family members
* Being excessively admired with no realistic feedback to balance you with reality

I will add more insights and perceptions into the development of this anomaly in subsequent chapters based on 25 years of personal experience and close observations as well as revelations given to me by the Spirit of wisdom, light, and truth.

The Victim

A lying tongue hates its victims, and a flattering mouth works ruin.
(Prov. 26:28)

Narcissistic Victim Abuse is the name given to describe the resulting trauma and often long-term wounds a victim incurs when subjected to a narcissistic perpetrator that ensnares and begins to destroy their unsuspecting prey. It is:

> abuse that has been caused by someone with this personality disorder. It is *very real*, yet because a person with NPD is often not medically diagnosed, the narcissistic individual goes undetected in society (home, workplace, organizations, social settings, etc.), and the victim's plight is often unrecognized.[8]

It is never okay or justifiable to abuse another person for any reason!

> God has called us to peace, not to torment. You can love someone who has evil, but you do not have to be a victim.[9]

---

[8] Jeni Mawter, "Jenimawter.com," *Jenimawter.com* (blog), October 22, 2012, https://www.jenimawter.com/narcissistic-victim-syndrome/.
[9] Henry Wright, *A More Excellent Way to Be in Health* (New Kensington, PA: Whitaker House, 2009).

Available Treatment—Both Secular and Spiritual

When you have NPD, you think there is nothing wrong with you because a personal flaw wouldn't fit into your self-image of power and perfection. Therefore, individuals with this mental illness usually only seek treatment when they develop symptoms of deep depression or find that they are having difficulty coping with daily life. If they pursue treatment, the most effective option is long-term psychotherapy with an experienced therapist and sometimes medication to help with specific troubling and debilitating symptoms. Honest acknowledgment of an individual's negative behavior(s) as well as a desire to change is a prerequisite for any positive course of action. These are the findings, perspectives, and avenues of treatment from a secular point of view.

I have been impressed by the amount of accumulated medical information and in-depth knowledge that those who treat narcissists (or their victims) have uncovered through counseling sessions as opposed to living with them for lengths of time. This is because *true* character traits are often hard to glean from a pathological liar who is accustomed to living a double life. I concur with the experts in this field that if a person is truly willing and desirous of change, that a heart and mind can be retrained and restored to a place of balance, wholeness, and healthy self-love. I believe in the necessity of modern medicine. I have been a grateful recipient of all the knowledge and understanding of the human body and mind that physicians have acquired as I have undergone several surgeries and have sought counseling to help me through some of the lowest times over the years. Also, I have several dear friends who provide healthcare in different fields of expertise and pour themselves out to offer a healthier, balanced, and more fulfilling life for the good of others.

One of them has been a clinical psychologist for over 40 years. She has shared with me that she has never counseled an individual who has come into her office and outright acknowledged that they had NPD, but I am sure that she has treated many people for symptoms related to the mental illness. A narcissist will sometimes agree to short periods of counseling when their spouse or significant other insists on some course of positive action or threatens to leave them in their frustrated desperation. This agreement will usually be short-lived, as most narcissists use counseling as just another form of manipulation to appease their victims in order to get them to stay—at least until they are through with them. Ask me how I know! When appropriate, my friends (mentioned above) now incorporate both medical knowledge of the human body and mind as well as their spiritual understanding of how faith is an integral part of our ability to be healed, with credible and miraculous results. I personally believe that all of our knowledge and understanding of our world and everything in it are gifts from God and acts of grace.

For the LORD gives wisdom;
from His mouth come knowledge and understanding.
(Prov. 2:6)

I read what I believe to be fascinating insight from a psychotherapist by the name of Dr. Gabriel Byrnes. He notes:

> Listening, I think, is one of the most profound compliments that you can pay to another person. To truly listen and to feel that you're heard is deeply fulfilling in a deep human way. This awareness of listening is an act of empathy (the ability to share in another person's emotions, thoughts, or feelings). Hearing the story of another human, and deeply listening to that story, is an act of compassion, altruism (unselfish concern for the welfare of others), and love. It involves losing yourself and experiencing a "vicarious introspection" into the life of another human being. To truly hear a story is an act of empathy. Acts of generosity, empathy, or altruism light up a primitive part of the brain that is usually associated with pleasurable actions like eating good food or sex. When focused on others instead of ourselves, we experience a pleasurable biological response which is a win-win for everyone. It could be a cure for narcissism.[10]

I was both excited and encouraged because his medical knowledge

---

[10] This quote came from Storylineblog.com/2015/06/12/narcissist/, which is no longer an active blog link.

ran parallel with his understanding of the human soul's need to be *heard*, seen, known, and loved by another human being extending empathy and basic human kindness, which the Holy Spirit had revealed to me. I also thought his proclamation that incorporating and encouraging this selflessness in the treatment of a narcissist could have very positive and life-changing results! Although this man's insights and thoughts might not stem from any source of faith, they actually fit in well with my personal beliefs and Christian perspective.

As a woman of faith, I have a different perspective from many people because I believe in a more powerful source of miraculous change over a mentally ill person's heart, soul, and mind. It is my belief that human beings were not created with any defect of the body, soul, mind, and spirit; I believe that mankind was made in the very image of God and, therefore, perfect. Not that humans were the exact replica of God in all His fullness, divinity, and glory, but rather, we were imprinted with the perfect character traits of God, which are whole, holy (sinless), and good.

> **Then God said, "Let us (Father, Son, Holy Spirit) make man in our image, after our likeness." And God saw everything that He had made, and behold, it was very good.**
> (Gen. 1:26, 31, parentheses added)

Everything that God made was good, whole, without spot or blemish —perfect. It was only after mankind "fell" in the garden of Eden (this will be discussed more in a subsequent chapter) that sin, death, corruption, hate, defect, sickness, infirmities (of body, soul, heart, and mind), as well as the exalted "self" came into being. In Ephesians 2:3 it is written,

> **...we all once lived in the passions of our flesh, carrying out the desires of the body and the mind, and were by nature (fallen nature) children of wrath, like the rest of mankind** (parentheses added).

But God had a plan to restore humanity to its former state, and that plan was Jesus Christ. Many historians and scholars from the earliest times in history who did not acknowledge Jesus as the Son of

God still affirmed that He was a relevant figure who did miraculous things during His time on earth. The New Testament is filled with recorded miracles alongside His message of salvation for those who would believe in Him as the One who came to save them from their sins. His ministry work and mission here was not only to free people from the bondage of oppression, abuse, injustice, and every kind of physical ailment but also to set them free from the dark torment that encased their hearts and minds, thereby ruling over their lives. Jesus did so many marvelous and supernatural acts. There were so many people He had compassion on and healed because of His great love for every human soul.

One miraculous story that stands out for me is about a man who had been tormented by demons (unclean spirits of Satan's realm) for many years.

> **And no one could bind him anymore, not even with chains (restraints to keep him from harming himself and maybe others). Night and day among the tombs and on the mountains he was always crying out and cutting himself with stones...And Jesus asked him, "What is your name?" He replied, "My name is Legion, for *we* are many."**
> (Mark 5:4-5, 9, parentheses added)

How tormented this poor man was by darkness and inner pain, most likely despairing that he would ever be in his "right mind" and heart again. But Jesus had mercy and compassion for this hopeless and desperate man, and cast the unclean spirits out.

> **The herdsmen fled and told it in the city and the country. And the people came to see what it was that had happened. And as they came to Jesus and saw the demon-possessed man, the one who had had the legion, sitting there, clothed and in his *right mind*, and they were afraid.**
> (Mark 5:14-15, emphasis added)

This newly freed man was so grateful to Jesus for breaking the chains of bondage and torment that had become dark strongholds in his mind for so long (blinding him from seeing truth and reality), slowly destroying him and deeply disturbing those around him, that he wanted to stay with Him always. Wouldn't you?

> **But Jesus said, "Go home to your friends and tell them how much the Lord has done for you, and how He has had mercy on you." And he went away and began to proclaim in the Decapolis how much Jesus had done for him, and everyone marveled.** (Mark 5:19-20)

This is an incredible story of one man's tormented heart and mind, which had left him in a hopeless cycle of darkness, self-harm, and brokenness with no restorative solution available to him. Many people had tried to help him but failed to both restrain him and free him from the strongholds in his mind. Only Jesus, in His selfless love and power over sin and man's physical, mental, and emotional ailments, had the authority to break through the darkness and set this man free so he could once again live in sanity, peace, and wholeness.

This story speaks directly to my heart in a very personal way on two levels. First, Jesus set me free from personal torment. This anguish didn't stem from my own darkened heart but was superimposed on me by my husband's dark soul and tormented mind as he systematically projected onto his "object" that which he loathed about himself. There were many times when his insane behavior made me feel as if I was becoming crazy, and I had to cling very tightly to who I was in Jesus Christ to keep from being swallowed up in my spouse's mental illness. Narcissism is a deeply sad and dark place for those who reside in self-made deception. Narcissists convince themselves so completely that they are "all right" when, in reality, their hearts and minds are "all wrong."

Although my husband has abandoned me (his *now* ex-wife) and fractured his family, he has no guilty conscience or remorse about what he has done because he has convinced himself that he is above reproach in the eyes of both God and man. How do I know this? Because I asked him. He believes he is in right standing with God even though he has completely reneged on the vow he made to me and his commitment to our family. Furthermore, he has not one shred of guilt connected to his cold and unjust actions of abuse toward me or others. It is written in Jeremiah 17:9, **"The heart is deceitful above all things, and desperately sick; who can understand it?"** This is the heart of a person separated from their Creator and not saved by grace.

Only God can truly know and understand our hearts and minds. **"I the LORD search the heart and test the mind..."** (Jer. 17:10). When abandoned to its own devices, a heart of flesh is left in the dark and deceitful ways of the selfish man under the curse of the Fall. But the Word of God tells us that when we give our hearts to Jesus and surrender our life to Him,

> He says, **"And I will give you a new heart, and a new spirit I will put within you. And I will remove the heart of stone (hard, cold, detached) from your flesh and give you a heart of flesh (soft, compassionate, connected)."**
> (Ezek. 36:26, parentheses added)

My heart is not left in deceit and darkness because it has been made new in Christ. Narcissists are pathological liars. The Bible says that he who lies is not of God but the devil:

> **You are of your father the devil, and your will is to do your father's desires. He was a murderer from the beginning, and has nothing to do with the truth, because there is no truth in him. When he lies, he speaks out of his own character, for he is a liar and the father of lies.** (John 8:44)

A person can't have it both ways and walk in the truth; one either lives and walks in the Light or in the darkness. Of course, as fallen people, we are not *always* going to live, act, and react perfectly at all times; it is the *intentions* of the heart, mind, and soul that make the defining difference. Even if at times a person's actions appear "good and right," if on more occasions than not an individual is living and walking in a way that is not fitting for a believer or in-line with God's Word, then that person is only deceiving themselves (and trying to deceive others) because God never compromises with darkness.

> **And this is the judgment: the light has come into the world, and people loved the darkness rather than the light because**

26

their works were evil. For everyone who does wicked things hates the light and does not come to the light, lest his works should be exposed. But whoever does what is true comes to the light, so that they may be clearly seen that his works have been carried out in God. (John 3:19-21)

Jesus is the only source of all true light!

I bear witness to the truth that Jesus doesn't need weeks, months, or even years to free us from the mental, physical, emotional, or spiritual bondage we find ourselves trapped in within this fallen world. The transformation takes only a moment of relinquished will and the openness of a surrendered heart and spirit, which allows the blessed freedom of our Lord to enter in. I will leave you with this declaration:

But Jesus looked at them and said,
"With man this is impossible, but with God all things are possible."
(Matt. 19:26)

3
Step Programs:
The Ladder to Healing

I AM VERY grateful that there are so many people in this world who still devote their precious time, skills, talents, energy, passion, and knowledge in their respective fields to help and heal others in need. It gives me much hope knowing that, in our increasingly inward-focused world, there are still so many hearts of compassion focused outwardly on the pain and suffering of others. There is a wide range of treatments and support systems offered in the field of medicine, many in the form of what are known as "Step Programs." When I think of a program laid out in this format, I envision a ladder on which individuals climb—one step at a time—until they reach the top, or the desired target they are aiming for. The positive side of these programs is that they offer an optimistic and constructive strategy for documenting progression, serving as visual aids that lay out personal goals and record accomplishments and improvement. They are reminders of where we were and how far we have come. They encourage us that we are making headway as we keep moving forward and upward, one rung at a time.

The negative side to these programs, though, is that they are also a constant reminder to us when we struggle and can't seem to get onto the next rung. They serve as a reality check when we lose our footing, loosen our grip, slide backward, fall, or just jump off altogether—and find ourselves back at the bottom of the ladder. These step programs can also make us extremely nervous and cause stress before each next appointment, weekly meeting, time we have to step on the scale, or urine test or blood draw. We need regular accountability for sure; this helps to encourage us in those moments when we are alone and struggling with temptation, knowing we have to answer to someone.

Our habits and addictions are so strong that we often need to have restraints placed around us (like on our computers, phones, in vehicles) or actually upon our bodies in the form of bracelets on wrists and ankles to keep us from harming ourselves or others. Our unhealthy behavior patterns and habits (in every form: food, alcohol, smoking, drugs, gambling, pornography, excessive social media intake and video gaming, etc.) cause temptations that are powerful forces! **"The spirit is indeed willing, but the flesh is weak"** (Matt. 26:41). Our human weaknesses are so great a draw that the Bible warns us to flee from that which tempts us because to expose ourselves, even for a moment, can send us tumbling down our ladders. And yet, if we are confronted with a temptation we cannot avoid, the Bible also promises that:

> **God is faithful, and He will not let you be tempted beyond your ability, but with the temptation He will also provide the way of escape, that you may be able to endure it.**
> (1 Cor. 10:13)

Blessed assurance! Nevertheless, we need to be aware that the tempter prowls around day and night like a lion looking for prey, and he will not rest until his appetite is satisfied at the expense of a weak moment in our flesh. Note that you will never be tempted by God:

> **Let no one say when he is tempted, "I am being tempted by God," for God cannot be tempted with evil, and He himself tempts no one. But each person is tempted when he (she) is lured and enticed by his (her) own desire. Then desire when it has conceived gives birth to sin, and sin when it is full grown brings forth death (spiritual death).**
> (James 1:13-15, parentheses added)

A big part of any type of healing and recovery is acknowledging our weaknesses; this is called humility. Unfortunately, a spirit of humility is not something frequently taught in our modern society. We equate humility with weakness with about as much negativity as we equate being submissive (the submitting of someone or something to another) with oppression. But in actuality, the definition of being "humble" is:

Humble
Having or showing a consciousness of one's shortcomings (deficiency); being modest (not vain or boastful, reserved, decent, unpretentious); to lower in pride.

I wonder what would happen in our society if we brought these two beautiful words back into our sphere of learning and practice; how they could radically change our personal lives, marriages, children, schools, workplaces, churches, communities, and world for the better! The forces behind narcissism and addictions like pornography are that an individual *cannot or will not* fully acknowledge or see the truth about their weaknesses, shortcomings, pride, and vanity; they have an inability or desire to willingly surrender to what is good, decent, and right. Instead, individuals are taught (and then subsequently often teach) to feed their vanity and boast of their right to do so without surrendering or giving heed to the needs of those who love them and desperately need them to be humble, decent, and selfless. We desire to be strong and self-sufficient, take what we want without asking, and do what we want without conscience or consequence. Everyone is a winner and gets a prize—except, that is, for the unfortunate, "weaker" loser. After all, for a narcissist, it really is all about me, my "selfie," and I!

On the flip side, however, the entire Christian message and core principles of our faith are centered on humility and surrender. Although with the statistics of pornography, narcissism, materialism, consumerism, etc., within our churches today, I would go out on a thin limb and say that we are apparently not practicing these basic principles of our faith very well. I perceive that these shortcomings might be slightly diminishing our positive impact upon our world and in bringing about the Kingdom of God here on earth as it is in heaven (Matthew 6:10). I think we might be boasting of great things, but that, consequently, some of our salt may have become tainted and not worth much more than to be thrown away (Matthew 5:13).

If we were honest, though, in looking back on both world and biblical history, men and women who I feel made the most positive and progressive changes in our world for the betterment of many were the most humble people. World leaders who were more concerned about the people they *served* while in their appointed positions and spheres—instead of being preoccupied with how they could elevate and empower themselves—had great influence over the hearts and minds of the people they were leading. Their ability to humbly see, hear, know, and care about the people under their authority was both encouraging and motivating.

The Bible says that Moses was the most humble man who walked the earth (Num. 12:3), yet I certainly would not ever consider Moses a weak man. He went before Pharaoh, one of the most powerful men during that time in history, and bid him to release God's people from captivity—not once but 10 times! Upon their release, it is recorded that Moses left Egypt with "**about 600,000 men on foot, besides women and children**" (Exod. 12:37). He then led this multitude (which increased over time) through the desert wilderness for 40 years. Of course, God was the real power behind it all, but Moses still had to allow himself to be used in his limited human body with both a strong spirit of leadership as well as a spirit of surrender and humility. That doesn't sound like a weakling to me. Sometimes we can barely tolerate being home all weekend with our disrespectful and whiny children. Can you even imagine what it must have been like to lead and "parent" a huge mass of often-stubborn, whiny, and disobedient men, women, and children for 40 years—in a desert, no less! Where is the Tylenol®?

But our greatest example of supreme humility and surrender for all time is found in none other than Jesus Christ Himself, the incarnate God. I could write about His life overflowing with these beautifully exemplified and expressed character traits, but I have not enough paper, ink, words, or life left in me to do so! I will attempt to encompass just a fraction of the enormity of it—of *Him*—in a few powerful Scriptures:

* "Come to Me, all who labor and are heavy laden, and I will give you rest. Take My yoke upon you, and learn from Me, for I am gentle and lowly (humble) of heart, and you will find rest for your souls." (Matt. 11:28-29)

* ...at the right time Christ died for the ungodly, but God showed His love for us in that while we were still sinners, Christ died for us. (Rom. 5:6,8)

* Have this mind among yourselves, which is yours in Christ Jesus, who, though He was in the form of God, did not count equality with God a thing to be grasp, but made Himself nothing, taking on the form of a servant, being born in the likeness of men. And being found in human form, He humbled Himself by becoming obedient to the point of death, even death on a cross. (Phil. 2:5-8)

* And He...knelt down and prayed, saying, "Father, if You are willing, remove this cup (of crucifixion and death) from Me. Nevertheless, not My will, but Yours, be done." (Luke 22:41,42)

* "I can do nothing on My own. I seek not My own will but the will of Him (God) who sent Me." (John 5:30)

* Therefore it says, "God opposes the proud, but gives grace to the humble." Submit yourselves therefore to God. Humble yourselves before the Lord, and He will exalt you. (James 4:6,7,10)

* Clothe yourselves, all of you, with humility toward one another, for "God opposes the proud but gives grace to the humble." Humble yourselves, therefore, under the mighty hand of God so that at the proper time He may exalt you.... (1 Pet. 5:5,6)

[All words within parentheses were added.]

So I think we are seeing a pretty good picture of both God's strong dislike of pride and His great pleasure in one who is humble and willingly surrenders their life unto Him—even His own Son. We also see that these qualities were not wrought in weak men but rather in the strongest, bravest, and most heroic men: noble leaders who would give all to protect, provide for, and save the people they loved. Our ultimate leader-by-example is Jesus Christ, who sacrificed even to the point of stretching out His innocent hands and taking the nails for your sin and mine!

You might be scratching your head right now and asking yourself, *"What does all of this talk about strength, pride, and self-sufficiency versus humility and surrender have to do with the topic of Step Programs as tools for help and healing?"*

Well, I felt it would help us to fully picture the vision impressed upon me and gain clearer understanding. Sometimes we need to take the "scenic route" to appreciate the whole landscape of a particular area instead of going directly to our destination.

From the onset of this book, I have tried to earnestly communicate my passion for bringing about enlightenment, knowledge, understanding, hope, and healing to *all* people who have been abused or oppressed by various disorders, addictions, injustices, etc., regardless of whether you are a believer or nonbeliever in the Christian faith. Although I expressed that a large portion of this labor of love would come at the issues from a biblical worldview, I am very aware that many individuals reading this book may not share my faith. Even so, I am very passionate about your plight and wholeheartedly desire your freedom from oppression. Although the majority of my healing and the avenues sought for it have predominantly been through fellow Christians as well as direct spiritual healing, I also received wonderful and effective care—especially for chronic physical pain—from those outside my faith, for which I am very grateful. However, since I am addressing these issues from both perspectives, and this book is also my testimony, I feel that I need to share my personal experiences and what I believe to be true regarding each avenue to wholeness.

No matter how much physical strength or stamina, intelligence, sophisticated technology, expertise, ingenuity, etc., that we have, I think we would all agree that the human body, mind, and even our technical prowess has its limits. We are, after all, only human. And although we may be extremely passionate about, committed to, devoted to, knowledgeable about, or even an expert in a particular field, there comes a time when we are all at the end of ourselves and can do no more. Our best efforts can be wonderfully productive, effective, and healing, but they are still finite. All human beings—even if they are in a wonderful season of health, have harmonious relationships, are successful and prosperous, and feel basically happy and content overall—struggle at times. If you dig just a little bit, I am pretty sure you will find something in their life (past, present, or looming in the future) that was/is causing some stress, anxiety, misgiving, discomfort, or pain. I know a lot of people, and I truthfully couldn't name even one who isn't, personally or somewhere within their sphere, dealing with some form of struggle; it is just part of the reality of a fallen world (a world after the Fall).

The doctor treating you most likely has their own doctor treating them; the chiropractor or massage therapist you go to probably have their own physical aches and pains that they are seeking relief for; the counselor you are seeing for emotional distress while, let's say, working through the pain of a divorce, may be experiencing their own anxieties while going through their own divorce or other trauma; your financial advisor may be filing for bankruptcy; your lawyer may be fighting their own court case; the person heading up the local Step Program for addictions or other recovery/medical needs may have a child, spouse, or friend going through their own Step Program. The scenarios are endless because the breadth, width, and depth of our human weaknesses, sicknesses, and brokenness are without limit. However, the beauty in our broken state is that *if* we can get ourselves to a place of genuine acknowledgment of and acceptance about our imperfect condition and into a place of vulnerability, humility, and surrender, *then* we are in the optimal position to begin the steps toward real hope and healing.

> "You must surrender to a breaking that must happen
> if you want any of your brokenness to heal."
> —Ann Voskamp, Wife, Mother, Homeschool Teacher, Writer,
> and Activist With Compassion International
>
> "In order to change we must be sick and tired of being sick and tired."
> —Author Unknown

The World and an All-Sufficient God

The Ladder: My Vision

This is what I saw: A desperate person laying at the bottom of a deep, dry well who was hungry, thirsty, exhausted, lonely, rejected, and abandoned—completely at the end of themselves. The world sees them and wants to help. People with appropriate training have great plans, and ideas, and their heart's desires are genuine in their attempts to get this hurting person out of the pit.

A team of experienced personnel are sent to the opening of the well, they lower down a long ladder, and one person descends. They have with them some water bottles and a few protein bars that they set before the needy individual and encourage them to drink and eat of its nourishment.

Let's make this personal for a moment...

Although the life-giving and strengthening necessities are now available to you , within arm's reach, you are still too weak, sick, exhausted, depressed, distraught, and without enough hope to even partake of the essential offerings. With much coaxing, the one with you then lifts you to your feet and helps walk you to the bottom of the ladder. The person waiting at the top is calling you to come, to keep facing forward, and to begin pulling yourself up, one rung at a time. The person still behind you is encouraging you as well, to keep looking up and to remain focused on your goal as they cheer on your struggling efforts to rise out of the pit of despair that you have fallen into.

You attempt to place one weary foot and shaky leg onto the bottom rung with the helping hand of the motivational speaker, and you begin your tentative and harrowing climb. They have wonderful and devoted intentions to see you progress, but they are motivating you from with*out*, and you are still so very empty with*in* that you cannot muster up the courage, strength, motivation, endurance, or hope to make yourself climb out of the deep pit into which you have fallen (or been pushed) over the edge.

You also don't know what awaits you at the top, past the rim, outside the little circle of light barely visible to your distrusting and discouraged eyes:

* Will there be more pain? Suffering? Rejection? Abuse? Neglect? Ridicule? Bondage?
* What will happen to you once you emerge into the unknown on the other end? Progress is slow and painful. Fear, doubt, insecurity, self-pity, pride, resentment, and the unwillingness to forgive (yourself or others) keep holding you hostage and pulling you backward into the pit of despair, depression, and heartsickness. Or...maybe this isn't your first trip up the ladder, and your last attempt at rescue, healing, wholeness, freedom, and renewed hope was disappointing at best.

Hope deferred makes the heart sick. (Prov. 13:12)

Thankfully, many people do emerge and enter back into full health, life, and relationships with renewed energy, creativity, life goals, focused vision, and victory! Some of them can make a clean break from the past, the addiction, the abuse, life's injustices, disappointments, and the bondage of sin, darkness, depression, fear, and hopelessness. I am so encouraged by their perseverance and *will* to be well and free. Unfortunately, though, many people never attempt the climb, or they give up halfway to the top, or they reach the top but have nothing solid to grab hold of and slowly slide back into the pit. They lay at the bottom of that dark pit with the world's offered help before them and never reach out to take it—or die trying through their own self-effort.

I went down to the land whose bars closed upon me forever;
yet You brought up my life from the pit, O LORD my God.
(Jon. 2:6)

The LORD your God is with you, He is mighty to save; He will take
great delight in you; He will quiet you with His love; He will rejoice
over you with singing.
(Zeph. 3:17)

This is the way of faith: An individual who acknowledges Someone higher, wiser, and more powerful than themselves. They seek the Savior and then ask Him to rescue them from the pit and their silent desperation. He *always* comes. He looks down through the small hole of light with eyes of compassion. He *sees* you are empty and humbly surrendered in the pit, that you are at the end of yourself. He *hears* your cries and groans for help. **"I called on Your name, O LORD, from the depths of the pit; You heard my plea…"** (Lam. 3:55, 56). He *knows* exactly where you are and what you need in order to get out. He *loves* you enough that He gave up His own life to save yours. He puts the ladder down the deep pit of brokenness and despair and climbs in Himself. He not only brings you water, but He also lifts up your weary head and gives you your fill of its life-giving refreshment. He not only supplies the needed nourishment, but He also feeds you until you are satisfied. He doesn't simply lift you to your tired feet, set you upright on your wobbly legs, and tell you to climb up the ladder while He watches from above or encourages you from behind. No, He gently picks you up and places you upon His strong shoulders. He effortlessly carries you up the ladder, out of the pit, and then lets you bask in the warmth and beauty of the sun/Son.

You see, like a good shepherd who goes out to find and rescue his lost and/or injured sheep, our wonderful Shepherd, Jesus Christ, searches for you. There is:

*   *no place He won't go to find you*
*   *no pit too deep He will not climb into*
*   *no place too dirty or shameful where He won't touch you*
*   *no past too dark and dingy that He can't erase*
*   *no sin too great that His precious blood can't cleanse*

He finds you where you are at, just as you are, and only longs to care for you, heal you, and bring you safely home.

But help doesn't stop there. Once you get to the top, He won't leave you. He doesn't schedule your next appointment in a few weeks nor sign you up for His "Steps to Recovery" program that meets every Tuesday evening. He stays with you day and night, around the clock, 365 days a year (366 in a leap year!), with no weekends off, holidays, sick days, or paid vacation. He is *always* on call and *never* puts you on hold. He stays with you, heals you, cleans you up, and makes you new. He redeems your past, your identity, your reputation, your worth, and your life from the pit (Psalm 103:4). He transforms your heart and mind and makes all things new (Romans 12:2; Isaiah 43:18). He does *all* of the work. He gives you the power to break all addictions and strongholds in your "old" life, as well as the ability to surrender the "self" life so you can live fully and freely in Him alone. He marinates you in His perfect love. As you confess your sins, He erases them from His memory (Heb. 8:12). He remembers them no more, and neither should you. He gives you the power and grace to forgive those who have hurt you and sinned against you, as well as the crucial ability to forgive yourself. He fills in all of the old potholes and destructive "ruts" in your mind that once led you down broken paths called "trouble and pain" while following blindly after sin in the darkness. Are all of these promises just another fantasy? A trick of the mind? Magic? No, but they *are* a miracle!

This is my life testimony, and I bear witness to its truth. Jesus saved me twice: once from eternal hell and once from the pit of hell I call silent desperation. He redeemed my life from that pit. He took off my shackles and set me free. He bound up my wounds, healed my broken wings, and taught me how to fly again. He exchanged my fears, tears, bitterness, frustration, and mourning with tears of gratitude, joy, and peace. After 25 years of narcissistic abuse and in the wake of my personal "exodus" toward freedom, He redeemed my life without one day of counseling, Step Program, or a prescription drug. He restored me in months that which normally takes years or even a lifetime to recover. The world's resources may be able to get you out of the pit, but they can't keep you there. My deepest passion is to offer this freedom to all who will hear my testimony and choose the new life and healing that only Jesus offers you. He truly is the way, the truth, and the life (John 14:6). He is the one-way ticket out of silent desperation and into a renewed life of quiet strength.

Come fly with me!

Footprints in the Sand[11]

One night I dreamed I was walking along the beach with the Lord. Many scenes from my life flashed across the sky. In each scene I noticed footprints in the sand. Sometimes there were two sets of footprints. Other times there was only one set of prints.

This bothered me because I noticed that during the low periods of my life, when I was suffering from anguish, sorrow, and defeat, I could see only one set of footprints. So I said to the Lord, "You promised me, Lord, that if I followed You, You would walk with me always. But I noticed that during the most trying periods of my life, there was only one set of prints in the sand. Why, when I have needed You most, have You abandoned me?"

The Lord replied, "My Child, I love you and would never leave you. The times when you have seen only one set of footprints are the times when I carried you."—Jesus

---

[11] Ella H. Scharring-Hausen, June 6, 1922. (While this poem has been attributed to many people, over the years, it is believed to have this authorship.)

4
Becoming Lovers of Self

For people will be lovers of self....
(1 Tim. 3:2)

A S PREVIOUSLY DISCUSSED, the psychological and scientific factors surrounding the question of how and why people become "lovers of self" can seem complex and filled with differing opinions, shades of gray, and holes in the narrative. Yet I believe that, at its core, the answer is really quite simple. As with so many other dilemmas and problems in our world, communities, workplaces, churches, families, marriages, etc., the answers are not as complicated as we'd like to make them out to be. Having the will, cooperation, and disciplined motivation to do what is necessary to live out the answer and make it a reality is the hard part.

Whether you believe in the Father, Son, and Holy Spirit, or not, I believe that the answer to the above question boils down to one powerful word: LOVE! Now, before your feathers get ruffled and you say, "I thought the *problem* was love—*too much love*," then I will quickly add that it is "love for God" and "love for others" and *not* a warped love for self that is the complete answer. The Bible revealed the solution to this fallen human condition thousands of years ago. The Old Testament addresses this question when (through divine inspiration) Moses wrote in Deuteronomy 6:5, **"You shall love the LORD your God with all your heart and with all your soul and with all your might,"** and in Leviticus 19:18, **"...you shall love your neighbor as yourself...."** In the New Testament, Jesus reiterates this most important commandment (with only slight variation):

And you shall love the Lord your God with all your heart and with all your soul and with all your mind and with all your strength. The second is this: "You shall love your neighbor as yourself." (Mark 12:30-31)

Both the Old and the New Testaments make it perfectly clear that when we get our eyes and minds off ourselves (our wants, desires, ambitions, and even needs) and instead focus on those around us, we will really become positively productive! As some researchers and mental health professionals call this psychopathic disorder, or spirit of narcissism, an actual "epidemic," I believe it is of paramount importance that the tide of self-love be turned before we are awash in a world devoid of basic human kindness, compassion, and selfless love.

...because they do not change and do not fear God.
(Ps. 55:19)

I expressed in the Introduction of this book that I had been enlightened to the elementary need in all mankind to be seen, heard, known, and loved. I believe that these four core elements were implanted in our human hearts as a means of rousing our desire to seek, know, and love God, foremost, and then to carry forth that same desire to know and love our fellow man. The original design for the "love cycle" has become terribly broken and increasingly warped with each passing generation, having been turned inside-out so that we are *injecting* into ourselves that which was meant to be *projected* outward onto others in expressions of love, kindness, nurturing, empathy, etc. What was designed to shine forth from us, now shines inward in such a way that so many want to stand in the spotlight as the "stars" of their own one-man/woman show. This unnatural phenomenon is really nothing new; it has been evident ever since the Fall of mankind in the Garden of Eden, and like a tiny snowball rolling downhill, it has gathered both speed and size ever since.

I realize that some readers may not be believers in the Christian faith, but I ask you to please stay with me on this because I think some basic points and truths, which will come forth from this

42

discussion, could be very beneficial in your understanding of how a person came to be able to use, abuse, manipulate, and coldly dismiss your life, hopes, dreams, and love without a conscience. As I stated earlier, I believe that any knowledge is power, shining truth and wisdom into our blind spots and lack of understanding. So, without going into too much theology, I will attempt to offer some elemental answers by which to consider how human love became so awry.

God gave His people many commandments, laws, and rules to live by, which were laid forth in the Old Testament. Contrary to some popular beliefs, these were *not* meant to keep people oppressed, depressed, or in bondage. God knew that *if* we would follow them, we would actually reap the benefits of good health, prosperity, peace, joy, love, long life, and freedom. But because Adam and Eve exalted themselves in a moment of pride and disobedience, exchanging God's perfect love and care for them for a lie they thought would raise them up to a higher position, they lost it all. At that moment of fatal decision, the world fell from perfect love and freedom into the bondage of sin, evil, hatred for others, and self-centered love. The whole rest of the Old Testament (the books in the Bible written *before* Jesus's birth: B.C., "before Christ") points us to the answer and only antidote for all our ills, and that *is* Jesus Christ.

Only through Jesus and His selfless, loving sacrifice, which required Him to give up His own life in order to save ours and take away the sins of the whole world, are we now empowered by the Holy Spirit to be elevated back to the status of sons and daughters of our Father, which had previously been lost to us in the Garden. This very important "key" that opened the door for our salvation and the gift of eternal life is also reiterated throughout the New Testament (the books of the Bible written *after* Jesus's birth: in A.D., *Anno Domini* [Latin term for "in the year of the Lord"]). The combined force of the Scripture gives us knowledge—and therefore power—to understand our present loveless condition. So, when one considers that the original mandate and desire for this beautiful gift of love was to give it away and project it outwardly in expressions of love and not

43

selfishly hoarded within ourselves, we realize that the core of narcissism is an issue of the heart and mind gone awry. It creates within an individual the inability to selflessly love both God and one's neighbor (in the Bible, the word "neighbor" conveys not just Dan and Sue next door but everyone in the world besides yourself). Considering this, I think perhaps God was trying to establish something really crucial in His deep desire for *all people* to live within relationships centered on selfless love, nurturing, compassion, and harmony…without trying to destroy one another within and without.

> **And then many will fall away (stumble) and betray one another and hate one another. And because lawlessness will be increased, the love of many will grow cold.**
> (Matt. 24:10,12, parentheses added)

To love God with all our heart, soul, mind, and strength means that we should focus on *Someone* above and outside ourselves. A deep awareness of and desire to respect, honor, and love both God and others would then spring forth from our hearts without effort and withholding. Our relationship with our Father God was meant to be a mutual give-and-take of love, honor, respect, and trust, which would include a perpetual desire to be seen, heard, known, and loved. The constant infilling of this selfless love poured out by God through Jesus would keep us so filled to overflowing that it would then naturally spill out onto everyone around us: our spouse, children, siblings, extended families, friends, neighbors, church body, coworkers, etc. It is a beautiful yet simple design that would keep each person's "love well" filled, thereby maintaining a balanced continuum of feeling loved and loving in return.

Out of that endless source of love would flow the desire to truly see, hear, and know those around us in a selfless way. We would no longer use knowledge of others as tools for manipulation or abuse, or to rob and ultimately destroy them. We humans think we can attain this form of selfless love on our own, and maybe we can for short periods of time with great effort, but our core is basically selfish in nature. If we were truly honest with ourselves and genuinely took the time to examine our hearts and ponder the *motives* behind what we believe to be selfless actions of love, we would most likely discover that there is a selfish (or self-righteous) motive hidden (no matter how small) beneath the surface of our perceived selfless love.

Now, don't be too hard on yourself; you can't help it. None of us can do the impossible without God and the help of the Holy Spirit. Even though the first time the command came that God's people should love each other as themselves was given in the Old Testament, because of our fallen human nature rendering us unable to keep this mandate to love one another selflessly, we needed a solution beyond our finite selves that would equip us once more with hearts capable of such sweet and natural inclinations toward unconditional love. This is where Jesus, in all of His humility and obedience, enters center stage, bringing with Him both perfect love and infinite power, yet without all of the modern-day pomp! He holds the key that unlocks our hard and closed heart chambers, allowing the unhindered flow of the love cycle to begin circulating among us once more. The truth is that—*apart from the love of Jesus Christ and the power of the Holy Spirit*—we are incapable of loving one another with genuine selflessness and unconditional love. That is why Jesus had to come to earth, to die, and to live again—so that He could live *in* us through the Spirit (sent to be our Helper *after* Jesus's ascension into Heaven) to both empower us and exemplify for us how to love selflessly again!

God is love.
(1 John 4:1)

Anyone who does not love does not know God, because God is love.
(1 John 4:8)

Beloved, if God so loved us, we also ought to love one another.
(1 John 4:11)

Sadly, it was prophesied thousands of years ago that this **narcissistic epidemic** would touch our world and many people living during this time, which the Bible refers to as "the last days." There is a whole list of character traits human beings would be manifesting with greater and greater frequency, resulting in much distress, dysfunction, and disharmony. Do you want to take a wild guess at what state of the heart and mind would be first on the list? I will quote the answer directly from the source:

> **But understand this, that in the last days there will come times of difficulty. For <u>people will be</u> *lovers of self,* lovers of money, proud, arrogant, abusive, disobedient to their parents, ungrateful, unholy, heartless, unappeasable, slanderous, without self-control, brutal, not loving good, treacherous, reckless, swollen with conceit, lovers of pleasure rather than lovers of God...always learning and never able to arrive at a knowledge of the truth. (2 Tim. 3:1-4, 7, emphasis added)**

I do not know about you, but that list makes me a little bit sick to my stomach—well, maybe more than a little bit! Can anyone, in truth, read the above list and deny that this is the unchangeable reality of our world, nations, communities, workplaces, schools, homes and families, and individual natures today? I know I can't. Narcissism is invading every corner of the world with increasing intensity and deepening darkness as modern culture *feeds the beast* with the promotion of "it's really *all about me*" messages.

These imprudent teachings are being instilled into the very essence of too many of our youth at the most crucial years of developing their identities, which will remain through all of their adulthood, impacting future relationships, subsequent families, and whole societies. The scope of it is daunting but not hopeless *if* we begin to truly acknowledge this mental illness for what it is, making conscious and concerted efforts to turn the tide of misguided and destructive self-love and reverse it from the inside-*out*—where it belongs! Knowledge equals responsibility. Knowledge is powerful—but only if it is acted upon.

> **...because they exchanged the truth about God for a lie and worshiped and served the creature (self) rather than the Creator...**
> (Rom. 1:25, parentheses added)

5

The Fruit Doesn't Fall Far
From the Tree

**"So, every healthy tree bears good fruit,
but the diseased tree bears bad fruit."**
(Matt. 7:18)

**Behold, children are a heritage from the LORD,
the fruit of the womb a reward.**
(Ps. 127:3)

A S LAID FORTH in the previous chapter, we see that it is the
common belief of experts in the field of mental illness that
narcissism is bred and fed beginning in a person's childhood; I concur
with this estimation. But I believe that the precursor to this anomaly
is sin that entered God's created order after human beings attempted
to exalt themselves above His sovereignty. It is my belief (based on
the Scriptures) that ever since that fatal decision, we are now all born
with a sin nature and are basically selfish creatures, but we also still
bear the image of our *selfless* Creator God as well. The question then
becomes, "Which part of our nature is going to be fed more: the
selfish or the *selfless* part?"

I also believe that narcissism has been a part of world history
since almost the beginning of time when the firstborn son of Adam
and Eve, Cain, killed his younger brother, Abel, during a jealous rage.
A man that should have been his younger brother's most ardent
protector became his unjustifiable foe—a disturbing yet truthful
illustration of the awful consequences that resulted after the Fall of
mankind into sin and dysfunction. That Cain somehow felt entitled to
rob his brother of life shows an exaggerated sense of his own

authority and power. He also had an absolute disregard for his brother's right to live out his life, dreams, plans, and purpose. Cain didn't seem to feel any sense of guilt or remorse for his actions either; he demonstrated no empathy for his parents' loss nor, after his unwarranted rage subsided, a sense of loss to himself. He killed without a conscience. And, when he was questioned by God as to where his younger brother was, he had the audacity to outright lie and tell Him he didn't know, with callous indifference—a natural-born liar! Cain's ego had somehow become inflated and thus blinded him with self-deceptive notions of entitlement and superiority.

Although Adam and Eve had exalted themselves to be *like* God, their son exalted himself *as if he were a* "god." By making himself a "god" in his darkened heart and mind, he assumed that he had the right and authority to decide the fate of his brother. Ever since, history has recorded thousands of times over this ever-increasing force growing like a cancer inside the heart and mind of too many people—the sense of entitlement to destroy the lives of other people (in a myriad of ways) without a conscience or remorse for the pain, sorrow, tears, loss, and devastation left in the wake! Just thinking about the parallels from this first family's experience and then my own—as well as the countless victims over the centuries since— brings a chill to my bones.

> **...we all once lived in the passions of our flesh, carrying out the desires of the body and mind, and were by nature children of wrath, like the rest of mankind.**
> (Eph. 2:3)

Balancing the Scales Again

> **Blessed is the nation whose God is the LORD.**
> (Ps. 33:12)

I made so many mistakes as a parent! Thank God that He considers and understands our weaknesses and human limitations, leaving us a wide margin of grace and mercy to live and work within. God has laid forth very wonderful guidelines in His Word that teach and encourage parents how to raise and invest in their children in a healthy, balanced way that leads them throughout their lifetime. They need this rearing in order to someday become (if meant to) good spouses, parents, neighbors, and citizens, as well as to carry forth the cycle of love and respect for all. Again, readers who are not believers in Christ yet may still be desperately seeking answers, I hope that you will find these next pages helpful in gleaning more powerful knowledge and wisdom for yourselves, your children, your grandchildren, and anyone else in your sphere of influence. I applaud your perseverance and hunger for the power of knowledge and truth!

We are all products of our environments, whether positive, negative, or a sampling of both. I have the advantage (or disadvantage depending on the day!) of seeing in my lifetime the dramatic changes brought about through the explosion of new technology (now I am telling my age). While growing up, our family had one television (yes, it had color!) and one rotary dial telephone with a stretched-out cord that we always got tangled up in as we tried to see how far we could get for a little bit of privacy. A cell phone, WiFi, a laptop computer, cable television, etc. was something so futuristic that it was only dreamed about while watching *The Jetsons* (now I am *really* giving my age away!). Although technology has brought amazing advantages to our modern-day world, it has also fueled much evil and resulted in many disadvantages in the lives of both children and adults alike.

I am not going to delve into that very much but only as it pertains to the subject of narcissism and self-love.

Now getting back to the Stone Age…okay, who didn't love watching *The Flintstones*? A child's major influences just a few decades ago were their everyday experiences in the home with their families, their friends (real friends—not the hundreds of Facebook "friends" they will never really see or know), their neighborhood, in school, at church, etc. Their exposure to the world was much narrower and limited to a smaller sphere of influence. Although our family was one of the few families in the neighborhood that attended church regularly, almost all of the kids I grew up with still shared similar values and generally accepted moral guidelines of what was considered good and bad, right and wrong. There was an unspoken code of ethics and moral values that overshadowed our lives whether we were believers or nonbelievers. We obeyed and respected our parents and other adults, our teachers, and those in authority (for the most part—nobody's perfect!) with hearts and minds that just accepted these expectations and boundaries as normal, healthy, and good.

But a subtle yet tangible shift started taking place as our culture began to slowly look more inward at our *own* needs, wants, desires, happiness, and personal goals as *self-satisfaction* became more paramount than the once-treasured core of marriage, family, and community as a whole and harmonious unit. Wives and mothers who were once solely devoted to their marriages, child-rearing, and homes started going back to college and entering the workforce. Newborns and young children were often being reared by strangers without an intimate and deep-love connection to them in daycare settings and preschools. Children began experiencing separation anxiety on a whole new level, as well as deep-rooted fears during crucial years of development. Divorce became more prevalent and accepted, and the family unit started falling apart and becoming scattered.

Technology became increasingly affordable and attainable, which birthed a growing staple of news, programs, and newer forms of entertainment, opening up the world around us at an ever-increasing rate. God was taken out of schools and other public places, and with Him, we also lost our higher moral standard of living and governing authority. Suddenly we had Nobody or nothing besides *ourselves* to be the standard for what was deemed good or bad, right or wrong, healthy or unhealthy, just or unjust, etc. When we removed the Author of the guidelines that taught us honor, justice, respect, love, and basic human kindness, we also stripped away the authority and respect God had so lovingly and wisely given to parents to help guide and teach our children within healthy, productive, and safe boundaries that would feed and nurture their *selfless* love nature and respect for others.

Children, obey your parents in the Lord, for this is right.
Honor your father and mother that it may go well with you....
(Eph. 6:1-3)

Human beings, in their increasingly self-exalted state of heart and mind, broke the beautiful and balanced cycle of selfless love that generated the necessary light and ability by which to truly see, hear, know, and love their neighbors (all people) as themselves. This ultimately turned that light inward, with a growing focus upon self, and began feeding the insatiable appetite of our *fallen* ego and self-love. The joy of giving became the joy of taking at the expense of others. As the "it's really all about me" mindset has taken root like a fatal disease, the rotten fruit has become evident in every facet of our broken lives, relationships, communities, nation, and world. It consequently strips people of their identity, health, finances, hopes, dreams, and precious time here on earth while withholding love and basic human kindness. This escalation of warped self-love kills them both figuratively and literally with little or no guilt or remorse.

So, I ask these extremely important yet perilous questions: How did we become lovers of self? How do we stop the epidemic of narcissism from taking root in our children's hearts and minds? The answer, I believe, is once again both simple and difficult because we have placed so many obstacles in its way. A world without a sovereign God who establishes a perfect standard to work within

will have millions of answers,

which will stem from the hearts and minds of millions of people,

who will have millions of their own solutions

—many very good and honorable, yet tainted with that little portion of selfishness inherent in every fallen human being—

and nothing will ever be agreed upon or accomplished.

As a woman of faith, I believe the only answer with any lasting value is to turn back to our Father God in an attempt to reinstate and regenerate the original "love cycle" by loving the Lord our God with all our heart, soul, mind, and strength; only then will we be equipped to love our neighbors as ourselves. And the second part is that we need Jesus, for He alone is the embodiment of *true* and *selfless love*. When we turn once again to the epicenter of all things, the very essence of love and humanity found in Christ through the power of the Holy Spirit, we can earnestly make our way home and find the peace, joy, hope, acceptance, healing, nurturing relationships, and selfless love that we are *all* longing for!

Some Basic Steps and Principles for Rearing Healthy, Whole, and Balanced Children

For You formed my inward parts;
You knitted me together in my mother's womb.
(Ps. 139:13)

I have done many challenging things in my life such as serving in the active Army Reserves for ten years, employment as a legal secretary for attorneys in a busy downtown law firm, working in school districts, in-home care for the elderly, homeschooling our three children for eleven years, etc. But the job of raising children has been both the most rewarding yet also the most challenging of them all, as the outcome of the effort put in has far-reaching impact on their lives and overall future success. Having the will, commitment, and discipline to act purposefully, and the wisdom needed to do what is right and necessary during countless moments throughout each day in order to reap positive results for each child (as well as the family unit), is hard work to say the least! But no matter your faith, or the absence thereof, I believe that a few basic strategies and principles will prove beneficial to *all* children regardless of any other defining factors that influence their development.

Babies in their natural state are selfish beings. They have to be to survive because everything they need comes from someone else.

Without words, they make themselves seen, heard, and known by crying—sometimes often and very loud! As their basic needs for food, warmth, changing, nurturing, and human contact are met, they usually become less demanding because they begin to unconsciously trust that someone loves them and is going to care for them in their helplessness. I believe that even at this very tender stage and age, parents are already instilling a subconscious awareness of their *selfless* love, which is imprinted on the heart and mind of that child. But unfortunately, even at this helpless stage, too many infants suffer neglect at the hands of young parents not equipped to handle the grave responsibility and commitment that is necessary for full-time nurturing and child-rearing. Too often, parents seek their own needs and/or wants *first* (whether it be sleep, food, work, entertainment, an addiction, etc.). Consequently, the cries of the child that go unanswered are already instilling in their tiny selves a distrust of their new world, insecurity, vulnerability, and a yet unnamed fear that they are *not* seen, heard, known, or consistently loved by someone. Although I am not a medical expert, I feel I can speak some truth into this subject matter from personal experience pertaining to both scenarios.

I had the blessing of experiencing this firsthand with my own three daughters who were very content during their infancy, as I not only desired to respond to their cries for life-giving nourishment, (both physical and emotional), but I also experienced great joy in the selfless giving of both. In contrast, though, I also took care of an infant who was being reared in an environment where her physical and emotional needs were *not* being met on a regular basis, nor in a selfless, nurturing manner. The difference was very striking. Not only was she initially unresponsive to activity and noise around her because of a lack of attention, including voice and touch stimulation, but her beautiful eyes had a glazed look, were unfocused, and lacked the sparkle that a recognition of familiar faces and soothing voices bring. When she would cry with hunger, there was a frantic nature about it, and a look of fear would come over her tiny features. I came to perceive that her cries indicating hunger were more than just for food that didn't always come, but they were also the cries of a helpless baby who had gone without being heard and all of her basic human needs being met. The most amazing thing was to watch her slowly, yet steadily, as her physical and emotional needs started being met on a regular basis, become ever more responsive to voice and touch. A contentment settled over her as if she knew she was seen, heard, known, and selflessly loved. It was like watching a dried-up desert flower slowly open its lovely petals one by one after a steady rain and flourish under its life-giving sustenance.

My personal testimony parallels what has become common knowledge in maternity wards and is backed by documented research on how a regular supply of the elemental needs of an infant affects the growth and development of a child in powerful and life-altering ways. At this very vulnerable stage of development, I believe a child *needs* to be surrounded with *selfless love* from their parents and others intimately familiar with the infant, which will lay the foundation for future stages of growth that are crucial for proper brain development and emotional balance as their identity is forming. This neglect of basic care and selfless love by people intimately connected to an infant needs to be eradicated from every child's earliest experience of new life (whenever possible) to ensure that they have the optimal opportunity to grow into a healthy, whole, and well-balanced youth and adult.

There is a lack of growth, a withering in the body and soul of any human being—be it newborn baby or full-grown adult—who is neglected and deprived of love in one form or another. This longing for love is universal and ongoing throughout a person's entire lifespan. These written words are very personal to me as I endured long seasons as a victim of neglect, which included the lack of care, touch, and basic kindness. The withholding of love became evident as parts of my body and soul ached and withered to the point that I feared the damage would be permanent. It has only been through the combination of being removed from the loveless, toxic environment I was living in, together with the selfless acts of love and kindness shown through my children, faithful friends and family, and the ultimate Giver of selfless love (God, through His Son Jesus Christ), that my body and soul are being restored to full health and wholeness as deep healing and freedom allow me to move and breathe again without pain.

**"See that you do not despise one of these little ones.
For I tell you that in heaven their angels always see the face of my
Father who is in heaven."**
(Matt. 18:10)

The Training Years

**Train up a child in the way he should go;
and when he is grown he shall not depart from it.**
(Prov. 22:6)

I believe God instructs parents according to the above-referenced Scripture because He knows that this training and teaching is invaluable to both the parents and the child(ren) alike. As children learn to do things for themselves (whether they like it or not), it begins to build their confidence, self-worth, and sense of identity. As chores and responsibilities become more difficult, a child begins to build their reasoning skills, becomes more efficient with time management and expended energy, and develops problem-solving techniques as well as good coping mechanisms. Over time, these learned skills will foster increasing knowledge, understanding, and wisdom. This subsequent wisdom and confidence then propel the child to embrace new challenges, break out of their comfort zones, form and build upon new relationships, and enjoy the freedom to experiment (in healthy ways) to discover who they are.

When children acquire a sense of who they are apart from others close to them, they begin to develop their own personality traits, character, and attributes—the very qualities that make them uniquely their own person. When an individual is secure in who they are within, they are then equipped to develop healthy relationships with other people who are stable. These relationships are built on mutual admiration for the contribution of each person to the relationship without jealousy, strife, or the desire to overpower. Each individual brings their unique character traits into any relationship (marriage, parent/child, friendships, coworkers, etc.). Over time, the strengths and weaknesses of each person will become evident. An understanding and acceptance of these strengths and weaknesses can create a peaceable environment built on mutual respect as they work together with a spirit of tolerance, as well as positive attitudes and encouragement, in order to bring out the best in one another. As a person matures and acquires an appreciation for other people's unique talents, skills, and strengths, they should also be patient with and compassionate toward those individuals' weaknesses as well as their own.

God knows that a child *not* allowed or encouraged to develop in such a way will never truly discover who they are (a healthy sense of self) apart from their parents or others who have raised or regularly influenced them. These youth will be more inclined to carry into their adulthood habits and behavior patterns that have been unconsciously programmed into their being. These can often be negative in nature if they were not developed in an atmosphere of faith or with some ethical/moral standards that instill an inner conscience. It is a well-developed conscience that upholds the crucial character qualities of selflessness and empathy for others.

When the development of the conscience is compromised, there is no guilt or remorse for wrongdoing and/or harming another human being. Without well-developed coping skills, a *healthy* dose of confidence, or an understanding of who they are, our youth will neither be fully prepared nor capable of surviving and thriving alone outside their childhood environments. These underdeveloped areas within almost force our children and young adults to then cling to another who displays all or most of the character traits they lack and desire, as they grasp for the confidence and personal identity formed within others that are deficient or nonexistent within themselves.

Sadly, many children who are not mature in these crucial life skills essential for initiating and sustaining healthy, balanced relationships (due to excessive coddling and/or neglect and abuse) actually develop egotism (an attitude of selfishness, self-interest, and conceit), thereby viewing everything and everyone in relation to themselves. They are crippled in their ability to have flourishing and stable relationships because of deep-rooted insecurities and voids in who they really are. They try to hide behind masks and radiate an air of selfish autonomy (existing and functioning independently) while at the same time clinging desperately to the very source of their being—the person who becomes an extension of themselves. The *lucky* individual who gets to be their "host" needs to consistently find ways to maintain the strong character traits that were developed throughout their (the host's) life, qualities that drew the "created" narcissist to them in the first place, in order to keep up with the daily drain from what has now become a narcissistic, codependent relationship...ask me how I know!

In truth, narcissists are angry and ill-equipped children in adult bodies. Severe damage from the birth family or other caregivers is either a reality or is perceived as such by the narcissistic child/adolescent. This anomaly takes root when a child is given too much entitlement, overindulgence, and unwarranted praise, having been spoiled by a mother or father who idolized the child, just to name a few. It can also stem from abuse and neglect during the early stages of the developing ego. Either way, the narcissist's emotional development became impaired or paralyzed usually somewhere between the ages of five and seven.

Anyone who has been with a narcissist for a long-enough period of time will begin to detect the depth of their immaturity in child-like emotional responses, an apparent deficit in coping mechanisms, a lack of discipline in personal responsibility and commitments, and a lack of contribution to adult conversations. The narcissist often hangs out with and is more comfortable around little kids or in just remaining silent. Many of them will still have toys or other paraphernalia from their stunted age of childhood development, and these items usually have greater meaning to them than would be normally felt by a grown man or woman.

**Listen to advice and accept instruction,
that you may gain wisdom in the future.**
(Prov. 19:20)

Read C. S. Lewis's words on "Choosing Hell" from his book *The Great Divorce*:

> The choice of every lost soul can be expressed in the words "Better to reign in Hell than to serve in Heaven." There is always something they insist on keeping even at the price of misery. There is always <u>something</u> they prefer to joy—that is, to <u>reality</u>. Ye see it easily enough in a spoiled child that would sooner miss its play and its supper than to say it was sorry and be friends. Ye call it the Sulks. But in adult life it has a hundred fine names—Achilles' wrath and Coriolanus' grandeur, Revenge and Injured Merit and Self-Respect and Tragic Greatness and Proper Pride.[12]

JOURNAL ENTRY – December 9, 2016

This speaks greatly into the life of a narcissist as they really are children trapped in a grown-up body who want the thrills, pleasures, and privileges of an adult yet also desire and exhibit the freedom, irresponsibility, and coping mechanisms available to them as a little child. Thereby, the man and the inner child are always at war within; yet the true effects of that war touch every area of the narcissist's life and those near the battlefield!

---

[12] C. S. Lewis, "Better to Reign in Hell," in *A Year with C.S. Lewis: 365 Daily Readings from His Classic Works* (London: William Collins, 2013), p. 375.

6
The Reality of Fantasy
(Love Is a Battlefield)

T HE ABUSE OF children in our world is on the rise and continues to escalate at rates that should make the tears flow, the head spin, the stomach sick, and the soul consumed with grief. The reality of this degradation of our most valuable yet vulnerable earthly treasures should bring our hearts and minds into such a place of horror that tirelessly working to eradicate the following sample of shameful statistics should be one of our nation's top priorities!

* Over the past 10 years, more than 20,000 American children are believed to have been killed in their own homes by family members.
* The child maltreatment death rate in the United States is triple that of Canada and 11 times that of Italy. Millions of children are reported as abused and neglected *every* year!
* American children suffer from a *hidden epidemic* of child abuse and neglect.
* National child abuse estimates are well known for being under-reported.
* The United States has one of the worst records among industrialized nations for abuse cases.
* National Child Abuse Statistics—4 million child maltreatment referral reports; child abuse reports involved 7.2 million children, the highest rate of child abuse is in children *under age one.*[13]

I had to stop the research there; my heart couldn't take another minute of such overwhelming sadness, degeneracy, and evil!

---

[13] Michael Petit, "Why Child Abuse Is So Acute in the US," BBC News (BBC, October 17, 2011), http://www.bbc.co.uk/news/magazine-15193530.

I took the liberty of highlighting some above words that I hope you took note of—just one more *hidden epidemic* that is consuming our country and our world. Our culture has obviously lost its way within the many shades of gray. God help us!

A perverse heart shall be far from me; I will know nothing of evil.
(Ps. 101:4)

Being the victim of abuse as an adult yet still feeling so helpless and vulnerable at times over the course of many dark years, it almost consumes me when I think about these injustices committed against the children we bring into this world. The children who feel vulnerable and defenseless because they cannot control their environment or circumstances—nor can they protect their bodies if they are being violated physically and/or sexually—begin their lives with wounds that remain deep within. These are atrocities that no little one should ever have to bear. The subsequent shame, fear, distrust, and agony of conflict these abuses bring upon the tender heart and soul of an individual put them seriously at risk for lifelong scarring from the trauma.

Too many children are also emotionally/mentally abused through consistently harsh and degrading words of anger and criticism, neglect, unfair punishment, and the withholding of words laced with love, encouragement, and kindness. Because they are not able to physically leave their harmful environment or defend themselves, many of them often escape their feelings by controlling their thoughts about what is happening to them. Although young in age and without the words to put context to their emotions, little ones often begin to despise their lives and often themselves because of the vulnerability that renders them helpless and trapped within the cycle of abuse, internalizing the hopelessness of their situation. I believe that even at their young ages, they have an innate instinct that they need to escape their reality in order to survive, yet they also know that they can't survive on their own. Consequently, many children will flee their insufferable situations by altering them in their minds.

When they are old enough to conjure images, the daydreams begin; they take them away to a better place, a safe place without hurtful words, violation, pain, shame, loneliness, isolation, and tears. A daydream can be a wonderful channel and imaginative springboard for dreaming up marvelous advances for our lives. Did not all inventions begin with a thought or dream that was imagined in the mind and then made into reality by an impassioned and creative heart?

In the mind of an abused child, though, their avenue to daydreaming might be fueled by an active imagination or could perhaps stem from a person or place they have experienced that brings happy memories, comfort, and peace. It may center on a character they admire from a television show, movie, or book. The daydream could even evolve around a toy such as a Barbie doll, G.I. Joe, or action figure that they see as beautiful, handsome, and strong. They often reason that because these characters are perfectly formed on the outside, they must be perfect, happy, and brave on the inside. They may gravitate to the hero of a story, the one who always overcomes the "bad guys" and evil as they rescue the weak, hurting, and vulnerable people who cannot save themselves. As a child's painful situation continues to haunt them, they escape more and more into the daydream that they *can control*, and it begins to grow and take form. This "hiding place" enables them to cope with their truth, and in it they find the strength to face another day and keep their hope alive that eventually the abuse will stop or they will be rescued and safe once again.

But if the abuse continues, or even escalates, so will the daydreaming, as it will be on a continuum and become more elaborate as it strokes and soothes their hurting bodies, minds, hearts, and fragile developing egos. Consider this definition of "ego."

Ego
The self, the individual as self-aware; the part of the psyche (the soul) that organizes thoughts rationally and governs action.

Even without a degree in psychology, you can quite easily see how important the proper development of a child's ego is for balanced behavior, rational thought, and a proper evaluation of their self-worth. Also, being self-aware of their place within the family unit and world, as well as developing a healthy understanding of love (both self-love and love cultivated in other relationships) as they mature into adulthood, are crucial to an individual's self-esteem, security, and inner peace.

When long-term abuse continues, during which time the child is still maturing, the coping mechanism of daydreaming, the psychological "escape route," begins to develop a "rut" in the brain. This path eventually leads to the "scenic route," which merges into the world of fantasy and becomes more dangerous.

Fantasy then leads to a much more intense level of the unrealistic than a basic daydream. Another powerful force behind a fantasy is that it stirs up greater emotions, which stimulate the physical body and trigger deep passions and pleasurable sensations in the flesh. So now, as a person begins to feel *mentally* "good," this in turn entices the flesh to feel *physically* "good" and creates a kind of "high." This is why pornography becomes such a powerful addiction because once the mind can conjure images and scenarios that stir the physical body into arousal, the body associates the good mental thoughts and pictures with the good physical feelings, which, in turn, create pleasurable sensations and elevate how an individual feels about themselves in their secret life of fantasy. This becomes addictive because the mind/body connection activates our carnal appetites, which are at the core of all created beings.

Remember, our thoughts fuel our feelings; it all starts in the mind. Fantasy that is used as a daily coping mechanism and escape from negative and often abusive circumstances begins to overpower the senses as it fuels the ego and the self; eventually, it can become that person's perceived reality. Because the fantasy-turned-reality looks and feels so much better than real life, if left unchecked, it will slowly take over the person to the point that the illusion "becomes" their life and self. This begins to completely dismantle the divinely created *true* self and replaces it with a newly created identity that is more preferable to the identity that is oppressed and crushed under the weight of abuse or neglect—or perhaps was never properly developed because of various other circumstances. What initially started as a crutch to cope through the present moment, day, week, year, or a long season of recurring maltreatment, has now become the only way that person can get through life because they no longer know *who they really are*; they only know *who they have created themselves to be*.

I believe this is often where the "objects" or "sources" come into play for a person with NPD. Once make-believe characters and daydreams from childhood are no longer sufficient to sustain the fantasy within the maturing body without giving away the deep insecurities and secret life (as well as the need for developing higher-functioning coping mechanisms when adult life becomes more demanding), the created self—now known as a narcissist—must find an *object* (in other words, their victim). This object must match, as closely as possible, the created image of "self" in their mind. That is why I wrote about a narcissist "shopping" for their spouse or significant other like a car (ownership versus belonging); they know what they need to be able to "stay on the road and keep driving," so they must pick a perfect "make and model" to reflect and uphold the image their superego needs in order to be stroked, sustained, and feeling "high." They try to steal the identity of their *purchased* victim and wear it like a cloak. You can attempt to systematically strip away traits that another person possesses (causing much collateral damage along the way); however, you can never truly "own" something that is the nontangible essence or character of another human being—you can only mimic it and/or have it reflect upon you by close association.

An abused child, whether physically, emotionally, sexually, or a combination of all three, will most likely believe that there must be something wrong with them for another human being to treat them so badly (especially a trusted parent or a person in frequent contact with them). Even as an adult, I struggled for years believing that there must be some terrible reason why my spouse didn't fully desire to see, hear, know, or love me, and intentionally tried to hurt me. At times it made me question myself as a person of worth and feel very unlovable. Shame, loneliness, isolation, and self-loathing often become deep parts of our being when we are treated poorly and even inhumanely. Over time, these bitter roots, which start growing because of an inability to control one's environment, circumstances, or the inflictions forced on the physical body or emotional core, will often foster resentment against the abuser as well as negative feelings about oneself. This, in turn, may fester and deepen from fear to dislike to hate: hate for the abuser and self-hatred. This hate/self-hatred will eventually be projected onto the narcissist's unfortunate "object" (the victim of a victim), both of which are now paying the heavy price for a broken, abusive, and bitter past.

The abused child or young adult (now living with the mental illness of NPD or another psychopathic disorder that falls under this umbrella) will "create" someone in their mind, an illusion they can "become" that they admire and feel good about: someone who is strong, handsome or beautiful, capable, powerful, independent, and in-control. They rise above daily situations and circumstances that make them feel badly, unworthy, unseen, unheard, unknown, and unloved. They need these crucial elements of their essence met, so they create a safe and wonderful place where they can be.

This makes me think of the movie, *The Wizard of Oz*. The victim of childhood abuse and/or neglect becomes like the great and powerful Wizard, controlling their environment as well as everyone around them. Their temporary escape route becomes a permanent residence, and they don't know how to get back to "Kansas" anymore—nor do they even want to! What begins as a child's innocent, yet too often necessary, way of escaping the painful reality of their circumstances—if left unbridled and allowed free rein, becomes a consuming fire. They often fall in love with the created self and begin to worship their own image (become lovers of self). They have "turned the tables" and "changed the rules," now reigning over their own kingdom. They become a "god" in their own little world and fully use, abuse, and manipulate people to stroke an ego that now needs constant validation that they truly are who they believe that they are. Anyone or anything that threatens this reality needs to be pushed away, punished, broken down, destroyed, and eventually abandoned (literally and/or emotionally), replaced, or forced to leave as a means of the narcissist's survival.

I believe that the prideful arrogance of the narcissistic ego is, in truth, held up by incredibly deep and paralyzing fear because if *anything happens* to destroy the false identity, the narcissist believes that they have no true self (no real identity of their own) to fall back on. They know not who they truly are and feel they cannot exist apart from who they created themselves to be. During the course of my living nightmare being married to a person with NPD, I often felt as if I was being consumed, dying, or would "be no more"; that was not a physical death but rather a withering of the heart and soul.

In the mind of an individual with NPD, deeply ingrained within their psyche, it seems that they believe another dark lie: that if the person they have created and based their entire life on is "destroyed" (by learning the truth about them), they will physically die with their fantasy. I can't imagine living within that all-consuming fear and deep self-bondage based on a lie and self-deception. It sadly yet truthfully doesn't surprise me that as statistics of abuse and neglect of our precious children rise to epidemic proportions, the stronghold and dark spirit of narcissism is escalating into an epidemic problem as well. I believe they run parallel to each other, feeding the beast with ever-increasing portions of fuel for the ever-demanding self (ego) that has woefully been misled into its own pit of hell—yet cannot see truth to save itself!

Take no part in the unfruitful works of darkness, but instead expose them. For it is shameful even to speak of the things that they do in secret. But when anything is exposed by the light, it becomes visible, for anything that becomes visible is light. Therefore it says, "Awake, O Sleeper, and arise from the dead, and Christ will shine on you." (Eph. 5:11-14)

The Pendulum: Two Extremes Can Lead to the Same Results

Time keeps on ticking, ticking, ticking…into the future.

I certainly wouldn't put myself in the category of someone who has a high IQ, but I also do not think it takes a rocket scientist to determine that many Americans live a lifestyle of overindulgence. When such a large portion of our citizens pay for a monthly storage unit (sometimes multiple ones) to accommodate all of their stuff, I dare say y'all may need to call the guys from *American Pickers* or *Storage Wars!* One of my favorite sayings on how to live a balanced life is "Everything in moderation."

But in keeping with the topic at hand, I would like to touch on the other extreme of the swinging pendulum that I believe can become a negative influence eventually leading to similar results as that of childhood neglect and abuse: *the overindulgence of a child.* I actually believe that overindulgence could be the fast-track (like the E-ZPass on the Thruway) to developing a narcissistic mindset in a child. Wherein abuse and maltreatment can lead a vulnerable and helpless child to seek shelter within a daydream or fantasy world, the overindulged child often has the fantasy world actually *created* for them. It is given to them on a silver platter. The castle with all of the extravagant toys and trappings of make-believe are placed around them before they barely even learn to walk or talk.

For little girls, the environment comes complete with princess dresses, sparkly shoes, crowns, jewels, magic wands; a princess bed complete with correlating sheets, pillows, wallpaper, curtains, wall hangings; princess toys, movies, books, video games; a princess cake with matching princess plates, cups, napkins; princess pajamas with coordinating bathrobe, slippers, washcloth and towel set; princess chair and footstool, etc. You get the picture.

For little boys, it is the superheroes who are strong and invincible with no limits to what they can do, where they can go, and what they can become. Sometimes their superpowers can even altar and control the minds of others and make them conform to their ways and succumb to their every desire. When did you ever see a superhero who was portrayed as a loving husband or with children they needed to care for and love? No, they are autonomous (one of the number one labels of a narcissist), self-existing, and self-governing as they operate above all restraints, answer to no one, and ultimately live outside of the world's rules and laws that only ordinary people have to abide by. Yes, they are often portrayed as the heroes in the story, but they usually decide the outcome and the fate of others, all within their unlimited forces! And certainly not every man or woman with powers acts as the hero while selflessly defending the innocent, vulnerable, and weak. Too often they abuse their powers and use them for evil and oppression, taking what they want without liability, accountability, or conscience.

In some twisted way, the "bad guy" often begins to garner our approval and/or sympathies for how they turned out as we try to justify their wrongdoing. Somehow we have been duped and lulled into making what is evil, wrong, and unhealthy *look* good, right, and healthy...even educational! We create "good" witches and "bad" witches—yet witchcraft, spells, curses, the occult, astrology, etc., are very real elements that are *not* meant for good no matter how we slice it, dice it, and display it on a pretty princess platter with a cute little black kitty beside it!

> **Woe to those who call evil good and good evil,**
> **who put darkness for light and light for darkness.**
> (Isa. 5:20)

The crux of these words is that I believe, as parents and

caregivers, we need to be more conscious of the influences that we allow to surround and inundate our children when they are at such important stages of their development, which is building the foundation for the remainder of their lives. What we call "child's play," if not monitored and guided within healthy boundaries, could have a much greater and far-reaching effect upon our children's developing hearts and minds (including their egos) than we could ever imagine. Food for thought—what we think is how we feel, and what we feel is how we act!

Before you go throwing this book into the garbage thinking of me as closed-minded, fanatical, or behind-the-times, let me clearly state that I have nothing against cartoons (well, most of them!), Disney movies, fairytales, Prince Charming and Cinderella, action figures, or a cute theme at your child's birthday party. My daughters had Barbie dolls and dress-up clothes, played make-believe, and watched children's movies, yet everything was in moderation. They knew for certain that they were deeply loved, special, and important, but they also certainly knew that they were *not* the princesses who could stomp around the house and demand their *servants* to wait upon them and give them everything that they desired or they would scream, cry, and pout for hours!

Of course, not all children who have been blessed with many nice things become narcissistic in nature. I believe the key to having an abundance yet remaining safe and secure in your own identity is knowing that you are loved, wanted, and cared for within healthy, structured boundaries, all wrapped up in an attitude of respect and gratitude. A child confident that the people in their sphere of influence see, listen to, hear, and know them as a unique individual, loving them unconditionally, has a *realistic* understanding of who and whose they are that fosters security, perpetuates happiness, and instills empathy for others. It is when the overindulgence is used as a *substitute* for time spent together with parents, while *not* receiving nurturing and comfort as well as guidance in building up a healthy self-esteem and respectful attitude, that emotional imbalance and an

68

identity crisis become instilled within their developing heart and mind. Too often, toys, gifts, and extravagant overindulgences are "guilt offerings," and our children know this! They are wiser than we give them credit for!

In my significant experience with children (my own and many others), I have learned that they are often content with very little in the way of material items but desperately need someone who really cares about, believes in, and invests selflessly in their lives. Truthfully, it has also been my experience that overindulgence for the wrong reasons creates the most unhappy and discontent children that I know. This makes my mother's heart very sad because I have found that raising my children has been one of the most rewarding and fulfilling experiences of my entire life, and unfortunately, many parents miss out on the joy of it. Too many children have everything they could ever *want* but are sadly missing what they really *need* to develop and thrive into healthy, well-adjusted, selfless, and loving adults. I believe that individually, within our family units, in community, nationally, and internationally, we can do *so much better* for the welfare of our children—now and for generations to come. I also believe that the most powerful weapon we have in our arsenal to turn the raging tide of narcissism is right within arm's reach and *must begin within our own homes*, by embracing and investing in one unique, beautiful, and treasured child at a time!

7
Ownership Versus Belonging
(The Object—A Possession Without Worth)

THE WORDS "OWNERSHIP" and "belonging" may seem quite similar in nature yet, in the eyes of the beholder, they can be as vastly different as day is from night. You may recall from the beginning of this book that in my marriage I began to feel like an "object" to my husband and not as a beloved wife; however, it would be many years before I ever knew the true nature of a narcissist. As I became educated on this surreal form of attachment, my feelings were affirmed in that the words "object" and "narcissism" often appear together in describing the relationship of a narcissist with their "object" of choice. I believe that having an understanding of the difference between feeling *owned* and feeling that you *belong* is important in both grasping the real character of a narcissist as well as in acknowledging your basic human need to be seen, heard, known, and loved as the unique and wonderful individual God intended you to be.

In ownership, there is a sense of possession, that which exists for or belongs to oneself. The word *possession* means to gain control over property or territory. Many of you who are reading this book *own* the book. You bought it for a price, and now it is your possession; you can do with it what you want. You can take good care of it. You can handle it with gentleness. You can enjoy it and find pleasure in what it has to offer you. You can take measures not to abuse it or tear the delicate pages. You can keep it as a reminder of why you desired it in the first place.

You can also destroy it. You can tear the pages out. You can blot out its words and mar its original beauty. You can hurl it on the floor or against the wall if you are mad. You can throw it away, ridding yourself of it. If you are tired of reading it, you can set it aside and never glance at it again. You can replace it with another book that you think you would enjoy more, one that would fulfill some unmet expectations or desires that this book just doesn't live up to. You can sell it for a price. It is yours, and no one can tell you how to treat it or what you can do with it. It is an "object" at your disposal, to cherish or destroy. You hold this same power and control over anything of which you take ownership.

Now, replace the book with a person, perhaps yourself. *This is the mindset of a narcissist.* The individual they set their sights on is not seen, heard, known, or loved as a person with thoughts, feelings, needs, and desires of their own; they are looked upon as a possession of the one who "bought" them. There can be no real and lasting commitment or attachment to someone we feel we can easily replace if they do not live up to or meet our expectations. In the darkened eyes of a narcissist, you are a possession that they own. They can use you, abuse you, and then dispose of you as they desire. This is the sad yet true reality of the victim of this type of abuse. Can you think of a greater detriment to the heart, soul, mind, and spirit of an individual (especially a spouse) than to be seen and used as an object *owned* by another person and viewed as a possession—arguably a more "sophisticated" form of slavery—knowing that one day you will have outlived your usefulness and be disposed of? This is exactly what happened to me!

> **...stand firm therefore, and do not submit again to a yoke of slavery.** (Gal. 5:1)

JOURNAL ENTRY – December 17, 2014

When I think of him or am near him, I think of only pain; pain in body, soul, mind, and spirit. Nothing more, nothing less...pain.

On the other hand, belonging to someone is vastly different; it is a matter of the heart and mind. The word *belong* means: "to have a proper place (it belongs here); to be a member with." When we feel that someone *belongs* to us, we then feel responsible for their care. For parents, the proper thought and heart toward (a) child(ren) we bring into this world is that they belong to us and are an integral part of our family now. Nurturing, care, protection, provision, and love are paramount. That child has an identity within that family and should feel safe because someone is committed to their overall well-being. They should go through life knowing and believing in their hearts that someone will be there for them in their time of need. This knowledge is extremely important to the proper development of a child and propels them into becoming healthy, balanced, and secure adults.

When a spouse or significant other has fallen to a place of being treated as an object *owned* by another and not *belonging* to that person, it strips away a crucial part of their identity as an individual who is needing and deserving of care, loyalty, and love. This expectation should be a spoken and unspoken essential element of the commitment made to one another. If you feel expendable when you don't perform at the level of another person's unrealistic desires/fantasy, or you can't live up to the expectation of the "owner" or "purchaser," it breeds much fear, anxiety, and insecurity. This will in turn influence every aspect of trust, your ability to be vulnerable, and ultimately intimacy. The object's need for close proximity and intimacy often breeds contempt toward them by their possessor. A process of devaluation is therefore in full operation throughout the duration of the relationship.

Although the object is seen as a possession, it is not prized. The sad truth is that in the eyes of the beholder, *everyone* around a narcissist *is an object*—either a source of narcissistic "ego supply" or cruelly neglected, ignored, and eventually discarded. This is the trunk from which every other malfunctioning branch stems and is the reason why a relationship of any kind with a narcissist ends up as rotten fruit. The simple yet profound difference between these words—to be *owned* or to *belong*—is the *key* to understanding the heart and mind of the narcissist! All other elements of this mental illness will begin to make sense and be made clear under this blazing light of truth.

There is little hope for someone in this world when they realize that they were bought as a possession (like a car)—disposable to the purchaser/owner after being run into the ground, stripped of their original value, and now having too many miles to be traded in. You may feel like you are good for nothing but the scrap yard. Many of you in this predicament will feel as if you have given your loved one (turned abuser) the best years of your life, and now you are left exhausted, empty, numb, confused, angry, and lonely. The thought of ever having the energy to start all over again can seem daunting and overwhelming, I know.

But I can offer you hope if your hurting heart and blurry eyes can focus long enough to see how very precious you are, despite how you may feel at the moment, to God. I can testify that after 25 years of living in the daily drain of my spouse's Narcissistic Personality Disorder, I have been in some of the darkest pits and at the bottom of the dry well, alone and near despair, wondering how I was ever going to get out of the broken mess and recover from all of the damage done to my body, heart, mind, and soul. But I can also speak with certainty that there is no place that you could find yourself— stripped down, beaten, robbed, and left for dead, where your heavenly Father cannot reach and rescue you.

I will never forget the morning I sat exhausted after another sleepless night of tears and anguish in the pit of my soul, when I read these beautiful words from my Father, spoken directly into my broken, lonely, and rejected heart:

> **"Fear not, for I have redeemed you; I have called you by name, you are Mine. Because you are precious in My eyes, and honored, and I love you...."** (Isa. 43:1,4)

Now, I want you to read those words from your Father God spoken about *you,* over and over again, until you own them as His precious child. Tears ran down my tired face as I soaked in the Truth that I was protected, saved, known, wanted, precious, honored, and loved by God. Of course, as a woman of faith for many years, I knew this in my mind, but in the depth of my silent desperation, I finally *really knew it* in my heart! And as I read my Bible, I became very conscious of all of the Scriptures that affirmed that I was a *prized* possession and *belonged* to the family of God. And this *belonging* meant that God was truly committed to caring for me, nurturing me, protecting me, providing for me, and making me feel loved like any good parent would do for their child. He doesn't cast us aside when we fail to meet His expectations, start to "malfunction," grow older, or become weary and empty. It is at these exact moments when He loves us all the more! Here are just a few Scripture verses taken from God's love letter to His beloved children:

* **"...I will not forget you [My child]. Behold, I have engraved you on the palms of My hands..."** (Isa. 49:15-16, bracketed content added)
* **The LORD your God has chosen you to be a people for His treasured possession...the LORD set His love on you and chose you...because the LORD loves you...** (Deut. 7:6-8)
* **...we are the Lord's.** (Rom. 14:8)
* **"I know My own and My own know Me...and no one is able to snatch them out of My hands."** (John 10:14,29) This is a God who will fight to keep you, not let you leave or cast you away!
* **See what kind of love the Father has given to us, that we should be called children of God; and so we are. Beloved, we are God's children now...** (1 John 3:1,2)
* **"Those who were not My people I will call 'My people', and her who was not beloved I will call 'beloved.'"** (Rom. 9:25)

This is just the appetizer, just a small taste of how precious you are in God's eyes as *belonging* to His family and as a *prized* possession in His loving heart. This was a significant turning point in my clearer understanding of how much I was seen, heard, known, and loved by my heavenly Father. This deeper knowledge gave me new hope, value, honor, power, courage, and respect for who I was in His eyes despite the people who still belittled me. Oh, I had years to go yet before God would reveal His plans to move me out of the pain of silent desperation and into the realm of quiet strength, but He was laying the groundwork for His perfect arrangements and timing. In the meanwhile, He gave me all the strength I would need to wait upon Him.

**Wait for the LORD; be strong, and let your heart take courage;
wait for the LORD!**
(Ps. 27:14)

8

Let Me Entertain You
(The Performance of a Lifetime)

"Narcissism is gross hypocrisy
saying one thing while doing another."[14]

I REMEMBER THE day so clearly when I came to the distinct realization, which made me weep great tears of sorrow as well as cry out incredulously, that I had helped create the narcissist I now lived with! Of course, he already had the hidden character traits ingrained in his conscious mind, but they were not yet polished, as he was relatively young by today's standards in both age and life experience when we got married. This was why I was patient and tolerant for many years. By "training" my husband through my words and encouraging him by my actions and character, I unknowingly exemplified how to interact with others in a way that was *normal*, acceptable, pleasing, and garnered him good favor, which stroked his ego and fed the inner beast of narcissism. Once he felt confident that he had mastered the skills needed to fool the people around him and had brought his narcissistic tendencies under very firm control, he felt less and less the need for his now undesirable object—that would be me.

Ironically, as layers of masks were being piled onto the exterior of my spouse, behind closed doors, he began to slowly peel off the original masks he wore in order to catch his beloved "object of supply" and lived more freely in his true character, which was a

---

14 CZBZ, "The Narcissistic Continuum," *The Narcissistic Continuum* (blog), November 15, 2013, https://n-continuum.blogspot.com/2013/11/narcissism-key-from-healthy-to.html.

whole new and disturbing discovery in itself! The void would grow deeper and wider between us as he turned ever more inward and cold toward me, yet worked all the harder to prove to the world that his "fake" identity was the "real" one.

JOURNAL ENTRY — November 22, 2015

I didn't sleep a wink last night, just tossed restless in Your arms and then moved from place to place until I gave up. I thought of the irony of my life with my husband. It—the truth of it—made me laugh out loud. I had groomed the perfect "N" (code I used in my journals for the narcissist). Unknowingly, while trying to support and love my spouse into being a committed and loving husband, father, son, brother, friend, and coworker; I taught him (or sometimes made him feel "guilty"—although I use that word loosely—as actually even in trying to make him feel remorseful or embarrassed for not caring about others, it only served as additional training in "normal," human behavior) how to be the perfect deceiver....yet still he remained completely unmoved and unfeeling under the surface of the mask.

He became "me" by mimicking my actions to receive his ego strokes, and could morph in and out of character at a moment's notice! I taught him so well that he deceives pretty much everyone except the "teacher" now! My eyes have been trained to see behind the masks (only after years of pain, lies, and manipulative abuse) the cold eyes and heart. It breaks my heart that his life is a lie to others as well as to himself. He has spun the web of deception so well that even those with the Spirit cannot discern truth. The cold, hard facts are that—if you are of no use to him for his personal gain, ego strokes, or pleasure—you are of no use! If people only knew what he says about them behind their backs or what he felt about them truly in his heart; they would be sad, appalled, and angry. But I stay quiet usually, as his false kindness makes people feel good, and he actually does nice things in his attempts to manipulate for his benefit. Hard to watch and know; I wish I didn't...but who would believe me anyway!

JOURNAL ENTRY August 3, 2015

Only You, holy Redeemer, could take the insanity of my life and give me the courage to make it look sane for the sake of others who desperately need to think it as such!

As a child, a healthy self-esteem (true self) did not develop in the narcissist so they construct and build up defenses to create a "false self" in public, and therefore the individual will exhibit behavior that is pathological (not real) in nature; someone who is uncomfortable within their own skin and disconnected from their inner peace. This is akin to wearing public masks. Wearing the masks is not only emotionally exhausting, but it also means that the narcissist is constantly on guard at being found out.[15]

These words affirm what I came to recognize in that, after social gatherings or events, the pattern emerged that my husband would disappear almost immediately upon people leaving our home or when we returned home from an outing. He would "check out," either in front of the television or just fall asleep; this would usually last for the duration of the day. I became aware, after many years of these now-obvious patterns, that he was physically, emotionally, and mentally exhausted from "performing" and needed to rest and regroup so he could be ready for the next grand performance when he had to step onto the stage. At this time, though, I still didn't know what lay behind the repetitive behaviors—I only knew the ongoing craziness of it all!

One of the reasons I was the lucky chosen object was because, with my very social nature, I could easily fill in lots of gaps and holes he knew he would leave void if left to perform completely solo, especially while still in the "training" years. If on the rare occasion he was alone with another individual, it would be with someone who could carry a mostly one-sided conversation or was not very social themselves and liked to "vegetate" in front of the television as well. I truly started to dislike social gatherings because I couldn't stomach the performances nor the aftermath of him being even more withdrawn and cold—absent in body, heart, and mind.

Indeed, all who desire to live a godly life in Christ Jesus will be persecuted, while evil people and impostors will go on from bad to worse, deceiving and being deceived.
(2 Tim. 3:12-13)

In the early years of our marriage, I was so hopeful about our

---

[15] Jeni Mawter, "Narcissistic Victim Syndrome - the Fallout of Narcissistic Personality Disorder," SlideShare, August 6, 2013, https://www.slideshare.net/jenimawter/narcissistic-victim-syndrome-a-powerpoint-by-jeni-mawter.

future together. I had so many dreams and plans of how we would nurture, grow, deepen, and explore this wonderful new season of life in this amazing oneness shared as a married couple. But as I touched on in the Introduction of this book, by our one-year anniversary, I had already detected that things were amiss—although I could never have fathomed where the root of my perceptions were stemming from. Before our first daughter was even born, I was already feeling lonely and the twinges of abandonment as he started going away more on the weekends for racquetball tournaments and Guys' Night Out. This left me home alone (after working full-time, long commutes, still in the Active Reserves, and now pregnant) to clean, do laundry, shop, cook, pay bills, etc. As the years went on, I survived by filling the voids with raising our growing family; keeping the house clean and organized, and running smoothly; planning social engagements; homeschooling our three daughters; carting them to extracurricular activities—all while attempting to keep my husband's attention on me, our marriage, and our family. Communication was an obvious weakness, although he was already making the promises that he would try harder at it as he said he wanted to *learn* how to talk better.

> **Like clouds and wind without rain is a man who boasts of a gift he does not give.** (Prov. 25:14)
>
> **For as he calculates in his soul, so is he.** (Prov. 23:7)

It would be many, many years before I would understand that narcissists are *trainable*, not teachable. A performing monkey at the circus can be trained to wear clothes and dance around, shake people's hands, do some funny tricks, and mimic the mannerisms of a person. You can change the cute little guy on the outside, but you can't change the internal forces that cause him—as soon as he is back in his natural environment and among other monkeys—to act like the monkey he is. The same holds true for a narcissist. You can train them to conduct themselves accordingly on the outside when in an environment that warrants them to act a certain way. This performance is not for circus peanuts, but their "treat" is more narcissistic supply in the form of ego strokes. But once they are off of the stage and back behind the curtain, they act like their *true* selves: the self-centered, self-loving, detached creatures that they are on the inside.

I spent years teaching (training, really), thinking, believing, hoping, and praying that it was all just a maturity issue, lack of responsibilities during his upbringing, poor example, a deficiency in discipline, lack of self-motivation, as well as inadequate experience in having to show others basic human kindness. He was a military man; couldn't he be both trained and taught? Didn't he have an ingrained desire to continually grow and learn? When training is repeated over and over, it can be performed on cue. This is what I unknowingly did in my desire to see my spouse become the man I just knew *he could be* if he would only see that we were worth the effort.

But narcissists have no desire for a permanent change of any kind in developing proper emotions, noble character traits, and rational behaviors. They just want to know the "normal" thing to do in any given situation, perform it on cue, and then move past the unpleasantness of the whole charade and get back to being themselves. Once a narcissist has the proper basic training, in time they can act with relative smoothness, especially if their faltering actions are laced with and distracted by developing a deceptive grandiose charm, adding in some humor with a joke or two, and using their good looks (if they are good-looking—but it really doesn't matter because they *think* they are anyway!). Everything becomes situational.

JOURNAL ENTRY — No date recorded

He tries to shroud himself...even going to the point of self-abasement—but it does not reflect the truth and reality of the inner man.

JOURNAL ENTRY — May 30, 2016

I was always there—still am—behind the scenes making it all happen, but I remain behind the curtain. That is okay; I have no real regrets—I really don't! I poured myself into everything, especially our marriage and daughters. The narcissist may take credit and the "bow," but he was never really in the show. Just showed up for pictures and to make all look good for the camera. Always disappearing when the cameras stopped rolling and the audience left. He sits for hours in front of the tv, shows up for dinner, more tv, then goes over to the neighbors to watch more tv, eat snacks and drink beer; back home again for tv, then bed, wakes up, and does it all over again!

In Hannah Whitall Smith's book, *The God of All Comfort,* she quotes the following excerpt, which I found very fitting for the topic at hand:

> A writer once said, "A man can never be more than his character makes him. A man can never do more nor better than deliver or embody that which is his character. Nothing valuable can come out of a man that is not first in the man. Character must stand behind and back up everything."[16]

I could train my spouse to act and do what was considered right, good, and normal behavior under certain circumstances within the scope of daily living, but I couldn't change the true character of the man I loved.

God grant me the serenity to accept the things I cannot change;
Courage to change the things I can; and
Wisdom to know the difference.
The Serenity Prayer

Even in laughter the heart may ache, and the end of joy may be grief.
(Prov. 14:13)

"Host"ess With the Mostest

"Deceivers are the most dangerous members of society. They trifle with the best affections of our nature, and violate the most sacred obligations."
—George Crabbe, English poet, surgeon, clergyman

Over the years, as the bizarre and insane became more

---

[16] Hannah Whitall Smith, *The God of All Comfort* (New Kensington, PA: Whitaker House, 2003), p. 279.

evident in my little world and as the narcissist grew ever more confident in his ability to deceive and still receive his steady supply of narcissistic "drug" (ego strokes and fantasyland), he also became more bold in his parasitic draining of the very host that had been training him. As I became more weak and weary from constant output with ever-decreasing input, the things that once filled me with purpose and outward distraction were coming up short. It would be at this juncture that I truly began to turn more and more to the Lord for help, strength, peace, understanding, wisdom, and love. Where the things of the world left me either empty or barely getting by, God never left me wanting for any good thing to see me through, even if on a moment-by-moment basis. As the silent abuse escalated to new heights, though, in order to survive the assaults upon my person (my high-spirited nature still not completely surrendered yet), I began to counterattack instinctively each impending blow, as I knew my resources and strength were waning. These acts of self-defense would leave me feeling even more isolated in my pain and loneliness by the deceived eyes of others that couldn't see truth and misunderstood what was *really* being played out before them.

> **His mouth is full of lies…his eyes watch in secret for his victims; his victims are crushed, they collapse; they fall under his strength. But You, God, see the trouble of the afflicted; You consider their grief and take it in hand. The victims commit themselves to You; You are the helper…call the evildoer to account for his wickedness that would not otherwise be found out."** (Ps. 10:7-8,10,14-15 NIV)

JOURNAL ENTRY – October 9, 2014

I suffer in silence. My suffering goes unnoticed as it hides behind a smile, a polished exterior, a heart that loves others. The blessing is that I still desire to relieve others who suffer with physical pain, the pain of loneliness and abandonment, the pain of abuse—the endless cycle of control that will not stop; the pain of deceit and distrust; the pain of shame. My abuser is wise; he leaves no outward bruises or scars. He speaks softly but carries a big stick. He beats me with his sly manipulations, quiet deceit, empty promises, bold lies hidden behind convincing words, the hours of loneliness and buckets of tears never cared about as they fell softly down my weary face. His manipulations spread outward like poison gas; invisible and deadly.

Shouts of anger would be better than endless silence. I have helped him be an abuser. I assisted him in his wicked ways by keeping hidden his secret life for the sake of many. It doesn't matter; no one really believes me anyway. The few I have felt I could trust with the truth are still blinded by the easy smile, warm handshake, silky words which tickle the ear, the seeming willingness to help. Oh, if they could see beyond the veil—but they won't. To see what is truth I would have to leave; I am the prop, the costume he hides behind. He knows I am faithful; although I doubt he knows how close I have come to leaving the stage. Only the Master knows the truth; most days this is enough, but sometimes I cave in my weariness. I always regret it; it only causes me more pain when people know and still do not care. So I keep moving forward, one step in front of the other. My faith is my hope and my shield. My life hinges on Your promises and faithfulness and endless love, my Lord God. Help me finish the race. Amen.

A seasoned narcissist will begin to *attack* their host or object more and more in public once they feel that they have built enough of a reputation of being a great, easygoing, charming, fun-loving person. They gain a newfound boldness and freedom to *act* more openly, confident that they can deceive others without raising any red flags upon their person—deflecting the negative attention upon the helpless host who becomes aware that they are trapped in a lose-lose situation no matter which route they take: whether they remain silent or institute a counterattack. I will describe a very common scenario that took place in my personal hell with my narcissistic husband.

He would spend days before some kind of family gathering making false promises, giving me the silent treatment (a favorite punishment of choice), lying about everything and anything possible from where he went during work hours to what he was looking at on the computer just seconds before I walked in and the screen went blank, to being cold in the wake of my tears or hot with anger that I dared to question something that he did or did not do. After 25 long years, the list and the scenarios are endless! By this point, he had barely looked at me or conversed much for days and hadn't given me an honest compliment or word of encouragement, or showed a shred of kindness, much less any physical contact or love.

Then the guests would arrive, or we would attend a social

gathering elsewhere. This very same man who had ignored and victimized me all week would now be hovering over me with unabashed devotion, helping me with my coat, pulling out my chair, complimenting my looks and wonderful cooking (which he had pushed around his plate and barely touched despite my hours in the kitchen—another popular punishment!), telling everyone who would listen what a great wife and mother I was. It was always a nice added touch when he played with other people's children like he was super-dad (even though he had given his children about as much attention all week as he had me), all the while being patient and laughing at all their jokes. He maybe would even help to clean up the dishes or rub my stiff neck, which by now would be extremely tense from trying to keep from screaming, running out of the room, or vomiting because the performance was making me sick!

After years of being expected to play the leading role as actress to the narcissist, my performance was becoming more forced, less convincing, or I just refused to play my part or speak my lines on cue. I would look around at the adoring audience and want to rip off his multilayered masks and reveal the truth, but I would realize that everyone's eyes were too dazzled by the one who played the leading role. Sometimes they were even envious of the recipient of such adoring love and sweet affections. They could only see me as the ungrateful costar who truly didn't deserve to be part of the wonderful show! Their sympathies would only increase and go to the one who worked so hard to win their approval and applause, giving the victimizer a standing ovation while they silently "booed" the true victim off the stage. I would then slink off into the backstage shadows of silent desperation: alone, unseen, unheard, unknown, and unloved. I hoped and prayed that my Father God would give me the grace, tolerance, and strength to go back onto the stage the next time I was called to perform for the sake of our family and others until He rescued me and set me free.

Most victims do not stay in the traveling show as long as I did. They either give up their acting career early, or they get kicked off the stage and replaced by a fresh, new costar who is oblivious to the narcissist's solo performance, eager to just be playing a supporting role next to the charming actor.

JOURNAL ENTRY — December 9, 2015

The sad thing about narcissists that people don't know is that they really don't care about anyone. People are just a source for his narcissistic ego; they have become unaware prey for the predator who is always searching to find people to stroke his ego and false identity. He has become good at following my lead. I am good fuel for his image. Too bad he doesn't care about his image with me. Crazy! I am his image to the world. God help me for helping him live a dual life in which I am the loser on both ends! I wish people could get off the fairytale train and hop into reality. Oh, yeah, my reality is different than others because they only see the side of my spouse he reveals. How special I am to have the "real" narcissistic man all to myself! I see the counselor today. At least she knows what I am dealing with and can listen to my insanity without trying to paint a rose-colored exterior where I have to try to fit into the fake role to make everyone else happy and not upset the applecart of their lives.

Whoever hates disguises himself with his lips and harbors deceit in his heart; when he speaks graciously, believe him not, for there are seven abominations in his heart; though his hatred be covered with deception, his wickedness will be exposed in the assembly. Whoever digs a pit will fall into it, and a stone will come back on him who starts it rolling. A lying tongue hates its victims, and a flattering mouth works ruin. (Prov. 26:24-28)

I thoroughly enjoy and am blessed by the writings of C. S. Lewis, who is often very profound. His way of presenting truth about life, faith, and fallen humanity is always very meaningful to me. I want to share an excerpt taken from a daily devotional that is a compilation of his many works published over the years; his words on understanding evil are as follows:

The right direction leads not only to peace but to knowledge. When a man is getting better, he understands more clearly the evil that is still in him. When a man is getting worse, he understands his own badness less and less. A moderately bad man knows he is not very good: a thoroughly bad man thinks he is all right. This is common sense. You understand sleep when you are awake, not while you are sleeping. You can see the nature of drunkenness when you are sober, not when you are drunk. Good people know both good and evil: bad people do not know about either.[17]

JOURNAL ENTRY — March 18, 2016

I believe this is exactly where my spouse is right now. He used to seem to have a small sense of his negative behaviors (but maybe that was all an act too), but now he doesn't have any conscience about his bad, unethical, and immoral behaviors. He isn't moved in the slightest way by his negative effects on others—especially me. He doesn't even flinch when I know he is lying, although he may break eye contact or fiddle with non-essentials. He has no compassion for people's physical nor emotional pain, even if he is the cause of it. He lives life as if he is above the natural realm of basic human thoughtfulness and kindness. His goal always is geared toward self-gratification..."What's in it for me?" This mindset is so foreign to me; so beyond the scope of my principles and value system. No wonder I feel like I have entered into the "twilight zone" when in his presence. I felt something "snap" into place today, and all of a sudden I let myself feel angry; mad at this whole dysfunctional marriage!

The final common element of human disturbances is "guilt." Guilt is "the sense of having lost one's core role structure." When someone's behavior is not consistent with their sense of self, they are likely to experience guilt. Kelly believed that if a person never developed a sense of identity, they would not suffer from guilt.[18]

This explains the lack of guilt or conscience within my husband or any other individual with Narcissistic Personality Disorder. They have never developed a core sense of self that would solidify their true identity, which is crucial to understanding who they are. This mental deficiency prevents them from having the ability to live in harmony within themselves and with others. There is no governing force besides what they themselves dictate as right, good, and acceptable—and even if that is entirely false, bad, and, in all good conscience, truly unacceptable, it matters to them not! Oh, how my nonsensical life is finally making perfect sense when I look at it

---

[17] Lewis, *A Year with C.S. Lewis.*

[18] Jess Feist, G. Feist, and Tomi-Ann Roberts, "Kelly: Psychology of Personal Constructs," in *Theories of Personality* (Maidenhead: McGraw-Hill, 2018), p. 583.

through the lens of an individual who operates completely without a conscience or sense of personal guilt!

> **O LORD, do not Your eyes look for truth? You have struck them down, but they felt no anguish; You have consumed them, but they refused to take correction. They have made their faces harder than rock; they have refused to repent.** (Jer. 5:3)

JOURNAL ENTRY — March 21, 2016

Dear God: I have been betrayed, lied to, and left alone when I have needed him the most. But there is no repentance, or guilt, or shame. There is no seeking of forgiveness or reconciliation efforts. He says he knows I will eventually leave, but there is no fight or sadness; I guess that is my clearest answer. I need to swallow my pride and accept my losses; I truly have no knight to fight the battle for my love. I see how much of his own pride is involved in this mindset and decision; that he would not feel me worthy enough to fight for—not love me enough to be my hero. He doesn't have it in him, as he is already defeated; the devil has defeated him, and he is down for the count. I certainly have tried to stir him up to be a warrior for us, but he is too consumed with himself and his needs to ever be able to see ours. Sad but true, I need to face it! But I know Your hand is in it all, God; You are sovereign over all. You see the end from the beginning, and I trust in You alone. You have done many beautiful things here and bore much good fruit. I praise You for Your mighty power and gifts of amazing grace.

> "Any betrayal is devastating because it is based on a relationship, often an intimate one. Those closest to you can hurt you the most."
> —Franklin Graham, American evangelist and missionary

Below are more wise words from C. S. Lewis:

> To love at all is to be vulnerable. Love anything, and your heart will certainly be wrung and possibly broken. If you want to make sure of keeping it intact, you must give your heart to no one, not even to an animal. Wrap it carefully round with hobbies and little luxuries; avoid all entanglements; lock it up safe in the casket or coffin of your selfishness. But in that casket—safe, dark, motionless, airless—it will change. It will not be broken; it will become unbreakable, impenetrable, irredeemable.[19]

---

[19] Lewis, *A Year With C. S. Lewis.*

JOURNAL ENTRY – July 3, 2014

The fact is that often when we make a choice out of love, we inadvertently also end up being handed suffering as well; personal pain. I have had to learn to guard my heart from those who carelessly mishandled it, causing it countless breaks, yet at the same time exposing it to new sources of love in order to keep it from becoming hard and cold. I have come to understand that this can only be accomplished through my Lord in Whom I can guard my heart and mind from pain—yet maintain my ability to love anew. I had once feared that I would lose my ability to love because the risk of trying again was just too great but could not deny the God of love who continually "woos" my heart to try again!

JOURNAL ENTRY – November 25, 2015

Lord, I thank You for the hard road, trials, tears, and pain. I pray it is completing Your work in me as it has made me strong in my weakness and reliant on You alone. As Psalm 42 reads: "As a deer pants for flowing streams, so pants my soul for You, O God. My tears have been my food day and night. Why are you cast down, O my soul, and why are you in turmoil within me? Hope in God; for I shall again praise Him." You are my hope in the turmoil within me—a perfect word to describe my state of being. But why? Is it an unyielding, unbroken spirit? Maybe.

Or as came to my mind today the fact that I am trying to live a double life like my husband—but on a different plane. By protecting his wrong and dark behavior before the girls, the family, friends; am I hiding a fox in the hen-house? A wolf in sheep's clothing? By not exposing the truth, I am living a lie—the very thing I detest! Was I feeling noble by protecting his reputation and image and by willing to be a "martyr" for the sake of the girls' safety and peace in order to not disrupt their lives and to keep things "normal" for them while I live in my "abnormal" world of hidden evil? Yes, I will call it evil as it is not of God.

But I want to ask as the Psalmist, "Where is your God?" while I eat my tears, which flow silent streams of pain. Please, Lord God, is it time to speak full truth and throw this blanket off the façade; expose truth in love? They are in denial, I know, and may choose to stay there; but they are also young adults now who need to process and see truth. Of course, I am often painted in a dark light, and I know there are consequences to the truth not received—anger and denial will flow. But anyone who knows me will be able to receive the truth and discern what is real. I can't believe my life is in this place sometimes.

But You write a better story and build better dreams. Help me to be strong in my weakness like Gideon, David, Moses, Esther, etc. I pray, Lord, that I have done more good than harm in showing this patient endurance, but is it time for truth and freedom? Is it time for the narcissist to be exposed and face his choices? I pray I have given it my all—everything I could to be poured out into preserving this unhealthy marriage from the beginning. I pray I have been faithful to the call as wife and mother to the best of my weak state. I praise You for all of the blessings poured out over me and our children despite adversity and tough times. Holy Spirit, Your divine discernment is crucial now. Please guide me in truth and love, and give me wisdom in all my ways that peace may be restored and God our Lord may be glorified! Amen.

> **I will praise the LORD, who counsels me; even at night my heart instructs me. I keep my eyes always on the LORD. With Him at my right hand, I will not be shaken.** (Ps. 16:7-8 NIV)

JOURNAL ENTRY of a vision dated March 29, 2014

In the wee hours of the morning, You gave me this vision with words to help express my feelings about my present circumstances—well, it really isn't just of the present but the past come to light: The visual involved a beautiful diamond ring, and this ring symbolized a marriage. The ring looked perfect, without chip or flaw. Many admired and even envied the perfect symmetry and sparkle of the outward appearance of the unique ring. But it was only a fake. What appeared to be a genuine diamond of great value, was really a fake imitation of the real thing. What appeared perfect and flawless was, in truth, filled with cracks and imperfections, which once exposed, greatly diminished its worth. Oh, how sad the news that what was thought a gem of great excellence was only a shadow of the real thing.

JOURNAL ENTRY — July 7, 2016

I realized this morning that You truly have done much healing already. The bitter resentment is gone and compassion is in its place. How could I not have pity on someone as lost as my husband; so disconnected from himself, others, and You. What a lonely and dreadful place to be; sustained solely on the life-blood of others with no real knowledge of self and the endless cycle of self-induced fantasy to stay afloat in reality. One false move, one faulty step, and he will fall into the abyss of nothingness with no way out.

*Personal Note: Within this chapter I have shared many journal entries that were written during a season of deep personal pain while living in desperation endured as the victim of silent yet very real hidden abuse. Although difficult to share, I felt that these raw words were the best avenue to express what is almost inexpressible to anyone who has not experienced firsthand this secret world behind the veil called narcissism.

Living in Shades of Gray: It's a Slow Fade

Too often, even seasoned Christians find themselves trying to hide from their heavenly Father. Because our thoughts, feelings, temptations, and fantasies are usually invisible to the eyes of the world, we think we have found a safe zone where we can hide behind walls of secret abandon. But if we take God's Word as ultimate truth—and we most certainly should—we would understand

> When the body of Christ begins to accept and live within the "shades of gray," trying to portray to the world one image while living out another, are we not also putting on a performance before God and man?

that there is no such thing as a secret hideaway from the eyes, ears, mind, and heart of God. Psalm 139 so clearly speaks into this truth, a vivid reminder that "no fly zones" are *not* an option in our relationship with our Father. When the Body of Christ begins to accept and live within the "shades of gray," trying to portray to the world one image while living out another, are we not also putting on a performance before God and man?

> **O LORD, You have searched me and known me! You know when I sit down and when I rise up; You discern my thoughts from afar. You search out my path and my lying down and are acquainted with all my ways. Even before a word is on my tongue, behold, O LORD, You know it altogether. Where shall I go from Your Spirit? Or where shall I flee from Your presence? If I say, "Surely the darkness shall cover me, and the light about me be night," even the darkness is not dark to You; and the night is bright as the day, for darkness is as light to You. Search me, O God, and know my heart! Try me and know my thoughts! And see if there be any grievous way in me, and lead me in the way everlasting!**
> (Ps. 139:1-4, 7, 11-12, 23-24)

> **"For nothing is hidden that will not be made manifest, nor is anything secret that will not be known and come to light."**
> (Luke 8:17)

JOURNAL ENTRY — August 1, 2016

While praying the Word and meditating on it, I was asking You, Lord, to bring truth and light to the world and to Your Church—both of which are often trapped in the "gray." To lift the veil of Satan's deceit from the blurry eyes of the unbeliever as well as the lukewarm believer. "I know your works: you are neither cold nor hot. Would that you were either cold or hot! So, because you are lukewarm, and neither hot nor cold, I will spit you out of my mouth" (Revelation 3:16). The word "gray" kept coming. Satan prefers the "shades of gray." There is a very popular book made movie out entitled Fifty Shades of Grey; its popularity says a lot about our culture and nature that is easily lured into the subtle, and not so subtle, enticements of this world. Most of us can perceive the "blackness" of evil and so avoid it...but we are blind to, disillusioned by, and drawn into the shades of gray—feeling the thrill of getting close enough to the edge of darkness to taste the forbidden fruits, but feeling we are "safe" because we don't fully jump in! We play with the gray areas because we believe God's love, grace, and mercy will always cover our selfish desires for the things of the flesh and this world. Like a comforting blanket we can wrap ourselves in when we want it—forgiveness bought with the precious and costly blood of Jesus Christ—to cover our sin and shame when we know we have gone too far; then throw it off when we feel we are in the "safe zone" again.

Satan is wily, often beautiful, and a superb tempter/temptress. "Say to wisdom, 'You are my sister,' and call insight your intimate friend, to keep you from the forbidden woman, from the adulteress with her smooth words" (Proverbs 7:4-5). Who is this temptress with lattice and colored linens and enticing perfume and seductive speech? Satan wearing "shades of gray," sin disguised in beauty.

"As a bird rushes into a snare; he does not know that it (the gray) will cost him his life" (Proverbs 7:23).

"Whoever is simple (lacking wisdom), let him turn in here! And to him who lacks sense she says, 'Stolen water is sweet and bread eaten in secret (the gray) is pleasant.' But he does not know that the dead are there, that her guests are in the depths of Sheol" (Proverbs 9:16-18).

Let me bring You glory and be a warrior and servant leader to rally the "troops" —the Church I love, which has fallen asleep in the gray zone. Amen. *Words in parentheses added.

Faithful are the wounds of a friend, profuse are the kisses of an enemy. (Prov. 27:6)

We live in a time where we don't want to judge the darkness too harshly because we may be forced to look at our own dark shadows and shades of gray that reflect the height (or lack thereof) of our personal measuring rods; I include myself in these words as I am not above temptation. Isn't it better for all if we could just ignore the "Standard" or force it to leave so that we can dim the lights just a bit and lower the bar just a tad or two in order to sleep a little more peacefully at night? And the enemy of our soul arrives shroud like a secret lover, sweet and beautiful, and woos and whispers, "Come, just a little bite…did God really say…?" And before we know it —bit by bit, which is hardly noticeable to self-deceiving eyes—we lower the bar just a fraction more, for there is happiness and earthly pleasure on the other side of the plumb line. No one will really notice. I tried it.

I tried to persuade my lonely heart and anguished soul in this matter so that I could enjoy just a morsel of the desired pleasures of the world, but I could not silence the voice of the Holy Spirit, hush the lie, or make something shameful "clean" through human reasoning. The momentary escape wouldn't be able to drown out the conviction of truth or comfort the conflicted soul. The silent tears that would stream forth through lowered lids couldn't wash away the shame of losing a piece of myself *if* I succumbed to the compromise. My whole life with my spouse had become a compromise: "If I give up this part of me, I get to keep this scrap!" I had my fill of compromise. I could not—nor would not—compromise my eternal soul; isn't it all we really have? **"Do not be deceived: God is not mocked, for whatever one sows, that will he also reap"** (Gal. 6:7). No matter what ground we think we gain when we fly in the face of God's Word and His standards, when we try to force the plumb line to suit our desires and feel comfortable in our many shades of gray, in the end…He will *always* have the final word.

> We have all become like one who is unclean, and all our righteous deeds are like a polluted garment. We all fade like a leaf, and our iniquities, like the wind, take us away. (Isaiah 64:6)

> "Do remember, the only thing that matters is the extent to which you (demons) separate the man from God. It does not matter how small the sins are provided they edge the man away from the Light and out into the 'Nothing.' Murder is no better than cards if cards (a 'small' sin) can do the trick. The safest road to Hell is the gradual one—the gentle slope, soft underfoot, without sudden turnings, without milestones, without signposts."
> —C. S. Lewis, *Screwtape Letters*[20] (paraphrased)

...God is light, and in Him is no darkness at all. If we say we have fellowship with Him while we walk in the darkness, we lie and do not practice the truth. But if we walk in the light, as He is in the light, we have fellowship with one another. (1 John 1:5-7)

Back in October of 2016, I was given a newsletter to read. It was put out by the Lancaster Presbyterian Church (the church I was brought up in, married in, and had our three daughters baptized in), which included a very insightful writing by Pastor Kelly. I had felt led to save it and find much of the content very fitting for the topic at hand as it exemplifies our love of gray. I will share some of his insights as well as quotes he included in his writing directly related to the condition of too many modern-day churches.

> The postmodern shift in the locus of authority *from* parental, governmental, ecclesial, biblical or even divine authority *to* the "self" is the dominant condition of the United States today. The insights of Cornelius Plantinga, Jr., are instructive when he indicates that "in an ego-centered culture, wants become needs (maybe even duties), the 'self' replaces the soul, and human life degenerates into the clamor of competing automobiles...self exists to be explored, indulged, and expressed but not disciplined or restrained."
>
> No one frames the implications of this shift to "self" as powerfully as David F. Wells when he warns that when "self" becomes the center: "Theology becomes therapy...The biblical interest in righteousness is replaced by a search for happiness, holiness by wholeness, truth by feelings, ethics by feeling good about one's self. The world shrinks to the range of personal circumstances; the community of faith shrinks to a circle of personal friends. The past

---

[20] C. S. Lewis, *The Screwtape Letters* (New York: Bantam Books, 1995).

recedes. The Church recedes. The world recedes. All that remains is the 'self.'"

He goes on to write, "The worship of the self is everywhere evident in what anthropologist Thomas de Zengotita calls 'MeWorld,' a world filled with 'millions of individuals *flattering themselves*, each living in its own insulated, personalized world.' "The star of the MeWorld is the self. The self is the glorified object of selfies, Twitter, and Facebook.

Jonathan Edwards identified unregenerate self-love with original sin in his *Miscellanies*. According to Edwards, "self-love minus the influence of the Holy Spirit equals original sin!"[21]

I certainly could not have addressed any of those poignant points better. Narcissism by definition is self-love. It is the adoration and worship of one's self. Unfortunately, it is also rampant within the Church along with its "partners in crime": postmodernism, relativism, materialism, and consumerism—that's a lot of "isms"! I believe, as do many others who are following the waves of current culture, that these *isms* are a great challenge within the Body of Jesus Christ, the supreme selfless One.

One sad statement that I heard from a few fellow Christians as my truth started filtering out was, "Well, aren't *all* men somewhat selfish in nature?" Yes, they are—we all are—but as I stated previously, as ones *called out* to exemplify our Lord who was and is the prime example of *selflessness*, those words should never spring forth from our mouth as an excuse or justification for the abuse of another or for self-exaltation. The only Being who should ever and always be worshiped by those who claim the faith is Almighty God through the name and person of Jesus Christ—Amen! In the song *"What If I Stumble,"*[22] DC Talk makes the connection that being a Christian in word only is not enough. The world can't recognize God if Christians don't live consistently with what they say that they believe.

[21] Pastor Kelly, [Church Newsletter], Lancaster Presbyterian Church, October 2016.
[22] DC Talk, "What If I Stumble?" *The Millennium Collection: The Best of DC Talk*, ForeFront, 2014.

JOURNAL ENTRY — July 4, 2016

Today is our country's 240th birthday. Wow, since our days of infancy we sure have grown into a prodigal child! Once a strong and moral nation under God, we have decayed and declined into a nation under "self," become our own little "gods" with a sad call to "Let the narcissists arise"! God help us! What we really need is a call to prayer as well as repentance and a turning away from evil. We need a revival, a purging, a cleansing fire to burst upon Your church and ignite us once again. Come, Holy Spirit, come in the power of the Almighty; the Lion of Judah who has already defeated the devil and sin that we still cower under and submit to like helpless lambs. Sound the call—Arise, O people of God, and shine forth the light and hope of Jesus to our dying world; our personal hope, our family's hope, our nation's hope, the world's hope.

Psalm 11:3 states, **"…if the foundations are destroyed, what can the righteous do?"** Unfortunately, the foundations of the Christian faith have been targeted for destruction since their beginnings through severe persecution, imprisonment, martyrdom, etc. These forces still rage against the Church to this day. Fortunately, though, as history clearly affirms time and again, something established on an indestructible foundation cannot be destroyed; that foundation is Jesus Christ, and He is the same yesterday, today, and forever (Heb. 13:8).

In the wake of my very difficult and painful walk alongside this epidemic called *narcissism*, I see it also raging across our world—infiltrating our marriages, families, communities, churches, and nations. I believe that we need to sit up and take notice of its destruction while there is yet light and truth to see it as the black spot that it is on the human heart, mind, and soul. The word "Church" is not meant to be just a noun; it is also meant to be a verb, an *action* word—a living, breathing reality. We, the Church Body, need to not just *learn* about our faith, but we need to *be* our faith; not just *look* like Jesus, but *be* Jesus. The people around us don't need to *hear* us talk; they need to *witness* our walk. It is not just about *doing much*, but rather about being *Jesus's touch* on the world. Jesus turned the world upside-down in three short years…let's get flipping!

We, believers and nonbelievers alike, need to throw away our glasses, the ones that taint our view with myriad shades of gray, and see this mental illness in all of its dark forms, attacking from every side without much resistance. This affects each one of us: man, woman, and child. This is not just a social or religious issue but an issue of freedom, justice, peace, and the right to be loved for *who you are* and not what another person deems you to be for their own selfish needs, wants, and desires. It is the right and fight for *all* people to be recipients of basic human kindness in our need and longing to be seen, heard, known, and loved as individuals of great worth!

"You shall love the Lord your God with all your heart
and with all your soul and with all your strength,
and with all your mind, and your neighbor as yourself."
(Luke 10:27)

9
A Spirit of Unbelief
(Our Deep Need to Be Believed and Believed In)

"Real doubt searches for the light;
unbelief is content with the darkness."
—Charles Jacob Mwenda

I HAVE COME to understand through firsthand experience that there are not many things that hurt a victim of any abuse more than to finally muster up the courage and make your already wounded heart vulnerable by revealing the hidden truth of the abuse, only to not be believed. Because I lived directly within my abuser's clever deception and didn't fully understand it myself for a long time, I knew that many people would likely have a hard time believing the truth I spoke, what my life was *really* like and the silent abuse I suffered from my narcissistic husband. Even so, it still hurt deeply when the time of revealing came. It is funny how you can wrap your mind around something, yet you still can't talk your heart around it.

I was kicked so many times when I was already down while bound to my marriage, that to be kicked again outside the direct realm of abuse was almost unbearable. To hear more silence and no words of compassion, and to see the looks of skepticism and unbelief just twisted the knife in me that much more. Now, with all due respect, if you have a history or reputation as a liar, deceiver, a stretcher of the truth, then you should probably expect some questioning looks as trust and character are earned—not free gifts. But if you have lived your life with integrity and built a reputation on a firm foundation as a trustworthy person, then to have people you know and love question your words or your suffering—especially when spoken through tears and obvious grief—is a deep blow to an already open wound.

> **I will walk with integrity of heart within my house; I will not set before my eyes anything that is worthless.** (Ps. 101:2-3)

If you thought you felt alone in your silent desperation and sorrow before, that pain is now intensified by the spurn and spirit of unbelief; feelings of isolation drop to a whole new level just when you thought you couldn't fall any farther.

> **I am like a desert owl of the wilderness, like an owl of the waste places; I lie awake; I am like a lonely sparrow on the house-top. All the day my enemies taunt me; those who deride me use my name for a curse.** (Ps. 102:6-8)

The most commonly used explanation for this unbelief was that they didn't see or hear any of this professed abuse before, nor know of it firsthand. This is where the phrase "hidden abuse" comes from. Do most abusive husbands beat their wives and children at the public zoo? Are loud shouts of verbal abuse usually heard in the local restaurant? Does sexual abuse of children happen on the streets in broad daylight? Are sweatshops operating in the public square? Abusers don't usually advertise or brag about their dark deeds done behind closed doors; that is why it festers and grows like toxic mold beneath the surface of what may "appear" as healthy, normal, and good. Abuse in its multifaceted forms has become such a part of our fallen world that we hardly give it much thought; we sadly almost accept it as "normal" along with so many other evils. But there is *absolutely nothing* "normal" or "acceptable" about any form of abuse against a fellow human being! And taking *any* abuse lightly is not only an injustice but adds enormous insult to the one already injured.

> **A bruised reed He will not break, and a faintly burning wick He will not snuff out. In faithfulness He will bring forth justice.** (Isa. 42:3)

These tender and comforting words are spoken of the Lord Jesus Christ, who is not only a compassionate and gentle Savior, but also a passionate seeker of justice for the oppressed and abused.

Although Jesus was sinless, He understands our pain and suffering for He endured in His flesh the sting of unbelief, rejection, abandonment, ridicule, loneliness, grief, and injustice, not to mention verbal, emotional, and physical abuse. He lived it all and knows it all, much more than anyone else in the world, for He hung on a cross— killed like a criminal—so He could free us from it all!

> **For consider Him who endured such hostility from sinners against Himself, lest you become weary and discouraged in your souls.** (Heb. 12:3)

Even self-inflicted abuse can be disguised and remain hidden for many years. For instance, a drug abuser or an alcoholic can function for years until the addiction grows into a problem that can't be concealed or tolerated anymore. An eating disorder can be disguised well with clothing, excuses, and lies until it becomes out of control and even life-threatening. Someone who self-mutilates can also hide their scabs and scars of pain underneath clothes until a stroke (purposely or not) goes too deep. I have heard of porn addictions going on for decades without exposure; this is an abuse against one's body, mind, and soul as well as anyone else affected by close association. Most all of us have something hidden—many things being rather insignificant, yet others devastating to the individual, to a silent victim, or to the whole family.

A few people have asked, "If this was *really* going on all of these years, why didn't you tell me?" As with many situations, the answers aren't always that easy and are as varied as the circumstances we find ourselves in. Many who are victims of abuse at the hands of their husbands or wives, though, I would venture to say remain silent for the sake of their marriages and families. Most of the women I know are very devoted to their spouses and passionately protective of their children and the stability and security of their homes while raising them; they selflessly suffer for what they hope will be the greater good in the long run. Also, some element of fear *always* accompanies any form of abuse; this adds to the silence of it. I had shrouded my private pain, not for my sake, but for the sake of our daughters and even for my husband's reputation. It was always my prayer that I would find the "hidden key" that would finally unlock the iron door to my spouse's heart and all would be well; then, no one would ever have to know about my abuse and silent desperation lived out behind closed doors. Preserving our marriage and our family was of utmost importance in my life as a Christian; to me, these things were not expendable. My vow was an unchangeable commitment and sacred matter sealed before the eyes of God and man—yet another thing once treasured that has eroded in this modern-day culture that I deem tragic. God knew my heart. He also knew that the only way I would *ever* walk away from the abusive situation was if He commissioned me to go and then paved the way for my freedom.

Let them know that this is Your hand; You, O LORD, have done it! Let them curse, but You will bless! (Ps. 109:27-28)

Another answer to the above question might be, "I tried." In my personal situation I would test the waters from time to time. I would throw out the line with a few words that spoke of my marriage "troubles" or "chronic pain and intestinal issues caused by stress," but if I didn't get a bite (or even a nibble), I quickly pulled the line back in. When you live with someone who doesn't listen to you or ask questions because they don't really care about how *you* feel, what *you* think, or what is going on in *your* life, you develop a real sensitivity to these qualities in others as well. People who have endured some form of abuse or neglect know that when you are already hurting and your emotions are raw and fragile, you just can't open up even the smallest crack in the door to your heart if you think there is the slightest chance of making yourself vulnerable to more pain. It is better to stay safe and suffer alone than to be sorry you put yourself in a position that you sense could cause you more harm than any good.

Many have heard the phrase that pain and suffering either make a person "better" or "bitter." I have found that as the world becomes increasingly harsh and people's lives are more hurried, stressed, and fragmented, selfless love and compassion are in short supply. Many people have become bitter in their hearts. I know the taste of bitterness; it goes down hard and sits in the pit of your stomach like a rock. If you don't expel it, it becomes putrid and rots away at all that is good inside of you. When people find themselves in this place, they become so consumed with their own problems, struggles, frustrations, and personal pains that they can't see outward and into the window of another person's suffering. Truthfully, you really don't need to know many details about a person's life—just look in their eyes, the windows to their soul. If you have eyes that *will* see, no words are even needed to believe a person is in some form of pain or distress.

Jesus has these eyes. I asked Him to give me His eyes, His ears, His hands, His tender heart, and His wisdom and knowledge so that I could know and understand a fellow traveler's pain. I believe that only through Jesus and the new heart that He alone can give us, can a person become *better* in their pain. And then, even in the midst of our own grief, pain, loneliness, rejection, abandonment, etc., our hearts can be opened outwardly to see, hear, know, and touch the hurting places of our fellow man—our neighbors. If we allow them to, our needs give us the knowledge, wisdom, compassion, and love to first recognize the need of another, then spurring the desire to act in a selfless way to relieve it, if even the slightest bit.

Bear one another's burdens, and so fulfill the law of Christ. (Gal. 6:2)

You can't really see, hear, or know a person's pain and suffering unless you are willing to step into it—to get down in the trenches with them in the midst of their battle while still fighting your own. But this step is a dangerous one that many people today, in our hurried, busy, and self-consumed lives, will not take because knowledge equals responsibility. This could then lead to a form of commitment some do not want to embrace. Hence, we stay on the fringes of others' pain while wearing "rose-colored glasses" and stick to "safe" conversations: platitudes without depth or commitment. And so the silent suffering goes on. Millions of people live day after lonely day feeling unseen, unheard, unknown, and unloved. But the Lord—He *sees all, hears all, knows all,* and *loves all.* He is just waiting for you to come.

> **"Come to Me, all who labor and are heavy laden, and I will give you rest. Take My yoke upon you, and learn from Me, for I am gentle and humble in heart, and you will find rest for your souls."** (Matt. 11:28-29)

JOURNAL ENTRY – August 12, 2013

Only You see my inner pain and struggle. Even those close to me only see the outside, which usually appears healthy and strong. But You see truth. You see the games I am dealing with, the manipulation, and the constant drain on my soul. You see behind the mask the other wears that fools the world but can't fool the Spirit. You revealed this ugly truth to me because I asked You to. Now I desperately need You to help me live it out as this has severely shaken my hope—the hope that has kept me moving each day. I have been the glue that has held it all together, but I am coming unglued. Stay very near, for only in You do I live and move and have my being. Show me the way, and then give me the strength and will to follow it. Amen.

The good is possible only in the light of truth. Not truth as it is defined today by personal preference or popular consensus, but truth as it is, independent from opinions and emotions. And where goodness and truth exist, there you will find beauty.

We were created for a purpose. That purpose is not left to chance or whim, but was determined by our maker and written in our nature. Our purpose is to seek truth in order to discover and to act on what is good and beautiful in this life.[23]

---

[23] Excerpt from Patrick L. Sajak, Vice Chairman, Hillsdale College Board of Trustees; address given on May 27, 2017.

To Believe or Not to Believe, That Is the Question: Our Inner Conflict

I believe; help my unbelief!
(Mark 9:24)

You may be asking yourself why I am spending so much time talking about this subject of belief when it may seem somewhat irrelevant to the topic of this book. But for someone who has walked in the silent desperation of abuse or neglect, whether or not someone believes their claims or believes in them, is very relevant to their rescue and journey toward healing. A person's source of hope—and even the possibility of rescue—is centered on someone else seeing or perceiving their dire need, hearing their pleas for help, knowing they are in trouble, and acting upon that knowledge with discernment. They need people to believe that they are *worthy* of being saved. As I stated beforehand, it is detrimental to the heart, soul, mind, and spirit of a victim of abuse—when they finally have the courage or opportunity to reveal their suffering or to cry out for help and understanding (especially to those who know them)—to have their need and pain dismissed by doubt and unbelief.

So what do you do in this situation when you are asked to receive and believe a claim for something you have not witnessed with your own eyes, nor heard with your own ears, nor known through firsthand experience? I think you need to ask yourself the following questions:

* Who is this person making these claims?
* I may not have seen or heard these things they speak of, but do I *know* this person?
* Do I know this individual's character and history, and how they have lived out their life before me?
* What have I heard from their mouth and seen with my eyes in the past?
* Is this individual prone to rash decisions, gossip, telling tales, and unreasonableness?
* Are most of their other relationships harmonious or volatile?

105

* Can I believe this person because I believe *in* this person?
* Have they earned my trust, and/or have I entrusted them with something important and personal to me in the past?
* If they are a professed person of faith, have they lived out their faith before me?
* Can I perceive that the emotions and pain exhibited by this person are genuine?
* Would this individual make themselves so vulnerable before me, lay their reputation on the line, for a lie?
* Does the exposure of what is claimed have an advantage or disadvantage to them personally or to their family, to their immediate and future situation?
* Does the revealing bring more loss or gain?

If you can't seem to deem the claim as advantageous to the confessor, and can't really pinpoint a viable reason to not believe *in* this person through personal knowledge and experience, and knowing that almost all forms of abuse are hidden, could there then be a deeper reason or stronghold for your unbelief? Is the lack of compassion rooted deeper than you would like to admit? If you find you have a spirit of unbelief and still can't believe *in* someone who is worthy of your trust and support, then I both encourage and challenge you to ask yourself another important question: Why?

At this moment you might be thinking, "This woman asks too many questions. Why is she making this book about *her* personal situation now a source of *my* own inner reflection?" You might even close this book right now and throw it in the recycling bin or use it for kindling. But I hope not because I believe these are important questions for all of us to be asking ourselves, including me. I will share my own honesty regarding this topic. At one time, dealing with the response of others' disbelief *in* me would have been rooted (at least in part) in pride. Thoughts like this one would have invaded my pricked heart and inflated ego: "Don't you know what kind of person I am by now? Haven't I proven my trustworthiness to you? How could you believe him over me?" I would have felt justified in my thoughts and feelings because I had always tried to live my life as a "good" person (those are dangerous words and thoughts that stem from a deceitful heart!) and sought to treat others in the same way I desired them to treat me—and we should.

But then the conviction came into my prideful, hurting heart that, no matter how hard *I tried,* apart from Christ, there was no genuine "selfless" good in me.

"No one is good except God alone." (Mark 10:18)

And though I had submitted this part of myself that I did not like to the Lord, down in the depth of my fallen human heart, some remaining residue of these sinful thoughts still lingered in the dark. But I can tell you—speaking for myself, of course—that when (after almost 25 years of marriage) my husband could barely hide his relief that I was finally leaving and practically held the door open for me, there really weren't many viable traces of pride left inside me. I was deflated and at the end of myself. Yes, I still had self-respect; I always managed to hold onto that. But by this time, I didn't even have the extra energy for something as strong as pride. No—just more pain, adding insult to injury, and more rejection and abandonment.

I believe that we all should take the time to reflect on our own actions and reactions, and what is behind the thoughts and feelings that stream forth from our hearts. When we have a hard time believing what someone claims to be true, what is compelling our reasoning—and, if relevant—our unbelief in them? As in my case, I believe many people react as they do from the same root of pride. In the instance of a person with Narcissistic Personality Disorder, because of its bizarre nature, which is covered with layers of masks to disguise a person's true self, many people are incredulous that someone could have "pulled the wool" over their eyes for so long without them ever detecting it. Trust me: There isn't anyone who doesn't want to admit that truth more than the victim who fell for the narcissist in the first place!

Victims can often spend years berating themselves for being

played a fool and for falling for such a scam before they can make peace with themselves. To think that someone we trusted and maybe even came to love could purposely trick us so cleverly for their own selfish gain is very insulting and hurtful; the victim knows these feelings all too well. This is one of the things that really got under my skin once I knew the truth that my spouse was playing with the hearts, minds, and trust of others—people I knew and loved. It tore me up inside. People only saw my displeasure and, because they couldn't understand or consider the source of it, I knew they often labeled me as a controlling and intolerant wife.

I would be remiss if I wrapped this chapter up without including the following testimony.

As a woman of faith, I have been blessed with an amazing circle of Christian friends—sisters in Christ—who have literally prayed me through this most challenging and life-changing season of transition. But even with the closeness we shared, it was still a slow and cautious process to finally reveal the full truth of the state of our marriage (the mental illness behind the mask), as well as the anguish and spiritual conflict I was in. That, in itself, reveals how very deeply a person enmeshed in this type of disorder begins to be wary of anyone or anything that could cause them one more ounce of pain, feelings of rejection, or unbelief. It was in my sheer desperation, having an acute understanding that I could not get through the coming changes and challenges in my life without outside support, that I confessed the whole truth. And their reaction? Nothing but the most beautiful outpouring of compassion, support, loving-kindness, hugs, tears, and prayers.

What caused this acceptance of truth when not one of them had personally seen or heard any of the silent abuse I divulged about a man they all knew to some degree? The answer: They *knew* me. They had observed my character inside and outside the church. They listened when I spoke and weighed my words. They knew my deep commitment to my husband and love for our family, as well as my love and commitment to each of them. And though I often struggled with my flesh, they knew my deep love for God and my devotion to Jesus Christ, my Lord. I also came to realize that it is much easier for Christians to believe in that which is not visible, as the essence of faith is believing in that which is unseen, unheard, and unknown except through spiritual eyes, ears, and an enlightened heart. I will always be deeply grateful for these amazing sisters and friends who *believed* me and *believed in* me at such a crucial time when I needed both!

> **Now faith is the assurance of things hoped for,**
> **the conviction of things not seen.**
> (Heb. 11:1)

> **Jesus said to him, "Have you believed because you have seen Me?**
> **Blessed are those who have not seen and yet have believed."**
> (John 20:29)

10
Stolen Identity
(A Fox in the Hen House)

**"You shall not steal; you shall not deal falsely;
you shall not lie to one another."**
(Lev. 19:11)

LIVING LIFE UP close and personal with an individual who has a
Narcissistic Personality Disorder systematically strips away the
identity and self-worth of the victim (spouse, significant other, child,
etc.), and adds a whole new dimension to our modern-day concept of
identity theft. The objective of the narcissist is to plunder as much of
the victim's "goods" as they feel are of value to them. For any readers
in a relationship with a narcissist, this would include all of the
character traits of yours that they most desire to claim as their own,
all while trying to project back onto you (the target of their warped
objective) all of the weak and unsavory character traits that they
despise within themselves. The longer you are in a relationship with a
narcissist, the more you will begin to see and experience the
calculated robbery of your unique identity. They may begin to use
words and phrases that are common to your vocabulary and style.
You will most likely recognize this immediately because they will
sound foreign coming from their mouth.

A narcissist will also begin to mimic your actions and
reactions in certain situations when they realize that they produce
positive results or well-supply their egos. You eventually become their
teacher as to what are the "right" and "good" ways in which a *normal*
person with a *conscience* would or should act or react in a particular
situation. These spontaneous reactions are not natural to a narcissist,

who is programmed to respond only to their own selfish needs and desires. They are not correctly connected to their own emotions and thereby can't recognize the natural response that should emanate from them toward others. Over time, if you stay in the crazy relationship long enough, you will feel as if you are having conversations with yourself instead of with someone with their own thoughts, ideas, style, and personality. Your thoughts become their thoughts, your feelings become their feelings, and your opinions become their opinions—yet without any real depth of personal connection, passion, or understanding. For example, if I stated an opinion about a political stance, my husband would wholeheartedly agree. If I changed my opinion about the exact same stance the next day (which I did from time to time just to test his response), he would agree with it just as wholeheartedly. This became a given in any sphere of interest; it made conversation dull and empty of any real exchange, depth, bonding, or intrigue.

One thing most narcissists will *not* do is show any esteem for or promote you in any way, *unless* it benefits them in some manner. They do not want you to have any sense of who you are or your own worth or true identity, apart from what they are "creating you to be" based solely on their personal needs and for perpetuating their "false" identity. If they do validate you, it is for the sole purpose of later tearing you back down. This makes them feel powerful and in control of the very essence of you. Sometimes, though, they will promote you or give you praise in public arenas to prove to themselves—and any audience at the time (whether personally known or unknown)—that you are worthy of being with them. This show of attention is really only used to elevate and stroke their ego as having "caught" such a wonderful trophy, thereby attaining the status of a lucky and loving husband (wife, significant other, etc.) and/or devoted father (mother)—yet another mask and act of deception.

JOURNAL ENTRY — March 23, 2015
As my identity was slowly stolen from me, my strong spirit was the only shred of who I once was; I clung to it like a child clings to the one thing that brings them some measure of comfort and security.

It would be many years before I fully realized the depth of the invasion of my person, which is by definition, my personality, my "self." By the time I truly understood how thoroughly I had been plundered, I was quite empty and drained of who I once was as an individual. If any of you reading this has ever been robbed by a thief who invaded your home or other personal belongings, you know the feelings of vulnerability, violation, and loss. I remember the strangest sensations that came over me when I was a young girl and my grandparents' home had been broken into. Drawers were dumped out all over the floor, and the contents of cupboards and closets were strewn everywhere; it seemed that every square inch had been rifled through and stripped of value. It was truly frightening and made me feel sad, mad, and numb all at the same time. These objects were such a part of my grandparents' lives; irreplaceable items that were worked hard for and saved for (such as family heirlooms). The remains were carelessly discarded as worthless by the detached individuals who had invaded. Many items that were valuable to my grandparents, which were of sentimental more than monetary value, were taken or broken and could not be replaced. They never felt safe in that house again and moved shortly thereafter.

Similarly, when a person is violated in any way, there is always a sense of loss...whether physically, emotionally, mentally, spiritually, or some combination. A part of my grandparent's lives and identities had been stolen, and all that was left behind lay stripped and abandoned by the thieves who discerned what was of value according to their own selfish needs and wants. Likewise, a narcissist ransacks your identity, steals what they believe has the most worth to themselves, and then leaves scattered behind all of "you" that they do not deem valuable or relevant to their created, false identity. This is how I felt as the victim of my narcissistic husband, except that the thief was not an unknown stranger without connection to my life and heart.

I had lived beside him all of those years, entrusting him with anything of value that I had to offer of myself, only to discover that I had been robbed and left stripped of almost everything I had been so willing to freely share with him in the building up of "us"—not the breaking down of me. If it had been a one-time bank robbery, that would have been easily noticed; however, it was more like a trusted employee who works for a successful company for many years and who *appears* to be loyal, yet is actually slowly stealing the company's precious assets and putting them into their own private account. The drain is calculated and slow in order to not alert suspicion until the day the bottom drops out and the company owner realizes that they have been scammed all along!

JOURNAL ENTRY – March 15, 2015

My main observation is the truth that I am almost unrecognizable to myself. Much has been stripped away by the Lord, and that is good. But much has been stripped away from my husband, and that is bad and has left me with an identity crisis—"Who am I now; where did Deborah go?" This is a narcissistic characteristic; to strip their "source" of their identity—their person—and take it upon themselves as they have no identity of their own. You do not readily see it happening and then one day you wake up to find that you are missing. It is like a slow leak; a dripping away of yourself until you realize your well is dried up.

Added later that same day:

"The greatest form of punishment that can be handed out to another human being is not acts of aggression, but to be ignored and to be subject to the slow, painful effect of neglect. This destroys the other person. It makes the other a nonperson."[24]

Healing With Hope: Finding Yourself Again

> "I once was lost, but now am found; was blind but now I see."
> "Amazing Grace" by John Newton

---

[24] This was an excerpt from a devotional I added in my personal journal but didn't record the name of the person behind this profound statement. It is extremely insightful and offers truth that deeply touched my sore spots.

So how do we retrieve that which has been stolen? Well, it is pretty difficult but not unheard of. Occasionally you hear of a happy ending in which stolen items are either returned because of guilt or reward, or because of hardworking police officers or detectives who track them down. Unfortunately, retrieving the stolen identity of the victim of a narcissist is not so easy. First of all, it is not a tangible thing that can be found and returned like a stolen wallet, jewelry, or car. The attempted robbery is of the invisible essence of a person, their unique character, who God created them to be. Stolen along with that are their hopes, dreams, peace, happiness, years, and often their health and sanity, to name just a few. The ability to trust again, and to allow themselves to love and be loved, is sometimes hindered for the rest of their lives. The dissolution of a marriage or long-term relationship resulting from the fallout of a narcissistic union, often leaves deep wounds within a victim's broken heart—wounds that never quite heal. But I am here to tell you, "Do not despair!" There is help available to you in two spheres: the world's remedies and that found within a living faith. I would like to speak into both realms, as it is my fervent desire to reach *all people* who are lost in silent desperation and to help them to find hope, healing, and strength again!

As I wrote earlier in this book, narcissism has become such a problem in our modern culture, growing to epidemic proportions. This, of course, has spurred the medical community into action. Psychologists, psychiatrists, and trauma counselors are seeing the results of this devastating mental illness as more and more victims are seeking treatment for the pain, loss, and brokenness left in the aftermath of this anomaly. As I also stated previously, professionals working in the mental health field are recognizing this victimization as definitive abuse and have started treating it as such. There are many licensed therapists who are specially trained in Narcissistic Abuse Recovery and will often recommend, in addition to any one-on-one counseling, support groups with others who have been in these unhealthy relationships.

"Processing the unreality of a 'fake relationship' is one of the first steps toward progressive action."[25]

For me personally, facing this truth about my marriage and life was extremely difficult, yet it was also a positive step toward seeking answers and avenues of healing. The main focus of restorative healing in the medical realm seems to be psychotherapy, grief work, and trauma recovery. Also, "understanding the elements of the toxic relationship helps so that patterns are not repeated in the future."[26] The victim of a person with NPD can exhibit one or more of the following primary symptoms:

* Disassociation (to disconnect or separate)
* Trauma
* Post-Traumatic Stress Disorder (PTSD)/flashbacks
* Avoidance of personal interaction
* Anxiety
* Anger and bitterness
* Sleeping and eating difficulties
* Memory loss or impairment
* Constant fatigue
* Depression
* Lost sense of self
* Confusion
* Hopelessness
* Loss of interest/detachment
* Self-harm

During the last few years when I was still living within the confines of this mental madness, I went to one counselor who didn't seem to take my husband's Narcissistic Personality Disorder seriously (I saw him only once!). Still another counselor took it very seriously and knew a significant amount about what it was like for me living in the midst of it on a daily basis. What a cool drink of water that was

---

[25] Contributed by Andrea Schneider, "Recovering from Narcissistic Abuse, Part I: Blindsided," GoodTherapy.org Therapy Blog, June 17, 2013, https://www.goodtherapy.org/blog/blindsided-recovering-narcissistic-abuse-relationship-0607134.

[26] Schneider, "Recovering from Narcissistic Abuse, Part I: Blindsided." Another helpful website: https://www.linkedin.com/pulse/20141030165049-141613845-narcissistic-victim-syndrome-and-how-to-help-victims-heal/

for this parched and weary soul! One thing that an informed and sensitive counselor will recognize is that this abuse is a serious stripping away of a victim's identity, and one should "first and foremost, always *believe* the victims. Never blame them or discount their stories."[27] As I wrote in the previous chapter, I know the insult (to what is already an incredible injury) that is added to a victim when they are not believed, believed *in*, or taken seriously. Many professionals have made great strides in tackling this very complex and multifaceted mental illness, and I applaud their dedication and efforts in helping and healing the victims of this often-debilitating abuse.

As a veteran of this abuse (not even knowing what many of my symptoms were related to for almost 20 years), I had to take the "scenic route" on my road to healing. Even though I was a woman of faith throughout those many years of abuse (and subsequent physical and emotional ailments), I didn't initially turn to my faith for healing of the body—only for strength and healing of my heart and soul. When I sought treatment from traditional medicine, more often than not, my symptoms were treated as independent issues instead of professionals looking at me or them as a whole. When I needed care and relief for physical pain, physicians looked for injuries of the body. MRIs, x-rays, and CT scans revealed many physical problems that were often labeled as injuries from my time in the military as well as the repetitive physical work I had always done. I had chronic intestinal problems that were sometimes debilitating in nature as well.

As my life became more hectic, ministry calls more challenging, my marriage more stressful, and the manifestation of the bizarre more frequent, my symptoms in every realm escalated to points where I could barely move or breathe without some form of pain. I was eventually diagnosed with severe acid reflux and celiac disease and put on a special diet. I also suffered on and off for years with insomnia, mild bouts of depression, issues with anxiety,

---

[27] Donna Hines: narcissist survivor, speaker, writer, and advocate for the abused.

restrictive breathing, and chronic fatigue. It took some time for me to understand that most of them were rooted in long-term abuse. Of course, I can't blame all of my medical issues on abuse, but it became a prevailing factor in not being able to achieve prolonged physical healing or being well in mind, heart, and soul.

As the medical community became perplexed and sometimes frustrated with my inability to achieve lasting pain relief and wholeness, they began offering me fewer natural options and more drugs to either cover up the pain or help me deal with the emotional aspects of my declining health. At times I became very thin, to the point where family, friends, and acquaintances would look at me with expressions of shock and worry. I knew they were concerned that I had an undiagnosed illness I was dying from—and I was—but the outward appearance of my flesh was only the visible manifestation of an invisible mental illness causing my heartache and soul pain. Although I was not a fan of prescription drugs and often sensitive to over-the-counter medication, I briefly experimented with some prescribed medications to see if they would help me function at a higher level. But they always made me feel worse, and I could never quite make peace with that course of treatment. My philosophy has always been "let's get to the root of the problem" and not just cover it up to relieve my symptoms.

The same was true with the emotional aspects of my healthcare. Often the world tells us we need to use the "power of positive thinking," and this is certainly one key to better health and healing in every realm. I am by nature a very positive person, and that is why being subjected to such a negative atmosphere was so difficult. I would fight daily against the dark clouds in an effort to let the sun burst through into our home and lives. But when I was at my lowest points and had to confront the attacks of the enemy every day, I had barely enough energy to muster up sufficient strength to get out from under the covers and slide off the edge of the bed—much less enough power of positive thinking to get me through a whole day!

As the long-term abuse began to affect my memory and ability to think clearly and stay focused, some days I had to really concentrate to make a pot of coffee, take a shower, do loads of wash, pay bills, and think about dinner. The brain power I needed to homeschool our three daughters was enough to drain the already low wattage. Those who suffer from insomnia, chronic fatigue, daily physical pain, and anxiety mixed with depression know the battle each day can be just to survive. I praise God for the warrior spirit He gave me, which kept me marching on until such time when I was able to fully yield my spirit over to His authority, strength, care, and healing.

Although I think there is a time and a place for prescription medication to help us through painful, difficult, and low seasons, I am also a fervent advocate for people to live in freedom whenever possible because they have conquered and/or been healed from that which kept them in pain and bondage in the first place—not to just numb the physical and emotional pain with temporary relief when there is a greater solution. The whole purpose of this book is to offer those who are in *any kind* of bondage—be it abuse in various forms, pain, oppression, neglect, addiction, fear, etc.—true freedom! There is a huge difference between really living and just existing, between true freedom and short-lived moments of escape. [*Side note:* Several years after I was diagnosed with celiac disease, in conjunction with other autoimmune disorders, I began to reject the "claim" of disease upon my body. As my faith deepened, so did my understanding that Jesus bought and paid for not only our salvation but also the healing of our illnesses and diseases:

Bless the LORD, O my soul, and forget not all of His benefits, who forgives all your iniquity, who heals all your diseases. (Ps. 103:2-3)

After I had been diagnosed, yet before I was rescued from my abusive marriage, I had been retested and completely cleared of celiac disease. Many of my other chronic symptoms have since been eradicated. I strongly believe that entrusting my health into the Lord's healing hands and my eventual removal from the toxic and abusive environment I had lived in for so long were the key factors in my recovery. This is just my personal testimony and not indicative of the depth of another individual's faith, belief system, or medical circumstances.

"I came that you may have life and have it abundantly."
(John 10:10)

"So if the Son sets you free, you will be free indeed."
(John 8:36)

JOURNAL ENTRY — March 17, 2015

I turned a bend in the road this week. I still cannot see any end to my pain, but I trust that You are there going before me; removing traps, debris, and evil. You are my divine provider and protector; I will not fear. You are giving me back my identity and preparing me for a new season of service and grace. I do not want to waste another day, month, year, thought, or unheard word. You are Jehovah Rapha our God who heals.

Mirror, Mirror, on the Wall...

How do we reclaim who we are? How do we find ourselves again? How are we able to look in the mirror and say to our reflection, "Hey, I know who you are! Welcome back! I missed you!" A mirror is a funny thing; it compels some to look into it and others to turn away. Mirrors say a lot about how people view themselves, both outwardly and inwardly. Mirrors reflect the true image of a person, like a camera captures only what it sees on the outside: the exterior of a person, place, or thing. But the mind can trick the eyes to see what isn't really "real," and our perspective of truth can be easily distorted. This happens when a person develops an eating disorder. I know several lovely ladies who succumbed to this devastating and sometimes fatal disorder because they couldn't see their unique beauty but only an unrealistic reflection of their physical form; many inner and often deeper mental and emotional strongholds accompany their reflected image. When we try to imitate what the world portrays as the "perfect" man or woman, not only is it an unrealistic pursuit, but it is also shallow in nature and of no lasting worth. The answer to our identity being reclaimed isn't found in the outward reflection—although to see a sparkle in your eyes again and a smile on your usually sad and drawn face is a good outward sign of an inward renewal process taking place!

Truly knowing who we are again after we have been robbed of our identity must come from deep within, at the core of our being and existence. Too many people, both Christians and non-Christians alike, connect what we *think* is our true identity to that which defines us on the outside. Do we wear the "right" labels, live in the "right" neighborhood, drive the "right" vehicle, send our children to the "right" schools? The outward labels that can overshadow our true identity are not always sewn onto our clothes, printed on our purses, visible on the watch we wear, stitched onto uniforms, pinned to fabric, or hanging around our necks. Often they are letters added before or after our names or nicely imprinted on documents hanging in frames on the walls of our home or office. When serving in the military, identity is often associated more with a uniform, hats, bars, stars, and stripes rather than with the man or woman wearing them. I am not implying that there is anything wrong with these labels that reveal what a person *likes, has achieved,* or *does,* but they do not define who they truly *are.* We need to get beyond the exterior and begin to explore the interior of people; this is necessary if we are to see, hear, know, and love one another. We must also have this crucial awareness about ourselves.

If outward labels and identifying factors are all you really know, even about yourself, then what do you do when they are stripped away, stolen, or abused by a narcissist or other individual who ravages your identity? Who are you after being drained, discarded, and abandoned like the used-up host of a parasite? Who are you when you age and youthfulness is a past memory, are laid off or fired, divorced, widowed, retired, become impoverished, or are marred in some fashion during the course and harshness of life? How do you find yourself again when you're empty, alone, and stripped bare of who you once were—lost in your vulnerability, hopelessness, and pain caused by another, circumstances, or personal choices? Unfortunately, I don't really have a good and solid answer to this question for those without faith in Someone (God) who is greater than this life—often one of perpetual sorrows amid a sprinkling of happiness. I looked at the things of this world and found them wanting. Yes, they can offer temporary pleasure and distraction, and can numb our hurting hearts. But when they leave, run out, wear off, or chain themselves to our ankles like shackles, they become just another form of pain, misery, and bondage. And I longed to be free—my heart and soul continually cried out, desperate to be restored to wholeness and freedom!

> **Oh that I had the wings of a dove! I would fly away and be at rest.** (Ps. 55:6)

All I can offer to others who walk in my worn-out shoes is to share what I did, how I survived my identity crisis. I finally stopped fighting and running away from the problem. I turned around, ran toward, fell on my knees, and laid down my exhausted head, crying upon the lap of the One in whose image I was made in: my Father and my God. I went to the *heart* of who I was, who I was created to be like. The only true reflection of myself was and is found in Jesus Christ, the visible incarnation of His Father, our Father.

> **Then God said, "Let *us* (Father, Son, Holy Spirit) make man in our image, after our likeness." So God created man in His own image; in the image of God He created him; male and female He created them.** (Gen. 1:26, 27)

This is the *only identity* that is truly safe, that is woven into the fabric of our very being. I learned, the hard way, that it can be trampled upon, damaged, tainted, marred, scarred, and hidden, but it *cannot* truly be stolen!

> **For You formed my inward parts; you knitted me together in my mother's womb. My frame was not hidden from You, when I was being made in secret, intricately woven in the depth of the earth.** (Ps. 139:13,15)

122

We often have to peel away and relinquish many layers of masks, labels, titles, worldly possessions, false images, and negative experiences to get reacquainted with the core of who we are as we fight our way back to reclaim our identity and freedom. That was one unexpected jewel I found during the arduous journey of reclaiming my true identity—*freedom*! I felt more free in being *who I was created to be* than I ever knew in being who I wanted to be or who I thought I was. I could not know this true freedom in what I was expected to be for others: in what an abuser or oppressor manipulates us to be—and what fear holds us back from becoming. Giving your life fully to Jesus and the will of God is *not* restrictive bondage as our modern culture would often like to portray about the Christian faith; rather, it is a freedom gained in the most real and tangible way this side of heaven. Trust me, after 25 years in narcissistic bondage (my private little hell on earth), I know what it is to live in truth and freedom!

I both challenge and encourage each one of you, no matter who or where you are—believer or nonbeliever—to make a mental or visual list of all of your identifying labels (of your own making or those placed upon you by an outside force). Can you find your true identity underneath the layers? We cannot (with honesty) be deeply and clearly seen, heard, and known by others

> If you allow yourself to receive God's amazing grace, you will not only retrieve your stolen identity, but you will also find that the man or woman who emerges from the ashes is a better "you" than you ever dreamed possible!

unless we can identify with who we truly are. Until we can reclaim and lay hold of the image we were created to reflect, we can never be sure of whose image and identity we are gazing at in the mirror. Once you know without any confusion or doubt who you *really* are, not only can your identity never be stolen from you, but you can be healed, made whole, set free, and unstoppable! If you allow yourself to receive God's amazing grace, you will not only retrieve your stolen identity, but you will also find that the man or woman who emerges from the ashes is a better "you" than you ever dreamed possible!

> **...to give unto them beauty for ashes, the oil (blessing) of joy for mourning, the garment of praise for the spirit of heaviness....** (Isa. 61:3)

JOURNAL ENTRY – March 17, 2015

I realized this past year was the most emotionally and spiritually trying of all; I never felt so empty, numb, and willing to give up on our marriage. But in this deep place of loneliness, rejection, confusion, and brokenness, I saw a light—a flicker of hope. These women's conferences put a spark to my almost extinguished wick and started to fan a flame. I began to see a new woman arising, empowered by the Spirit of grace, mercy, and love. A new identity emerging; still myself and yet somehow changed. A confidence that had long been stripped away. Purpose renewed rising out of the ashes; beauty from pain.

Stuck in the Rut:
The Well-Worn Road That Leads to Nowhere

Most of us do not realize the power of our thoughts. I didn't for many years. Because humans are emotionally wired, we often think our thoughts stem from our emotions or feelings, but it is just the opposite: Our emotions and feelings are *ruled* by our thoughts. I heard people on a Christian radio program talking about this one day, and it stopped me in my tracks—literally! This is very profound and worthy of looking at more closely. You might be thinking, "What does this have to do with the topic of our identity?" I believe it is of great importance when it comes to seeking, finding, and reclaiming our identities, our true selves.

So let's test this hypothesis out with an example often said now as a cliché but one that actually has a real impact on the way we think and feel. The expression, "I am having a *bad* hair day" may resonate here more with women. If we *think* that our hairstyle looks really great, our color is just right, and our tresses appear healthy and shiny, then we *feel good about ourselves* that day and our mood is somehow much lighter. If we *think* that our hair looks terrible, won't cooperate with our efforts, feels dry, looks greasy, is frizzy, lacks luster, and that our gray roots might be showing, then we *feel* unhappy, annoyed, depressed, frustrated, and maybe even ugly and too embarrassed to go out. I am sure many dates and plans have been altered or canceled over the years by those who just couldn't make their hair look "good enough" to go out in public! What we *think* about our hair, skin, weight, clothing, etc., can have a *huge impact* on how we *feel* about ourselves and the subsequent emotions attached to those feelings.

I have noticed in the last few decades that even men are more concerned about their hair, skin, and clothing as our modern culture looks increasingly more toward outward body image than the inward character traits of a person. I believe that men (and even many women now) are prone to *feeling* good about themselves when they *think* that they have achieved their educational and/or vocational goals, or are financially successful and can afford a bigger house, drive nicer vehicles, wear designer clothes, eat at fancier restaurants, take more exotic vacations, etc. We need to *think* that we are successful before we can *feel* that we are successful; the gauge of our success is formed in our minds.

The same philosophy holds true with our identity. If for years a narcissist in your life systematically steals your identity and works tirelessly to devalue and drain you, squelches your self-esteem, abuses you physically and/or with harsh words, or punishes you with their absence, neglect, and silence (all while withholding love, support, and words of kindness and encouragement), you will most likely begin to *think* that you are unworthy of such basic human needs, and as a result, you may *feel* worthless, useless, rejected, and terribly unlovely. What we think and then ultimately feel is then reflected by the image we see in the mirror as well as the damaged (originally perfect) interior design woven into our created being.

As our negatively cultivated thoughts begin to consume our mind, they make what is often called a "rut" in our brain: a well-worn path to destructive thinking. This then perpetually feeds our negative feelings and subsequent emotions, which fuel depression, anxiety, bitterness, frustration, low self-esteem, and even hatred of ourselves and others. These prolonged, toxic emotions often promote damaging and deadly physical ailments, such as insomnia, chronic fatigue, high blood pressure and blood sugar, involuntary shaking, acute intestinal issues, debilitating migraines, elevated stress levels often causing panic attacks, and even suicidal thoughts and attempts.

For example, when I would *think* about my abusive husband arriving home from work and knowing what negative energy would enter along with him, my mind would already start producing the emotions that I automatically felt when I was in close proximity to the source of my distress. Often it was a mix of anxiety and stress rooted in fear of what I was going to be confronted with, and my body was already preparing for it, like a soldier in the battle zone tensing and waiting for the enemy that they *think* will be arriving soon. My body and mind were almost always in a state of alert and anticipation of an unseen attack, and that is why I began to experience chronic muscle tension, pain, insomnia, fatigue, PTSD symptoms, and the inability to heal. My thoughts were caught in a negative rut pattern, which, in turn, was controlling my emotions and feelings in a very unhealthy way, thus causing my chronic physical ailments. I knew that I needed to find a way to retain peace within, or I would never survive in my dysfunctional marriage. As I had already turned outward in my quest for answers and relief using the remedies of modern medicine and had found them inadequate for my desperate needs, I then turned inward to seek solutions and healing from my faith in my God, who promised to hear and help me.

> Incline Your ear, O LORD, and answer me, for I am poor and needy. Preserve my life, for I am godly; save Your servant, who trusts in You—You are my God. Be gracious to me, O LORD, for to You do I cry all the day. Gladden the soul of Your servant, for to You, O LORD, do I lift up my soul. In the day of my trouble I call upon You, for You will answer me. (Ps. 86:1-4, 7)

His divine power has granted to us all things that pertain to life and godliness, through the knowledge of Him who called us to His own glory and excellence, by which He has granted to us His precious and very great promises, so that through them you may become partakers of the divine nature. (2 Pet. 1:3-4)

Live not your life to attain perfection, but always strive for excellence.

What Did Faith Give Me That the World Could Not?

**The mind governed by the flesh is death,
but the mind governed by the Spirit is life and peace.**
(Rom. 8:6)

Our minds and our thoughts within the limitations of human flesh are only capable of doing so much by means of our own capacity to understand and reason. Likewise, no matter how healthy, big, and physically strong a person is, they have a limit to their capabilities to lift, move, and work. Even though people have succeeded in accomplishing many things that were once thought impossible, there are still countless mysteries in our world and beyond that we cannot possibly fathom. This is where the world has boundaries that faith does not.

Faith is believing in that which the human mind and senses cannot always experience, fully understand, or completely comprehend. Therefore, there is no limitation to notions such as hope in the hopeless, meaning in the meaningless, purpose in the purposeless, joy in the joyless, and love in the loveless. With faith, that which is lost can always be found. That which was thought dead can always be brought back to life. The key to opening the door of faith is *believing* in what can't always be seen with the eyes but can be envisioned with the heart, soul, and spirit. This is what kept me going, working, trying, moving, seeking, learning, hoping, praying, and loving when I knew nothing but pain, loneliness, and darkness in my marriage. **"Let him who walks in darkness and has no light trust**

in the name of the LORD and rely on his God" (Isa. 50:10). Faith offers us more because our redeemed identities in Jesus are not limited by our human capacity and power to be transformed and renewed, but rather are fueled and empowered by an all-powerful, all-knowing, and infinite God!

The Scripture quoted above from Romans 8:6 is so very insightful because it reveals the tendency of our minds to be governed (ruled, controlled, and influenced) by the flesh, which, apart from a higher power and authority, has a tendency to fall into the rut of well-worn thought patterns that lead to dead-end, negative thinking. Because we are rebellious in our fallen nature against the higher thoughts of God, our minds are inclined to seek the gutter instead of the high road that leads to a more fulfilling life, peace, and positive thoughts and emotions.

> **We destroy arguments and every lofty opinion raised against the knowledge of God, and take every "thought captive" to obey Christ.** (2 Cor. 10:5)

To get our minds out of the rut and begin to take our thoughts captive in obedience to Jesus Christ, we have to align them with our *true identity*, which is rooted and grounded in our Creator God who patterned us after Himself. This is a matter of our free will; it must be surrendered.

> **...assuming that you have heard about Him and were taught in Him, as the truth is in Jesus, to put off your old self, which belongs to your former manner of life and is corrupt through deceitful desires, and to be *renewed in the spirit of your minds*, and to put on the new self, created in the likeness of God in true righteousness and holiness.**
> (Eph. 4:21-24, italics mine)

For those who are reading this book who do not know God as your heavenly Father or acknowledge Jesus Christ, His Son, as your Lord and Savior—but you feel in your heart that He is the only way to forgiveness, reconciliation with the Father and others, salvation, renewed life and restoration of your true identity, and the giver of eternal life—please turn to the back of this book now and pray to give your life and heart to Jesus. In doing so, I promise that you will be on the right path, which leads to new life and true freedom this side of heaven and for all eternity. You will *never regret* the choice you made this day!!! (See "Believe to Receive" after the Appendix.)

>**...that they should seek God, in the hope that they might feel their way toward Him and find Him.** (Acts 17:27)

For those who are already Christians but find yourself like I was—stuck in a rut of negative thoughts and emotions that were, in turn, consuming my life and causing more harm to my already broken body and heart—you need to reset and renew your weary mind so that you can claim complete restoration of your true identity. **"Do not be conformed to this world, but be transformed by the renewal of your mind..."** (Rom. 12:2). What you think about yourself determines who you are. You become who you tell yourself you are, or in the case of narcissistic abuse, you become who *they tell you* you are or make you feel like. You defeat yourself before you even begin a new day if you carry negative thoughts in your mind; even just one can be deadly poison to your true identity. But how do we change this?

For a professing Christian, it is by putting things in accordance with who you are in Jesus Christ! You are a child of the Most High God, co-heirs with Christ, a member of the royal priesthood, and the Bride of Christ. You need to start identifying yourself as one *set apart* for the will and purposes of God, designed specifically for you to accomplish during your lifetime here on earth. If we spend our days lost in abuse, hidden behind masks, surrendered to circumstances as if we haven't already had our victory in Christ, then we shall surely remain in the tomb with Lazarus. This is how I once felt, like the walking dead, zombie-like as I moved throughout too many of my days. How many of us walk through our days like this—the appearance of living but really just going through the motions?

Routines of daily life got me through many days when I was too numb to think outside the box of my structured plans. This kept me feeling semi-normal, yet it was a far cry from real life and truly living! Our daughters were my major source of motivation to keep my feet on the floor and my body upright when I often wanted to pull down the shades, pull up the covers, and bury myself in a warm, safe cocoon of darkness. My faith was the unseen yet palpable force surrounding me, mercifully allowing me a short respite from time to time, but then gently yet firmly reaching down and pulling me upward with invisible hands of grace, courage, and power.

> **He reached down from on high and took hold of me; He drew me out of deep waters. He rescued me from my strong enemy and from those who hated me...the LORD was my support.** (Ps. 18:16-18)

Strangely, I never felt deeply depressed or even that life was not worth living. By grace through faith, I was still able to find joy in even the smallest of things, like my hot morning coffee, the fresh air of a new day, the songbirds ushering in the dawn with their unique choruses, the sunrise over the trees, or the glistening of fresh-fallen snow. The sleepy faces of my daughters as they slowly descended the stairs. My quiet time with the Lord, even if it brought tears. If you can still be moved to tears, whether in joy or sorrow, then you know you are alive. It is when you are so removed from your feelings, when you no longer are able to feel emotions that bring tears, that you should check your pulse. Your tears are so precious to our Father God that He sees each one and keeps them in a bottle.

> **You have kept count of my tossings (wanderings); put my tears in Your bottle. Are they not in Your book?** (Ps. 65:8, parentheses added)

Jesus walked our walk, felt our pain and sorrow, and cried as we cry. He came to earth to *identify* with us so that we could then have *our true identity* in Him! If you let Him, God will take away your dull, lifeless eyes and give you back your sparkle. As He did with Lazarus, dead in the tomb, Jesus will also cry out your name in a loud voice, like He did to me:

"Deborah, come out!"

Then you will arise, be unbound from your graveclothes, and emerge from the darkness into a full and vibrant life, secure in your renewed and true identity, which can *never be taken away again*!

11
Created to Be Creative

In the beginning...God created...
(Gen. 1:1)

I AM ONLY now, one year past my personal exodus that separated me from my abusive husband, beginning to understand the depth of our great need as individuals to be intentional about cultivating our creative expression. We all have the capability and innate desire to be creative, having gifts and talents to various degrees that are truly limitless in their scope. But what is the engine that drives our need to outwardly express our inward creativity? As a woman of faith, I believe it originates from our Father God, the Creator of all things. **"In the beginning, God created the heavens and the earth"** (Gen. 1:1). In Genesis 1:26, God expresses what He desired to create using His infinite wisdom, knowledge, power, perfection, and beauty: **"Then God said, 'Let us make mankind in our image, after our likeness.'"** With His last stroke of creative energy, God literally formed, and then breathed life into, a man and a woman made in His own image. He then implanted His very nature within them. The whole act of bringing forth life in every form, from the heavens to the depths of the sea, were ultimate expressions of creativity. **"The heavens declare the glory of God, and the sky above proclaims His handiwork. Day to day pours out speech, and night to night reveals knowledge"** (Ps. 19:1-2). The whole earth proclaims His creativity and sings of His glory!

Some people express their creative nature through talents and gifts more easily or often than others, especially if their natural abilities and learned skills become their vocation and are more relevant to their daily life. I am personally very aware of the need for this outlet now, whether as a vocation or just for stress relief and inner healing, since I left the toxic environment I was living in, which limited my ability to express myself in many ways. Over the years, as my life became a mere struggle to endure some days while serving as mother (and often father), homeschool teacher, spiritual mentor, disciplinarian, laundress, nurse, comforter, motivator, taxi driver, gardener, "butcher, baker, the candlestick maker" (okay, I didn't make candles!)—there was little time or energy left to even think about being creative! When you are in survival mode, treading to keep your head above water while trying to prevent your world from imploding in on you, being creative in positive and expressive ways is not even on your to-do list. I am sure I am speaking to many of you right at this moment!

During fleeting seasons of peace over the last 25 years, the dense fog would temporarily blow away and clarity would return. At these moments, I could remember short periods when I did have the time and energy to express myself creatively by writing poetry and short stories, painting, making crafts—things that brought me joy—and I would grieve the loss. I longed to feel the passion and energy I had experienced then, which was a part of who I once was. The Lord would graciously give me short seasons to write again, my most prevalent outlet for creativity since my youth. In retrospect, I can see so clearly that these opportunities to write and share the fruits of it with others were yet another avenue God used to keep me looking outward and moving forward. In this way, He helped me from being swallowed up by the abyss of silent abuse and days of emptiness.

Only in my current situation of rescue and daily healing can I be still and peaceful enough in my fear-free environment of solitude, that the depth of this need for creative expression can once again be felt. The Lord has purposely guided me to a place where He is providing all of my simple needs so that I can write as my sole vocation and focus. Why has He spent so much time orchestrating my current circumstances to allow such favor? Not because I am more special in His eyes than anyone else, but for the exclusive purpose of writing His truth, extending knowledge, and shining light into dark and oppressive places that have become obscure in our harassed, stressed, disillusioned, meaningless, hopeless, and lost world—especially the silent world of narcissism. What greater ploy could the devil use against us than to keep us so busy, fearful, anxious, troubled, sick, exhausted, distracted, confused, addicted, etc., that we no longer have the time, energy, or clarity of mind to be the unique and creative individuals God intended for us to be? Just a generation or two ago, while I was raising our daughters, each day was filled with fostering creative energy and expression through play and using their imaginations. The freedom to explore and experiment within healthy boundaries allows limitless outlets for a child's budding gifts and natural abilities. But most children today do not have to use their imaginations, and neither do most adults. Technology and constant forms of entertainment, on many levels, have stolen our children's ability to learn through imagination with hands-on playing, stunting the heart and brain's ability to implement creative thinking and expression at a crucial time of development.

The root of this problem is very relevant to the essence of this book and the road from silent desperation to quiet strength. You see, one of the sole objectives of a narcissist is to strip away and steal the identity of their "object of supply." A huge part of that stripping away is wrought in their ability to dismantle you in such manner that you no longer have the energy, focus, clarity, emotional stability, or mental dexterity to be creative. Your creative expression is a huge part of *who you are*, and the narcissist does not want you to know *who you are* apart from what

> "In any battle between the imagination and the will, the will loses out every time."
>
> —Billy Graham

you *need to be* for their use and personal gain. When you have been stripped or robbed of your creative identity, you have lost a huge portion of your personality, character, and "self"—the very reflection of your Creator. The silent abuse of narcissism, as well as any form of abuse, neglect, violation, or withholding of love facilitates the systematic disassembling of a person's identity and degrading of self-worth (including, but not limited to, pornography, sex trafficking, slavery of any kind, forced isolation, etc.); it flies in the face of everything God desires for our lives and is the devil's playground.

Each day that I am given to write, a little more of myself rises to the surface as I embrace the joy and freedom of finding a large part of my identity again through creative expression. If you currently find yourself in a narcissistic relationship or other form of oppression that is stifling or robbing you of your identity and individualism, it is important to cultivate activities apart from your difficult relationship in order to maintain a sense of healthy identity while waiting for wisdom and guidance on how to proceed in a good and positive way toward freedom. (That is, unless you are in immediate danger, in which case you need to find a safe haven as soon as possible.) As much and as often as possible, find simple ways to take care of yourself physically, mentally, emotionally, and (if it applies) spiritually. This will help protect your creative identity.

Unfortunately, our society as a whole is systematically chipping away at this crucial element of our individualism, which, if used outwardly and productively, benefits all of the people we touch with our creative gifts and talents. Years ago, education was not just about the highest test scores and number of degrees earned, or what career you could have in order to make the most money or become famous. A good, well-rounded education cultivated the arts, literature, music, etc.; it supported and nurtured creative expression. I believe this is not only a great loss for the individual but also for society as a whole. It is a great loss within the church. Many people today (whether practicing a faith or not) are constantly busy, stressed out, and exhausted. Who has time to be creative and just have fun?

So often our extracurricular activities are laced with fierce competition and large commitments of time, and infringe on our much-needed sleep, downtime, as well as family time. Sadly, they often lose their purpose as the positive, restorative, and creative outlets that they were meant to be! When you take away the time, opportunity, and freedom for creativity and healthy fun, you breed a society of unhappy, unfulfilled, frustrated, angry, bitter, exhausted, uncompassionate, ungrateful, and hopeless "hamsters" running in the wheel of life. Take a leap of faith and jump off the hamster wheel for a while! Work into your hectic schedule this crucial element of who you are. We make the time to do other things that we deem important for our overall health, such as doctor and dentist appointments, exercise, counseling, massage and chiropractic appointments, daily devotions, fellowship, etc. I believe (as well as know from personal experience) that implementing time for some form of enjoyable creative expression, which is an important extension of "you," will do wonders for your sense of well-being.

I assure you that if you are purposeful about letting your creative juices flow, you will notice a difference in how you feel immediately as these long neglected or lost elements of yourself flow up and out of you with renewed passion and joy. All people are creative beings; throughout the world we see creativity in action displayed for us to admire, appreciate, and enjoy. The amazingly beautiful and unique architecture of the old buildings and mansions where I am currently residing while writing, together with their cultured gardens, are a feast for the senses and food for the soul.

The difference I find within the realm of Christian faith is that our creative energies are enhanced by the power of the Holy Spirit. He guides our unique abilities and talents in ways that not only solidify our identities in Christ but also direct and encourage believers to utilize their creativity to enrich the lives of others as well as glorify our Creator God. True creativity emanates from deep within, from the very essence of who we are. It originates in our thoughts but flows forth from the heart, thus revealing the true condition or nature of our hearts. I believe a raw genuineness about ourselves, apart from our masks and outwardly portrayed images, is revealed when we freely express our creativity unhindered—for better or for worse. What we produce outwardly is often an authentic reflection of who or what we really are in our inward being. Our creative energy can be used to birth works that emanate beauty, love, and peace, or it can be used to develop instruments of hate, destruction, and disharmony. Let us all desire to use our creative gifts of expression for good!

As in water face reflects face, so the heart of man reflects the man. (Prov. 27:19)

Some of you may be asking yourself, "How do I reclaim talents and natural abilities that have long ago become dormant, lost, or stripped away?" Take time to reflect upon what made you feel the most happy and fulfilled in the past. What did you do that brought people joy or garnered compliments that made you feel special and valued (seen, heard, known, and loved) when shared with others? Recall things you had a passion for at one time, such as singing, playing an instrument, dancing, cooking or baking, decorating, gardening, painting, writing, photography, pottery, woodwork, knitting or sewing, etc.; the list is as endless as the creative beings behind them! We usually have remnants, pictures, or mementos that grace our living space (or are in the back of closets, stuffed in drawers, in the basement, attic or garage!) of what had once given us joy, fueled us, offered a sense of satisfaction, and relieved stress in our bygone days.

Maybe you are not sure that you ever really tapped into them, or are not even aware of any creative gifts you have because they were never cultivated. In my personal experience, I have found the following few indicators pointing to my unique gifts and talents:

* When my creative energy is in action, I feel deep joy and contentment.
* I also have a strong desire or "pull" to be doing it and look forward to each opportunity.
* I find that I easily get caught up in the flow of it as the world fades away. I get "lost" in the moment as time, place, and even physical needs for food and sleep take a backseat to what is consuming my heart, mind, body, and soul.

138

* My spirit feels freer and lighter than usual, and I sense my true self more than at any other time.
* I know that when I am finished, even for a while, that I am doing what I was created for and that what was brought to fruition has some purpose and meaning beyond myself.

I believe the vision for our creative energy and what it produces is not only meant to bring us personal joy and fulfillment but is also to be shared with others. After all, what would be the true aim of creating something of beauty and purpose if it was selfishly hoarded and not displayed or given away for the benefit of our fellow travelers in this life? In retrospect, and even in the present moment, I realize that I am more freely creative when I feel the most loved, secure, content, and peaceful. I believe love is a very important part of creativity as we need to have positive fuel in order to create with passion. Creativity is an overflowing manifestation of what we have within us. If we feel empty, numb, unloved, and unlovely, how can we be empowered and impassioned to create something lovely with an energy and passion we do not possess? Love is the breeding ground for passion and desire. It stirs up the soil of our heart, making it fertile and ready for new growth and expression. Beautiful things grow out of well-tilled ground that has been fertilized with patient nurturing, time, and energy poured into it. But when the soil of our hearts has been neglected and becomes hardened by lack of use and tender care, what can be brought forth from it, except something dark and void of real life?

Our creativity is a huge and essential part of our identity. It helps to establish who we are as individuals as well as how we fit into the framework of our (healthy) marriages, families, church body, circle of friends, places of employment, communities, and world. As I have already alluded to, creativity is certainly a decisive element to an individual who has been stripped of their identity and consequently been unable to express themselves in this way, as they were forced to be someone they were not created to be at the hands of another. The resurfacing of my creative self has been a priceless gift of grace toward healing as well as empowerment in my efforts to move out from under the dark and oppressive forces that encased me in silent desperation. I am delighted to be entering into this new-to-me, beautiful, and *free* realm, utilizing my renewed strength through creative expression!

> "When I stand before God at the end of my life,
> I would hope that I would not have a single bit of talent left,
> and could say, 'I used everything You gave me.'"
> —Erma Bombeck

12
When Your Anticipation Becomes Anxiety

Why are you cast down, O my soul,
and why are you in turmoil within me?
(Ps. 42:5)

TRY TO IMAGINE a time, probably in those first years of
marriage, when upon separation from your spouse you couldn't
wait to see them again. You watched the clock and listened to hear
the car pull in the driveway and the door slam, letting you know that
they had arrived home. You greeted them with a genuine smile and
eyes that said, "I am glad you are home. I missed you!" Your spouse
returned your warm welcome with the same mutual joy and love, so
happy to finally be home with their favorite person in the whole
world. It may have been a long time ago when you last experienced
this wonderful feeling of anticipation, but I am sure it was once there.

Many people recalling these anticipated moments may now be
reexperiencing them with teary eyes, as the memory of what was once
a sweet part of your life is long gone and buried under layers of
painful homecomings. I understand. Instead of excitement about the
homecoming, or your own return from work or an outing, there is
now a growing dread as the clock ticks closer and closer to arrival
time. Your stomach churns, your throat constricts, muscles become
taut, and nerves feel raw and shaky as you brace yourself for the cold
indifference toward you in what should have been a moment of joyful
anticipation, now turned into pain.

Throughout the day you may have experienced a reprieve
from the "prison cell" as you breathed in deeply a bit of fresh air and
enjoyed the taste of freedom during those blissful spans of time out

from under the watchful eyes of the warden. Then the door opens, and your cell door closes and locks again. The bars of silence slide shut (or for others the verbal and/or physical abuse starts), and the strain of another long and lonely evening begins.

> JOURNAL ENTRY – February 23, 2015
>
> There was only one cloud hanging over the day. The cloud that follows me wherever I go. The silent presence which sucks out joy and tries to steal peace. I won't let him take this special place of freedom; I am sorry, but I can't. I need, like air and water, some places I can be free and feel fully alive instead of half-dead, where I do not have to pretend for the sake of others. Please allow me this small token of favor, my heart begs You! Give me places where my heart can be free and my worship untainted. Amen.

(The place of freedom I was asking God for was within the safe walls of the church, my sanctuary.)

A Remedy to the Rescue—Anxiety to Anticipation

So, where are you to go and to whom do you need to turn in your solitary confinement and silent desperation? Ladies and gentlemen, please do not turn to the things of this temporal world that are only short-lived substitutes and just as empty as the void you are already living in. So much of what this world offers are just fleeting entertainments that often leave you feeling more alone, envious, and rejected because they portray mostly unrealistic scenarios of daily life, love, and romance. This includes soap operas, reality shows, romance novels, Facebook, various dating/chat room websites, and pornography in its myriad forms. These alternatives to the "real deal" only make you more acutely aware of the unfulfilled longings within your body, as well as the unmet needs of your heart and soul.

These delusive portals paint a picture of easy and uncomplicated romance, which only serves to reinforce the message that you are a failure in your own. They further fuel the devaluing process already happening in a relationship with a narcissist as well as any other form of neglect or harassment. Replacing genuine love with written words and scenes of lust and dishonorable substitutes (in the flesh and within the mind) often leave you feeling more empty, frustrated, guilty and/or ashamed on top of everything else you are already coping with.

So, again, the question is: To where do you turn when your anticipation fades to anxiety? What do you do with all of this turmoil within your body, heart, and soul that yearns for peace, joy, and love once again? I cannot speak for everyone, but I can share with you the only risk-free place I have found.

The sole place I could run to without guilt, shame, regret, or more loneliness.

The only arms I could fall into and rest and be refreshed anew.

A place where my tears could flow freely and not be mocked or ignored, but rather be seen with tender compassion.

A truly safe person who I know sees me, hears me, knows me, and selflessly loves me—Jesus.

He is the long-awaited Lover of your weary soul and broken heart. **"He heals the brokenhearted and binds up their wounds"** (Ps. 147:3). He became my heavenly Husband. **"For your Maker is your Husband"** (Isa. 54:5). It was a slow turning, I admit, but He kept wooing me and gently turning my tear-stained face toward His beautiful face of love, compassion, and understanding until I could not resist Him anymore—and didn't want to. And when I did allow Him to be, not only my Lord and Savior but also my spiritual Husband, it was the first time I finally knew what it felt like to be unconditionally loved just as I was: weak, weary, bruised, broken, and hollow, with nothing to give Him in return but my love and my life. It was a relationship that would bring me the much-needed peace, hope, joy, and restoration that I so desperately desired without all of the guilt, shame, misery, and striving that I knew this world offered me. Although tempting at my lowest times, I also knew that any other worldly substitutions would only leave me where the narcissist attempted to take me all along: completely empty of myself except for feelings of self-loathing about who I had become under the administrations of his warped mind and guiltless manipulations.

Therefore, my devotional time literally became a time of relationship-building with the living Lord. It wasn't just picking up the Bible with a few spiritual readings and nice words to make me feel better for a little while, but rather, it was a time of anticipation as I waited for the Lord to arrive and greet me warmly. It was a peaceful period set apart from the day's duties that I devoted to Him, a genuine time of adoration and thanksgiving to the One who was saving my life, healing my heart, and loving me back to wholeness— piece by broken piece. I approached my time with Him as that of an excited wife who was watching the clock, listening for the car to pull in and the door to slam, and welcoming my beloved Husband home to sit with me awhile. As my faith grew, and with it a deepening spiritual relationship, I came to expect the Lord to show up...not in a demanding way but one of humble awe and joy that He would actually delight in seeing, hearing, knowing, and loving *me*!

Because I so often lived in oppressive silence, prayer and journaling became my spoken words back to our Father God and Lord who desires to have this intimate relationship—this "give and take"—just as much as we should (even more so) desire it with Him. When we call upon the Lord, He answers us. **"When he[she] calls to Me, I will answer him[her]"** (Ps. 91:15, brackets added). And when we draw near to Him, He draws near to us. **"Draw near to God, and He will draw near to you"** (James 4:8). These are not just platitudes and flowery words that entice the heart, but they are a living Truth that I bear witness to with my life's testimony as to how I survived the anxiety, insanity, and extreme loneliness while caught in the tangled web of a narcissist.

For He satisfies the longing soul, and the hungry soul He fills with good things. (Ps. 107:9)

JOURNAL ENTRY — September 10, 2015

I praise You that while I walk each day in a cloud of insanity and on shifting sand with the narcissist, that You are my solid Rock and Anchor and keep me from drifting away and drowning in the waters of disunity of heart, mind, and spirit.

Hope in God; for you shall again praise Him,
my salvation and my God.
(Ps. 42:11)

13
Praying the Word

...for we walk by faith, not by sight.
(2 Cor. 5:7)

THE FOLLOWING IS a testimony of how my belief in the power of standing on the promises of God, literally and spiritually, saved me and set me free. In my silent desperation—when I had met the insanity at every angle, spoken my heart's cry in every possible way imaginable, wept so many tears that my "well" was literally dry and not a drop could be squeezed out (not even by the IRS!), shared my pain to a face that was consistently cold and unmoved, and pleaded with every last fiber of my being, only to have my words bounce off deaf ears and hit the stone wall—I was at the very end of myself. I hardly recognized the weary, lackluster reflection staring back at me in the mirror. And even though marital communication was becoming increasingly nonexistent, God's Word spoke to me every day. I knew the Lord *heard* me because He answered my cries and calls for help when no one else heard or cared. I knew He *knew* me because His precious Word spoke intimately into my very heart day after day. I knew He *saw* my desperate attempts to save what I felt was sacred and worth every ounce of me.

It was during the last few, yet most arduous, years that I began to pray the Scriptures as prayers because, more often than not, I couldn't even think clearly enough (nor could I muster sufficient energy) to pray with any genuine focus or power of my own. This life-giving practice was the only way that I could keep my mind from wandering or just plain shutting down. Praying the Word of God started out as both a crutch to hold up my prayer life, which was consistently becoming inconsistent, and a way for my heart and mind to pray within God's will when I had no idea what God's will was. I figured that if I prayed God's Word, I was always going to be in His will whether I knew it or not! This spiritual discipline and lifeline quickly became my anchor as the winds of change were increasingly evident.

I began to *feel* the profound power of praying the Word in ways I never knew or felt before. This act of faith and devotion was truly life or death for me. I prayed for protection from my enemy(s), protection for our daughters, wisdom, knowledge, discernment, guidance, truth, justice, strength, courage, peace, forgiveness, grace, mercy, hope, rescue, and freedom in whatever way God deemed was right and just. He promised to fight for me; He even wanted to fight *for* me! He told me that I was precious in His sight! I couldn't remember the last time I felt precious, much less was told that I was. He told me I was honored—what was that? Chosen? Wanted? Loved? Oh, how I longed to be loved for who I was and not for who my spouse was trying to force me to be—an "object" of his own making that consumed his mind. And I *believed* every word God told me at a new and deeper level than I ever had before in my life as a Christian.

For years I had wanted to be able to memorize Scripture, but except for a few of the "classics" that most believers know by heart, it was a constant challenge and frustration. But now I *needed* to know what God promised me as His child because I was desperate and dying inside; this apparently is a powerful motivator! And the more I sought Him and prayed, the more I believed. The more I believed, the more He gave. And the more He gave, the more hope, like a flickering flame, began to rise ever so slowly from beneath the rubble. **"...a bruised reed He will not break, and a faintly burning wick He will not quench; He will faithfully bring forth justice"** (Isa. 42:3). And I became bolder in my prayers as, one by precious one, I claimed the promises that my God and Father was offering to me.

Let us then with boldness (confidence) draw near to the throne of grace, that we may receive mercy and find grace to help in time of need. (Heb. 4:16)

JOURNAL ENTRY — November 23, 2015

Father, I thank You that Your Word of life is so powerful that it can reach into the darkest places of our lives and minds with hope, love, and strength. May I always hear Your Word all the days of my life! Amen.

Jesus Christ is, in fact, all we truly need to be whole; He can completely fulfill our heart's desires. Our relationship with Him is multifaceted: both simple and complex at the same time. When we come to God, praying in Jesus's name, and desire to receive the promises laid forth throughout the holy Scriptures, we have to approach Him with the deepening wisdom and faith of a maturing Christian, yet at the same time with the open heart of a child. Jesus taught His disciples saying:

"Let the children come to Me, and do not hinder them, for to such belongs the kingdom of God. Truly I say to you, whoever does not receive the kingdom of God like a child shall not enter it." (Luke 18:15-17)

Through Jesus Christ, all who believe in Him become children of God by grace through faith (Gal. 3:26, Eph. 2:8). So why do I speak to grown men and women about becoming a small child before the Father? For several reasons. We embrace truth and promises given us more readily when we accept the words as a trusting child.

Think back to your childhood days. Did you not readily believe, without question, when your parents or another trusted adult promised you something? We fully trust these people in our lives until they begin to break the promises they have made to us (as so many unfortunately do, especially when a promise too often really means a "maybe, if I remember or if I feel like it later on"). This is devastating to both children and adults alike. What does every hurting, fearful, or rejected child really need during their lowest times and in their deepest sorrow? Is it not the love, protection, security, and comfort of a parent (or other trusted caregiver) who they know loves them deeply and unconditionally? In my silent desperation I finally, in all earnest, knew what it meant to cry out, "Abba! Father!" like a child who needed her Daddy (and a wife who needed her husband). By faith, I grabbed hold of God's promises and knew that He would not fail me or ever leave me. My husband had failed me and forsaken me so many times that it needed to be a supernatural act of faith for me to be able to trust another man again with my wounded heart, but Jesus Christ is no ordinary man! And when He sets His sights on you as His beloved, there is nothing that can ever separate you from the divine and faithful love of God, found in Him.

> **No, in all these things we are more than conquerors through Him who loved us. For I am sure that neither death nor life, nor angels nor rulers, nor things present nor things to come, nor powers, nor height nor depth, nor anything else in all creation, will be able to separate us from the love of God in Christ Jesus our Lord.** (Rom. 8:37-39)

Prayer, Power, and Preparation—The Exodus

> **I stand silently before the LORD and wait for Him to rescue me.**
> (Ps. 62:1)

> **...fear not, for I am with you; be not dismayed, for I am your God;**
> **I will strengthen you, I will help you,**
> **I will uphold you with My righteous right hand.**
> (Isa. 41:10)

At a particular time of deep prayer in the Word, while fervently seeking discernment and guidance for the future days ahead, I felt led more and more to fast while praying. I had to modify fasting somewhat due to low blood sugar at that time; however, the desire and urgency overshadowed minor limitations. As a side note, I recently discovered that the *spiritual root* of hypoglycemia or low blood sugar is *lack of identity* and *insecurity*, which causes anxiety and fear coupled with self-rejection, etc.[28] Imagine that: spiritual precursors for a medical diagnosis evident in an individual living with a narcissist

---

[28] Henry Wright, *A More Excellent Way to Be in Health*, p. 290.

who strips away their *identity*, causing *insecurity, anxiety, and fear*! Interestingly enough, I no longer have this ailment since my departure (exodus) from the source of it!

During one of my other times of fasting prayer, the Holy Spirit kept leading me to Jeremiah 29:11, a very well-known Bible verse pointing the reader toward a hopeful future: **"'For I know the plans I have for you,' declares the LORD, 'plans for peace and not for evil, to give you a future and a hope.'"** But as my mind was whirling with fleeting thoughts and trying to formulate plans on my own, the Holy Spirit kept emphasizing the words *"I know"* over and over again until my foggy brain finally got the message! I wasn't going to have *any* part in the planning of my future...for the Lord already had not only the plan but also the course of action that would bring that plan to fruition.

In that moment, while on my knees, I further relinquished my life, future, and finite plans over to Him. I was too tired to fight or think about it anymore. He had to get this soldier's heart, mind, and spirit into a place of absolute exhaustion for me to completely surrender my self-efforts. I could not figure it all out with my limited reasoning and human strength. God knew that my heart was in a place of honorable commitment to my husband, but His ways are not our ways, nor are our thoughts His thoughts (Isaiah 55:8). So, even if what He was revealing to me didn't fully make sense to my human understanding, it was His perfect plan for me.

I thanked and praised Him, and then waited every day and evening for Him to show up as He continually unfolded His divine plan and placed it in my heart. The Lord, who is unseen with the natural eyes, became more real to me than my husband, whom I saw every day.

> **I wait for the LORD, my soul waits, and in His Word I hope....** (Ps. 130:5)

> **Now faith is the assurance of things hoped for, the conviction of things not seen.** (Heb. 11:1)

JOURNAL ENTRY — November 11, 2015

I feel with every fiber of my being that You will seek justice for me—
somehow and in some way—and rescue me with as little pain to my beloved
daughters as possible. You are my Hiding Place, my Rock, my Hope, my
Promise, my Redeemer, my Healer, my Fortress, my Defender, my Master,
Lord, King—my Savior!

JOURNAL ENTRY — December 12, 2015

The Holy Spirit gave me all the help I would "let Him" when I was weary
and could not go on in my flesh. I guess I am not as surrendered as I want
to be; still fighting some battles, but I know He will win out (thankfully) and
set me free from the ongoing war. I do not have the will nor desire to fight
anymore; there is no gain in rebellion. I guess one of the final laps is giving
up the falsehood of our life together and letting the pieces fall where they
do. God will put them back in the right place. Facing the shame of failure
and rejection by some, and the "blame" for walking away from others. The
price of freedom. Hold me, dear Lord, lest I crack in pieces and be no more.
You will go before me and make the crooked places straight. God will
protect me as He prepares me for my biggest assignment yet as I surrender
fully to the unknown future. I praise Your holy and delightful name, Jesus!
My God is faithful and in Him all things are possible, and I can do them.
Amen.

JOURNAL ENTRY — March 14, 2016

I feel like I am very near the threshold of major changes in my life. I feel it
is crucial that I hear Your leading very clearly. As my emotions are raw,
my mind weary, and my strength depleted—please speak to me with
volume so I do not act on my own desires, fears, and human power. I just
don't trust myself or my heart right now. I need to listen only to the Spirit
within me so that I do not cause any unnecessary pain, trouble, grief, nor
miss the blessings in Your perfect will, plan, and purposes. Amen.

JOURNAL ENTRY — April 4, 2016

Heavenly Father, You are always so consistent and true to Your Word,
which I pray for peace and power. Again, I give myself to You in body, soul,
and spirit, and ask that You renew and revive my heart. Your Word is my
confidence; Your Son, my Anchor, and for this I am forever grateful. In
Jesus name Amen.

JOURNAL ENTRY — May 4, 2016

Even though You have shown me some of Your plan, I know it is best that I
do not know all that is ahead. If I did, I may run scared. Or maybe if I did

know, I wouldn't want to endure the next level of training but either remain or just leap forward, thereby missing many important lessons. This separation is going to stretch me in so many ways. If it was not for my faith and trust in You and Your strength—and the knowledge that I would fade away here like a neglected flower until I was no more or went mad...I would never be brave enough to take the risk or suffer the loss. Amen.

JOURNAL ENTRY – May 29, 2016

As I sought Your face in prayer this morning, even before arising, You made me aware of how it is Your grace and mercy alone that is completely sustaining me during this time of transition and preparation for letting go. You didn't "show" me what I would be like if You were not in the midst of it all, but I knew in my spirit I would be filled with fear, anxiety, and conflict—maybe even immobilized by it all! So, I receive and rest in this blanket of holy grace and protection, which You alone supply. I continue to move forward in Your provision and grace. To You be the glory! Amen.

JOURNAL ENTRY – June 14, 2016
(Written the day before leaving, my personal exodus)

Dear heavenly Father, my Abba, in Jesus' name I write in the Spirit:

I am strangely peaceful in heart and mind again, although my insides are a bit "wiggly"; it feels more like anticipation than negative feelings of fear or regret. I guess this has been such a long time in the making that I am just awakening to the fact that the nightmare is almost over and a whole new life is opening itself up to me. As I think about all of the women who are still trapped in the madness, I feel very sad and guilty that I have received such grace from Your heart and hand. Lord God, make my life worthy to have received this undeserved favor; that I use this freedom and gift of grace to help multitudes of others still in darkness and the bondage of this terrible silent abuse. I offer my life for Your good pleasure in honor and glory to You! Amen.

Looking back, I could never have imagined how the Lord would answer this prayer prayed from the heart of such a simple woman just longing to be free...and have that freedom give hope to others silently desperate.

JOURNAL ENTRY – September 14, 2016

Gracious God and Father, my thoughts are on my gratefulness for all You have done in and through me. Also, my answer to prayer that, by Your Spirit, I have been able to memorize so many verses, which have truly become woven into the fabric of my life! I prayed for this gift many times, but I wasn't focused or desperate enough for Your words of life as I have been these last difficult years. With a strong desire to pray within Your will, I felt led to pray Your Word which would always be within Your perfect will. I began to feel the strength, peace, and power in praying Your Word of truth, light, and life. I claimed the words and promises as my own as the Holy Spirit would guide me to what I needed to pray for. As my situation and needs changed, so did the prayers. I clung to Your Words with everything within to get me through these last few years—especially this year of letting go of my life with my husband. I couldn't have gotten through without the comforts and strength of the living Word; Your presence manifest in the holy Scriptures. I have made it my mission to not only share Scripture as led by the Spirit, but to encourage others to pray the Word as a means to draw near to You and to claim Your promises and open up the power within. Thank You for writing Your precious words upon the tablet of my heart. They are priceless beyond measure as they reveal You to me; Your heart to Your children! The Word gives us authority over the powers of Satan and darkness of which though it try—the world cannot deny. What a beautiful gift; this love letter from our Father God and King! Amen.

*As with previous chapters, I felt that inspired selections from my personal journals penned over the years spoke more clearly and with greater volume my testimony of praying the Word to release its manifold realms of protection, peace, and power!

14
Wanting and Waiting

Wait upon the LORD and be of good courage,
and He shall strengthen your heart;
Wait, I say, upon the LORD!
(Ps. 27:14)

O ur deepest passions are motivated by a living hope that our
longing will be fulfilled. For a professed Christian, the biggest
obstacle that can get in the way of retaining our faith and keeping
hope alive is being willing to surrender our heart's desire to God and
wait upon Him, all the while knowing it may never come to fruition if
it isn't part of His plan for our life. The challenge is in knowing that
we can have what our hearts and flesh truly desire in the "now"
(often only a credit card purchase, phone call, breath, or touch away),
yet we battle with every fiber of our being to relinquish it into the
Lord's hands because our longing and love for God are greater than
the desire of our mind, body, and/or anguished soul. A spiritual
conflict arises when we contemplate the cost of knowingly stepping
outside of God's perfect will and standards, which are established out
of love to protect and safely guide us, to satisfy a moment of longing
or acquire something we know is not His "yes"—at least not yet.

For a person of faith, the question that always needs to be
asked of our conscious self should be: "Is the fulfillment of this
momentary pleasure, acquisition, achievement, etc., worth inflicting
grief upon our Father's heart or to have His favor (His approval, not
His love) tainted?" For both believers and nonbelievers alike; the
question we need to ask ourselves is this: "What could be the possible
cost or repercussions to myself, my family, others, and my

conscience?" If all of our decisions and actions could be rooted in a *selfless* desire to both please and remain in good relationship with our earthly parents, siblings, spouses, children, friends, and other significant people as well as our heavenly Father—it would greatly minimize the guilt, shame, pain, stress, and conflict we too often bring upon our own souls and upon many others who become a part of our decision(s) by close association. When we do not make wise choices, the resulting consequence(s) greatly diminishes our comfort, peace, and joy to live free before our loved ones, acquaintances, and our Lord—even within our own skin. When we answer the call of the flesh (temptations to sin), knowing we have sneaked onto territory that has been posted for our own safety, just to taste the forbidden and to fulfill a longing that seems so unbearable until it is quenched and satisfied, we have stepped outside of God's will for us and enter unprotected.

Then, when we "come back to ourselves" (Luke 15:17) and realize what we have done, we often condemn ourselves for our weakness and lack of self-control, which robs our inner peace and the wellness of our soul, often stealing the peace of those around us as well. Even though the Bible says that in Christ we are therefore no more under condemnation (Romans 8:1), we so often set our own prison sentence. We do this either by not acknowledging, repenting of, and seeking forgiveness for what we have done to ourselves and to others, or by shackling our sin to our ankle and carrying it around like a ball-and-chain while forfeiting freedom bought with Jesus's blood—as if that were not enough payment. Someone who has already known the feeling of this self-imposed condemnation, guilt, and shame—over time and through much unnecessary pain and grieving—usually realizes that the momentary fulfillment of any desire is not worth the cost of losing one's peace and joy to walk freely in their spirit.

When we fall into unrelinquished temptation and sin and have a conscious awareness that we are dying (literally or spiritually) with no hope of recovery or rescue, then have an encounter with the living

Lord who redeems us and sets us free...that's when we truly understand the gift of amazing grace. Unfortunately and tragically—because narcissists operate without a conscience—they usually continue on their destructive course without conviction, guilt, or remorse for the ways in which they harm others, and ultimately, their own souls wither and die. Unless we fully surrender ourselves and our cherished possessions, passions, and even the people we love—we may never truly experience the depth or magnitude of pure joy that accompanies the fulfillment of our longing when the time is ripe to receive it!

You see, ultimate gratitude and joy are always found in the waiting! Unfortunately, though, in many instances, we have raised up a society of what I will call "the ungrateful." Because we live in an instant-gratification world, no one has to *wait* for hardly anything anymore. We have created the "drive-through" mentality wherein *waiting* not only breeds impatience but also very angry people, sometimes violently so. We have drive-through restaurants, pharmacies, grocery stores, doughnut and coffee shops, ice cream parlors, banks, gas stations, liquor stores, video stores, dry cleaning pick-up windows, porn shops, and even sex; we barely have to get out of our cars for anything anymore!

When I was a teenager, just about everyone I knew had a *used* older vehicle that they bought with their hard-earned and carefully saved babysitting money, by mowing lawns, shoveling snow, delivering newspapers, scooping ice cream, or flipping burgers. Young couples often lived in a small apartment for years before they could even think about buying a home; this was us. Many lugged baskets of laundry to the hot and crowded laundromat before they could afford to own their first washer and dryer; this was us also. Even to this day, I still want to kiss my washer and dryer out of happiness for their convenience, but I refrain! Yes, it was harder, more time-consuming, and often inconvenient, but we learned both gratefulness and patience in the waiting. We longed for the day when these practical yet meaningful conveniences and pleasures would grace our lives with simple joy. Waiting makes the fulfillment of the longing much sweeter and infinitely more satisfying. Fine wine is made in the *waiting*; it is the secret to its richness, bold flavor, and perfection as it slowly yet steadily goes from good to better to the best. This, too, is the essence of the fulfillment of a heart's longing— one that is cried for, pleaded for, prayed for, hoped for. Its sweetness is only intensified by enduring the pain, trials, and temptations of the wait, and when it is finally granted, acquired, or received, it will truly be an unimaginable oasis after our long desert wilderness experience!

Earlier I stated how important it is, as God's children, for our souls and overall well-being that we make decisions of relinquishment in lieu of acting upon our longings, especially when an unhealthy or unproductive consequence could occur in the aftermath. These positive choices bring respect, honor, and glory to our heavenly Father, thereby safeguarding ourselves from *thoughts*, which in turn lead to *feelings*—of distance, shame, and self-condemnation—within us and our relationship with Him. But this baseline for decision-making truly applies to anyone, regardless of any or no practiced faith. As an analogy, I think of the child who knows they have a test the next day but makes a choice to go outside and play instead of choosing to be self-disciplined and study for it. Compare this to the child who forfeits the temporary pleasure of playing to receive the greater reward of a good grade. The former child misses out on the lasting satisfaction that comes with deferring their present want. The child who chooses wisely and defers gratification does so with the hope and anticipation that the withholding of instant gratification is going to be worth the wait.

Often, the greater motivation to delay the fulfillment of our deeply desired longings is something or someone greater than ourselves. For instance, the child who is disciplined and exhibits self-control is not only rewarded with good grades and school honors but also the even greater reward of pleasing their parent(s) through their sacrifice and hard-earned achievements. The child, however, who does poorly on tests because of a lack of self-discipline and submits to their desire for instant gratification often feels ashamed and reluctant to show their parent(s) their test grades. One child enters the household jubilant and beaming, while the other is ashamed and feeling low in their spirit. These emotions are usually already exhibited *prior* to reaching the threshold of the door because they stem from the thoughts the child has about themselves (either feeling successful or a failure) *before* they are even confronted with the reactions from their parents.

Remember that our thoughts determine our feelings—not the other way around. That is why the choices we make determine not only our *thought* patterns about ourselves and others (whether positive or negative) but also the way we *think and thereby feel* about ourselves and others. The grade on the paper doesn't alter or diminish the love that a good parent has for their child, but it can have a very profound effect upon how the child views himself or herself. The exact same concept holds true for a child of God. God doesn't withhold His love from us when we do not make a good or wise choice; we just no longer *think* and thereby *feel* that we are worthy to receive it. This is a simplified example of how a deferred longing can make a significant difference in how our life's journey unfolds. We have to make a choice and determine if the prospective outcome of our deferred desire is worth the discipline, obedience, surrender, and pain that often accompany the wanting and waiting. I believe that the joy of knowing we endured and overcame the hardship, temptation, and tears to be rewarded with the "best" (instead of the "good enough" of the moment) will far exceed our expectations. For a believer, the sole source of this extraordinary strength and power to wait is the Holy Spirit.

Our longings keep us motivated, impassioned, creative, a visionary, and in forward motion—always striving and reaching for something greater and more satisfying than what is seen and available in the "now." It is the hope of something and/or someone not visible, yet we feel deeply in our souls and spirits that it is (or they are) just beyond our ability to see, touch, and experience. While we wait, though, it is important for us to live in and focus upon the present moment, to appreciate and cultivate all that is happening within and around us as we press toward the goal of the upward prize.

> **But one thing I do: forgetting what lies behind and straining forward to what lies ahead, I press on toward the goal for the prize of the upward call of God in Christ Jesus.** (Phil. 3:13,14)

When we forfeit the race, we lose much. When we choose the easy road instead of the one less traveled, we bypass much undiscovered beauty and many lessons and blessings to behold. **"Enter by the narrow gate. For the gate is wide and the way is easy that leads to destruction..."** (Matt. 7:13). When we settle for the drive-through meal instead of *waiting* for the gourmet banquet, the aftertaste will become bitter in our mouth, and our appetite will never be truly satisfied. When we opt for instant gratification of the body instead of waiting for the exclusive rights and delights of a unique, unblemished gem in marriage, our heart and soul will always wonder how it could have been...if only. But the good news is that, by grace through faith, there is *always* another race, and it is *never* too late to get back on the right and high road!

I believe that there should, and will always, be a longing in our spirit because our hearts were created to long for our Father God, whom we will not see until Christ comes again or we pass from this life into the next for eternity. But I am also convinced that, this side of heaven, there will be many longings satisfied when we patiently endure the refining that only comes through afflictions while exercising perseverance in the waiting. The core message of the entire Old Testament was the anticipation of and longing for the arrival of the promised Messiah, our Savior. The essence of the New Testament is the waiting and longing for His, Jesus Christ's, return.

> "Let us not seek to get out of the furnace before it has done its work. Let us not ask, 'When shall this trial end?' but, 'What is the trial sent to do in me?' And then let it have its perfect work."
> — Lillian G. Harvey, *The Fiery Ordeal*

Temptations in the Waiting Room

Our seasons of deep longing can be amazing times of spiritual growth and faith building, but they can also be very dangerous to the flesh, as they are the perfect breeding ground for temptation and sin. A longing is an intense desire that whets or stimulates our appetite to crave some kind of powerful need within us that will not easily be quenched until it is satisfied. The measure of a person's desire is vast in its scope. It could be a longing for spring, a vacation, a new house, a career change; these are transient things that are fulfilled outside our bodies and are often not as closely tied to the human heart and soul.

> "Love is the climax of my happiness, and the pinnacle of my pain. Love is the fire in my heart with an eternal flame."
>
> —Written by a youth on an American Indian Reservation

Even so, it is the deep longings that generate from within that can motivate our passions in a positive way during the season of wanting and waiting. On the other hand, they can also drive us to the pit of desperation, hopelessness, and all manner of temptations—even insanity and evil.

I think of so many couples who long for a child yet cannot conceive. It breaks my heart to hear their raw pain and the angst in their souls when this desire is not realized. With many couples, this longing eventually leads to becoming foster parents as well as adoption. Many other positive and wonderful things can spring forth as subsequent outlets for their unfulfilled desire. I am always overjoyed when I learn of couples who have either waited patiently in their longing and were finally blessed with a child, or those who went ahead with adoption and then conceived after years of fear, frustration, grief, tears—empty rooms now doubly filled with love! I can only imagine how many children who were once orphaned, put up for adoption, or rejected who have found their deepest need and desire fulfilled when welcomed into the hearts and homes of others whose own longings were also realized in full measure—even if through unique and unexpected avenues!

But I do not believe, no matter how strong a person we may think we are or even how faithful a Christian we may be, that during a long, dry season of deep and unfulfilled yearnings we are not tempted to find even the smallest relief for the pent-up desires of the heart. Because we were created with a longing for relationships implanted in our hearts, there is a hunger in many souls to experience a deep covenant relationship bound by love with another, as well as all of the human desires that go with that. This is a power source that compels both men and women in their searching, hoping, pining, wanting, waiting, and praying for fulfillment in these empty places. The longing isn't transient because it doesn't originate from without but rather from deep within us. It is a heavy burden to bear when it remains unfulfilled and can draw us into all varieties of unhealthy and even destructive behaviors if left to our own devices!

If Jesus could be tempted and tried in every way by the master of temptation (the devil)—yet without sin—what makes us think we are strong enough, immune to, or just too controlled and "good" to be tempted by the enticements of this world? This is when we are the most vulnerable! **"Pride goes before destruction, and a haughty spirit before a fall"** (Prov. 16:18). It is only when we truly get "real" with ourselves and with God, and admit our weakness and powerlessness in the wake of our longings bridled with temptation, that we can be empowered by Someone greater than our most noble self-efforts. I reckon that some of the greatest deficits in the world—including the Church Body of professed believers—are a lack of self-discipline, taking personal responsibility for our actions, and the crucial element of accountability (a believer's desire for forgiveness without repentance). We are so concerned with *appearing* like we "have it all together" on the outside, that we often allow our inner self to become disconnected, dysfunctional, depraved, depressed, diseased, and destroyed. It is the pernicious lie that has been birthed and passed down through the ages: First clean the outside of the cup that the inside also may be clean.

But Jesus said:

"Woe to you, scribes and Pharisees, hypocrites! For you are like whitewashed tombs, which outwardly appear beautiful, but within are full of dead people's bones and all uncleanness. So you also outwardly appear righteous to others, but within you are full of hypocrisy and lawlessness." (Matt. 23:27-28)

How misguided, really…to clean and polish the outside of the vessel to impress the shallow and transient while letting the inside of the vessel decay and crumble—our eternal souls. When we live in truth, we live in freedom. Release yourself from the bondage of self-sufficiency and self-righteousness; acknowledge your need for help, strength, patience in the waiting, and amazing grace. **"But He said to me, 'My grace is sufficient for you, for My power is made perfect in weakness'"** (2 Cor. 12:9). Be free and clean on the inside, so you can truly be clean and free on the outside!

I so clearly remember the afternoon when I sat opposite my husband and asked him point-blank if he had ever considered that I would be unfaithful to him because of all of the abuse, hurt, silence, rejection, and terrible loneliness he had made me live in. He didn't even think about the terrible question that had just come out of the mouth of his wife of at least 22 years; he just replied, "No." I just stared at him a few moments incredulously—although I should not have been surprised in the least—and finally said, "Then you are a fool." After his completely unemotional response, I reminded him of how desperately I longed for communication, companionship, physical and emotional connection, and commitment to our marriage and family. I also reminded him of how finding temporary fulfillment of some of these longings was just a click away, a phone call, or a "night out" with friends. Still no response of any kind—only cold eyes stared at me.

I would have liked to have convinced myself that it was solely because he knew me well enough to know I was a devoted, faithful, and committed wife and mother, that my vows before him and God were sacred in my eyes, and that I greatly valued my honor and integrity; all of this was true. That probably held some clout in his cool assessment of the deepest needs and desires of my heart. But I knew by this time that the deeper truth of the matter was that he viewed me as an "object of possession" without any real longings, passions, and needs of my own apart from taking care of his. He didn't truly see me as a breathing human being with emotional and spiritual needs or even those of the body. And even if he had an inkling of my needs, he relied too much on my integrity without taking into account the temptations that run rampant sometimes in our fallen natures. The only time he reacted in "normal" mode was when I told him that I had been sought after and flirted with right before his eyes, yet he did not even take notice (although it was often embarrassingly obvious). These words finally roused his anger, and he demanded to know "who"—not as an ardent protector of his beloved wife but based solely on his own ego and pride. Obviously irrelevant by this time, I remained silent. The sad underlying truth is that he was always so preoccupied with his narcissist "self," that he never even considered me as a truly connected part of his life worth jealous love, protection, or fighting for. I know I am talking to someone else who has been here....

JOURNAL ENTRY — January 12, 2015

As the ground is covered with hard layers of snow and ice, so my heart lies deep within layers of neglect, indifference, ignorance, selfishness, distrust, disloyalty, loneliness, and manipulations. It has been buried in a bullet-proof case to stay protected and alive. The deep cold has made it numb, beating but barely. It so desires to be unearthed; to breathe fresh air and bask in the warmth of the thawing sun. It longs to be free from the bonds of sin, pain, and the unmet desires; to beat fervently for God and a dying world. To live and love freely without fear of pain. Will this ever happen this side of heaven? Peace, glorious peace where art thou? Come thou Lover of my soul; my weak and weary heart waits for You! Amen.

Oh, how great the temptation in the desert! How close we get to the brink sometimes—the very end of ourselves. Thank God that He never gives us more than we can handle and will always provide for us what we need, not only to endure the temptations but also to be victorious over them!

> **No temptation has overtaken you that is not common to man. God is faithful, and He will not let you be tempted beyond your ability, but with the temptation He will also provide the way of escape, that you may be able to endure it.** (1 Cor. 10:13)

I came so close to leaving at times as I was suffocating and could barely breathe in the confined space and toxic air. But during each trial and test by fire I walked through in unfulfilled longing, the final exam always concluded with the relinquishment of my self-will just a little bit more. I always knew in my heart that I would come to regret—not so much the transient, weak moment of perceived freedom—but what that freedom would cost me. The ability to close the door and lock it behind me was grounded in the understanding and truth that my life was not "all about me" and my own needs; it was about my marriage vow, our daughters, my faith, my name, my reputation, and my honor before God. **"...for I am honored in the eyes of the LORD, and my God has become my strength"** (Isa. 49:5). The losses could never measure up to any temporal gain.

But be it known that I had absolutely no strength or power of my own to stand up against the temptations that crested and then crashed like merciless ocean waves against my broken, fragile, and lonely heart. No, I will not boast of my own strength over temptation and sin. **"If I must boast, I will boast of the things that show my weakness"** (2 Cor. 11:30). I solely relied on the power of the Holy Spirit and the Word of God to resist the seen and unseen forces that tormented and buffeted me during some of the lowest seasons of my life.

If we make our choices outside of God's perfect will, we forfeit His divine power and protection. If we stay within the boundaries of His will and wait upon Him, He is faithful to work on our behalf, often rewarding our faithful obedience with the deepest desires of our wanting and waiting hearts!

"Then you will know that I am the LORD;
those who wait for Me shall not be put to shame."
(Isa. 49:23)

15

The Voice of Silence

**For God alone, O my soul, wait in silence, for my hope is in Him.
He only is my rock and my salvation, my fortress;
I shall not be shaken.**
(Ps. 62:5-6)

VERBAL ABUSE IS a terrible thing. It saddens my soul when I am out in a public place such as a park, a store, in a restaurant, etc., and I hear a parent speaking harshly to their child(ren) with an anger that stems—not from the child's behavior—but from within the heart of the adult who is outwardly unleashing their own obvious inner pain upon the relative helplessness of the child. Occasional disagreements among people who live together in close quarters is normal, as we all struggle to compromise and live in harmony with our differing character traits, preferences, habits, and temperaments. Verbal abuse, however, is altogether different. Its purpose is to control by invoking fear, often with heightened volume, threats, profanities, and degrading words, which too often are accompanied by physical abuse. The victims of this abuse are targets for an angry person's bitterness, unhappiness, frustration, and maybe even self-loathing (often perpetuated by an underlying fear) that oozes off their sharp tongues with poisonous darts, penetrating the heart of the recipient and often injuring for life.

These cutting words are meant to break down a person's will to fight back, trample on their self-esteem, break their spirit, and wound their heart. It often builds negative strongholds in the abused person's mind concerning who they are, their place within the family, and feeling that they can never do anything right; it keeps them "walking on eggshells," so to speak. The abuse and the resulting confusion keep the victim(s) questioning why they can't be seen, heard, known, and loved just for who they are without having to strive to please another—be it a spouse, sibling, or parent (guardian) who they desperately want to love and be loved by, yet often feel there is a chasm a mile wide between them.

I have witnessed this up close and personal with children—a heart-wrenching reality for too many. Sadly, it is common for those who have been abused in this way to become abusers themselves because it is the only form of communication that they know; individuals typically become products of their environments. They carry their scars into every other relationship: marriage, parenting, vocations, and social arenas. We commonly live what we know unless we are fortunate enough to witness a more positive and loving environment outside our own spheres of influence.

The same holds true for the verbal abuse of wives by their husbands. It is devastating to their hearts and souls, as words spoken in anger strip them of the ability to feel safe with the very person who should be their most ardent protector. Many men fall victim to verbally abusive wives as well. Words may be forgiven but not easily forgotten. When cherished things are tarnished, or stripped away altogether by careless words and actions, the element of trust is badly damaged or even destroyed and is often hard to restore. Without *both* sincerely acknowledging and regretting our harsh words and actions (including physical abuse), a reinstatement of trust, security, and real intimacy is almost impossible. Trust is a sacred thing, and the wise guard it with wholeness of heart.

My understanding of verbal abuse, therefore, was always something that was projected outward against another. But after two and a half decades living within the bondage of forced isolation and the withholding of a regular and normal exchange of communication with my husband, the ensuing silence began to have a voice all of its own. It would take many years to slowly unwrap the attractive outer covering that disguised this manipulative and destructive form of punishment, laced with countless false promises, before I realized the heartbreaking truth. What I thought was just a serious lack of good communication skills between my husband and me, which I believed could be remedied with committed resolve and counseling, was actually being used to control and break me. When I would approach my spouse with this serious ongoing problem that was so terribly eroding our marriage and family stability, there were several classic answers that always accompanied my frustration, fear, pain, and tears:

- "I will try harder to talk more."
- "I just don't know how to communicate like you do."
- "I don't know big words."
- "You are much better at talking than me."—flattery often a manipulation tool to detour real issues
- "We'll talk later."
- "I just don't know what to say, and my words always come out wrong."
- "I can never say anything right."

But I wasn't requiring big words, fancy words, the "right" words, or even *a lot of* words; I just wanted and needed to hear *something* other than silence!

Language is universal. Every people group and culture since the beginning of time has needed some form of communication. It is not a novelty; it is a necessity for individuals to survive and thrive together. It is the foundation of every nation, society, community, and family unit. Communication comes in a variety of forms—but it always comes—as all people have an innate desire to be able to express their thoughts, feelings, needs, wants, and concerns. Organizations and medical institutions spend millions of dollars to initiate research, create, and produce (especially with the use of continually progressive technology) devices and new avenues in which people who are impaired in any way from the ability to communicate with others have every available means to do so. It is a non-negotiable springboard from which all other necessary elements of relationships and societies are established. The hunger in every human soul to be seen, heard, known, and loved is exhibited through some form of communication. **"I must speak, that I may find relief..."** (Job 32:20).

The voice of silence is the voice of neglect and forced isolation. This punishment is used to control the victim by withholding precious words of love, concern, companionship, and intimacy. Everyone has what is sometimes referred to as a "love language." Author Gary Chapman wrote a wonderful book called *The 5 Love Languages: The Secret to Love that Lasts*. This book describes in detail what he has gleaned after years of counseling couples on this essential and interesting topic. He outlines, based on an individual's personality type, what specific means of communication they typically needed to "feel" loved by their spouse. The purpose of the book is to equip partners, who truly desire to make their significant other feel loved, heard, known, and cared about, with practical tools in which to initiate more meaningful and deeper connections during daily communication. He shares beautiful insights he has discovered over the years that couples can easily implement in order to fulfill the particular needs of their loved ones, yet this effort also enriches the intimacy and joy in their own lives. Now, the warped mind of a narcissist *does seek to know* their spouse's (object's) love language—yet *not* with the intent of making that individual feel loved, seen, heard, or known but rather as a weapon of destruction against them. I will share my personal experience as an example within this chapter.

JOURNAL ENTRY — August 30, 2013

I wish that in a hundred words spoken, just a few were laced with truth. It would be better than the deafening silence—the "noise" of which I desire to flee far away from.

I have come to understand that silent abuse has a sound all of its own. This seems contrary to its definition, as silence is the absence of sound. This is true to the ears but not to the heart and soul. In the hustle and bustle of life, especially in the city environment I am living in while writing this book, the absence of any sound is very rare. When I lived in the country, however, while lying awake in the night watches or just before a winter's day dawning, I would listen to the deep silence and marvel at the absence of noise. During the formative years of raising children, the fleeting moments of silence were treasured. Years later, that absence of sound—of words I desperately needed and wanted to hear—would create such a gaping hole in our marriage that only an act of divine intervention could bridge the void.

JOURNAL ENTRY – April 2014
Silence in solitude is welcome and blissful. Silence in loneliness is heartbreaking and torture.

Unless you have experienced it personally, it is very difficult to explain this non-verbal abuse. In more recent years I have spoken to other women who have been subject to a Narcissistic Personality Disorder or other forms of forced silence and isolating loneliness. Although distressing to hear their personal stories, it has helped me tremendously to talk to those who *understand* the pain of it. In the early years of my marriage, though, I had no thoughts of something as insidious as narcissistic manipulation at play but only of two individuals struggling to find common ground in communicating. Knowing that open and honest communication came quite easy to me, I worked hard at being tolerant with my husband's lack thereof and chalked it up to a time and maturity issue. But after patiently explaining my deep need for more communication and connection with him during those early years, even suggesting the help of marriage counseling somewhere around the six-year mark (and many other times throughout our 25 years of marriage), there were only more empty promises and fewer words.

As the void grew, so did my loneliness, frustration, fear, resentment, and anger. In the middle of a long stretch of very difficult and demanding ministry calls upon my life, which ran parallel with raising and homeschooling our three children, having almost full responsibility of maintaining our household, and escalating personal health problems, the pot was beginning to boil over. The more the urgency arose within me to find a way through the brick wall around my husband's heart and mind, the more emotionally charged became my words of anger and pleading. No angle moved the aloof body language nor cold, unemotional eyes; this stonewalling almost drove me crazy. Nothing disturbed his eating, entertainment, or sleep. The boat was sinking, and our marriage and family were starting to go under, but there was no plug for the ever-widening hole, nor was there a life raft in sight. Where in the world was my "knight in shining armor"? Why would he not step up and save us? Why did he not want to get us out of the sinking ship and onto the safety of the shore? I began to loathe the way I felt in my heart and soul when I was around my husband. I longed for him to desire to be the man I believed he had the potential to be if only he could see what he was missing, losing, abandoning.

Somehow I made the "outside" of me look okay, even happy and peaceful most days; no one was the wiser. I would be remiss if I didn't state that I had wonderful and fruitful things happening in my life during these years of trial, for I found much joy in raising and teaching our daughters, creating a loving and welcoming home of comfort and fun, caring for others, and any acts of service I was called to do. These activities were my saving grace, the anchors that kept the underlying storm from blowing me away. But internally I was so confused, angry, resentful, lonely, weary, empty, numb, and filled with a deep grief I couldn't name—and yet I knew it was causing parts of me to die. Although I was aware that my attempts were futile, I couldn't give up. I couldn't let this precious family unit fall apart. I couldn't surrender all I had worked for and sacrificed so much to build, only to have it all crumble at my feet; yet I knew I was losing ground instead of gaining it. I hated feeling angry inside.

It would be many years before I understood that my narcissistic husband purposely provoked me into frustration and anger because that was another avenue of punishment and control; he *knew* I despised feeling that way. If he could goad me in private to a place of emotional distress, then I would appear a difficult and hard-to-please wife within our home and in public. Then he could look like the innocent victim, and I, the source of our conflicts. These mind games actually fuel the ego of the narcissist. If he could convince others, as well as himself, that my angry frustration was unwarranted, it only served to justify his heavy hand of punishment against me and increased its frequency.

> **The same type of scenario often plays out in the heart and mind of a porn addict who, in the wake of their addiction, neglects their spouse's needs, thereby leaving them lonely, distrustful, resentful, and feeling undesirable. When the spouse expresses their grief and displeasure, or turns inward in their pain and abandonment, it throws fuel on the addict's already hot fire and justifies their actions in their own eyes. In light of the fact that addiction to pornography runs almost parallel to narcissism in its epidemic proportions and subsequent destruction to the marriage and family (rampant both inside and outside the Church), I felt compelled to interject the comparison.**

By nature, I was always an upbeat, positive, easygoing peacemaker. I detest drama and unnecessary conflict. I also knew that my inner feelings of anger and stress were as toxic for my body and soul as the oppression raging against me, so I began to meditate on and seek its deeper source. It didn't take long to get an answer; my anger was rooted in fear. But fear of what?

- Fear of our family being broken apart by divorce—I couldn't even think about or say the "D" word for years, much less seriously consider it
- Fear of losing control—of the direction our marriage was headed in and that it would never get better
- Fear of failure—failing at our marriage and failing our children as parents
- Fear of the unknown—what would happen to us all?
- Fear of disappointing my Father God—not in a condemning way but in my heart, which longed to please Him with my faith and in the vow I had made before Him

I came to understand what I believe now as truth: *All* anger is rooted in some form of fear. This fear is initiated in the mind by negative *thought patterns*, which then affect our feelings and emotions with a conscious (or unconscious) knowledge that we are *losing control* of someone and/or something, including ourselves. My heart now also believes this to be true: The only remedy for eradicating both debilitating fear and consuming anger is *the complete surrender of all things we desire to control* that remain within the grip of our fears. In a later chapter I will share the journey to my surrender.

> **Because the LORD was witness between you and the wife of your youth, to whom you have been faithless, though she is your companion and your wife by covenant. Did He not make them one, with a portion of the Spirit in their union? . . . let none of you be faithless to the wife of your youth. For the man who does not love his wife but divorces her . . . covers his garment with violence [harm done while violating rights], says the LORD of hosts. So guard yourselves in your spirit, and do not be faithless.** (Mal. 2:14-16, content in brackets added)

Journal Entry dated July 9, 2015

I asked myself, "Why does it feel so difficult now, when I have been through so much else in the past?" The answer came—"Because you could be active, moving, involved, seeing and knowing. Now there is just silence, inactivity, and waiting!" Yes, this is definitely more of a challenge to my heart and soul. No one knows the depth of pain; only You. It feels as though a part of me has been ripped away and I have a big, gaping wound that will not stop bleeding or throbbing. It is only by Your strength and grace that I function each day without my mind going crazy. The loneliness remains and gnaws at my bones each day; it is oppressive and I can't breathe. I know I need to yield under it, but I can never seem to stay there. I need Your help. How can you feel full and empty at the same time? Joy and sadness beside each other? Peace and pain? Love and hate? I pour out these feeble words; who hears them? Some day they will be thrown out and be no more. Written in vain, though they somehow comfort now. This paper is the only one listening; the pen my instrument of pain. You, alone, hear my silent cries. How do You deal with us weak and helpless children? You are mighty to save even the least of us and make us great in Your eyes. Give me that love. Amen.

> **If the LORD had not been my help, my soul would soon have lived in the land of silence.** (Ps. 94:17)

Forced silence is excruciating. It is like the painful pressure beneath a blister that is only relieved when popped and allowed to drain. I see a profound parallel within this example when it comes to unexpressed words. I am not really focusing here on frivolous words that we speak daily that have little impact, meaning, or depth other than as outward expressions of our in-the-moment thoughts, feelings, and ideas. I am specifically drawing attention to the words that are needful—I will even go so far as to say *crucial*—to the maintenance, stability, trust, and depth of intimacy that should be present and preserved in our more personal relationships, but most especially in a marriage.

Only when a person is allowed the freedom to express themselves in an environment that feels both safe and inviting, do they truly sense that they are seen, heard, known and connected with another. Even though I have had the pleasure of this type of mutual relationship with my daughters and close friends, I have not rightfully had the delight of this beautiful and fundamental exchange of mutual intimacy within my marriage, the most important of all. I believe those who desire a covenant relationship with another are really looking for what is considered a soulmate. A soulmate is one with whom a person feels free to reveal their deepest thoughts, feelings, fears, secrets, shame, dreams, visions, needs, and longings within a realm of absolute trust and safety. This connection allows us to speak honestly, even when we know our words are opening us up to being vulnerable to the other person's response. Our hearts feel safe within their love, even if they do not always fully agree with or understand us. Unfortunately, when it comes to narcissism, this place of open expression and vulnerability is not used for encouraging, deepening, and building up but rather as an avenue for discouragement and tearing down. As I stated earlier, a victim's words become weapons in the hands of a narcissist. I will give the following scenario as an example.

I openly expressed to my husband my need for communication to feel intimately connected to him and that the lack of communication made me feel lonely and isolated. Instead of him taking those words and using them in ways that would fulfill these voids in my life and heart, he withdrew both himself and his words all the more so as to deepen the void. This tactic, of course, faithfully served its intended purpose in making me feel even more unworthy of the love and connection I so desperately longed for. Over a long period of time I began to see the behavior patterns form, as the more I openly and honestly expressed my needs, the more he withheld them. The more I asked him not to do or say something that hurt me, the more it was done or said. These patterns of abuse forced me into even deeper isolation and loneliness because I began to keep my needs unexpressed so that I wouldn't make myself vulnerable to his manipulative ploy of using my words as arrows to stab my heart.

It was a no-win situation because I was forced either to swallow all of my unexpressed words, choking me with unbearable pain, or to take the chance of expressing them again in silent desperation and hoping for a breakthrough—yet knowing I would have to live with any negative consequences. The inability of a person to express themselves, whether with words or physical action, especially in a relationship as intimate as marriage, is like being forced into solitary confinement without just cause. Communication is the key, the core, of any relationship; without some form of it there is no real connection. Like the flow of electricity when you flip on the switch and it brings light to the lamp, one is useless without the other. If there is a malfunction at either end, the other one suffers a loss. As with anything that we want to function well and run smoothly, there needs to be regular maintenance. With any form of neglect, over time, the results of that neglect will become apparent, even if it is a slow fade.

Give ear, O LORD, to my prayer;
and attend to the voice of my supplications.
In the day of my trouble I will call upon You,
for You will answer me. (Ps. 86:6)

The Voice of Silence

**I sought the LORD, and He heard me,
and delivered me from all my fears.** (Ps. 34:4)

Through my personal 25-year journey wandering in silent desperation, I have come to understand that a person will do almost anything to get some relief from the devastating silence, loneliness, and internal turmoil it brings: to be let out of solitary confinement and into the fenced-in courtyard—even if only temporarily. Wants become irrelevant, and overall needs are reduced to simply having the freedom to think clearly, move freely, and breathe deeply in peace. On a small scale, people in this kind of pain will stick a sharp object (symbolically speaking) into their engorged flesh to release the physical pressure of that painful blister I wrote about earlier. On a much larger scale, they will burn their flesh or slit open their skin with whatever sharp object is available to them to achieve temporary relief from the emotional and/or mental pain that is building up inside them. Without an outlet for unexpressed pain, they may feel that they will either burst open with it or be consumed by it.

This kind of pain is suffocating. Like someone drowning and crying out for help, we know we only have so much time left before we are too exhausted to keep treading water, too tired to keep fighting to stay above the surface, knowing the next wave is coming to push us back under. As a woman of faith, I had a safety net and anchor that many who find themselves trapped in this desperate place do not yet have. Scripture became my lifeline, my floating device, my anchor in the storm, my only source for hope of rescue. I will share just a few Bible passages that strengthened and encouraged me daily during some of the lowest seasons of my life:

* He reached down from on high and took hold of me; He drew me out of deep waters. (Ps. 18:16)
* Behold, God is my helper; the Lord is the upholder of my life. (Ps. 54:4)
* For my sides are filled with burning, and there is no soundness in my flesh. I am feeble and crushed; I groan because of the tumult of my heart. O Lord, all my longing is before You; my sighing is not hidden from You. My heart throbs; my strength fails me, and the

light of my eyes - it also has gone from me. But for You, O LORD, do I wait; it is You, O LORD my God, who will answer. For the LORD loves justice; He will not forsake His saints. (Ps. 38:8-10,15; Ps. 37:28)

* My soul clings to You; Your right hand upholds me. But those who seek to destroy my life shall go down into the depths of the earth. (Ps. 63:8-9)

* When you pass through the waters, I will be with you; and the rivers, they shall not overwhelm you; when you walk through fire you shall not be burned, and the flame shall not consume you. For I am the LORD your God, the Holy One of Israel, your Savior. (Isa. 43:2, 3)

* I wait for the LORD, my soul waits, and in His Word I hope…. (Ps. 130:5)

JOURNAL ENTRY — April 1, 2014

If I do not speak truth, I have no strife;

But by not speaking truth, I have no life.

So answer me Lord, what should I do?

I cannot please the man and also please You.

As You are just, faithful, and kind,

Place the key in my silenced heart and mind.

At one time I was very perplexed about self-harm and mutilation, always so deeply saddened by the acts; I still am. And even though I do not advise these dangerous acts as a healthy way of outwardly expressing and relieving inner pain, I finally understand the motivation behind them. Unfortunately, I got to a place in my silent desperation that I would do almost *anything* to get a verbal response from my husband, even goading him to anger in hopes of opening the expressionless and wordless mouth and breaking through his eyes that were either indifferent or stone-cold toward the pain and turmoil within me. Receiving harsh words in his anger would be better than nothing at all.

Sadly, toward the end, a part of me wished he would just hit me when I saw that his carefully guarded and controlled anger was boiling toward the surface. Even though I knew he could really hurt me, as he was much bigger and stronger than me, the thought of physical pain—something at least tangible and visible—seemed a much better alternative to the invisible silence that I was forced to live in. He tried that route early on in our marriage. He threatened me one day with a tight fist held high in midair, poised to hit my face, the face of a noncompliant "object." But I was a high-spirited German redhead, a soldier, and in that unexpected moment of decision, I looked him square in the eyes and said, "Go ahead, but you better make it good because it will be the first and last time you will *ever* have the opportunity to lay your hands on me again, as I will be gone and so will your children." He knew I meant it. In that moment he had to make a split-second decision as well, and he realized he wasn't ready to lose his trophy wife and "object"; he had too much to learn yet to be a more seasoned and convincing narcissist. So he lowered his physical weapon, which would be loud and draw too much attention, and put on the "silencer." This form of emotional and mental abuse, at least for me, would become much more insidious and toxic than I could have ever dreamed—a nightmare from hell that carried me to the lowest places in my heart, mind, and soul. But that same "high spirit" of mine would prove invaluable to my survival in the ensuing years, until at last it was broken—but not by him. It would be broken by the Lord, who would lovingly use that yielding to bring me from brokenness to victory![29]

> I love the LORD, for He heard my voice; He heard my cry for mercy. Because He turned His ear to me, I will call on Him as long as I live. The cords of death entangled me, the anguish of the grave came over me; I was overcome by distress and sorrow. Then I called on the name of the LORD: "LORD, save me!" The LORD is gracious and righteous; our God is full of compassion. The LORD protects the unwary; when I was brought low, He saved me. (Ps. 116:1-6)

---

[29] The Christian band Third Day wrote a song called "It's a Shame" that greatly resonated with the part of me that my narcissist husband had abandoned long ago. With its beautiful lyrics about loss, abandonment, and wasted love, it speaks so perfectly to my own situation.
Third Day, "It's a Shame," *Wire*, Provident, 2004.

...in all these things we are more than conquerors through Him [Jesus] who loved us. (Rom. 8:37, content in brackets added)

I have lived with chronic physical pain, oftentimes debilitating in nature, for over twenty years. Chronic pain can be all-consuming to the one who bears it. Sometimes to just function and pull through the day or night can be physically, emotionally, mentally, and even spiritually exhausting, frustrating, and depressing. These symptoms often run parallel with emotional and mental pain. Fear can become a large part of physical pain as well: fear of the unknown and fear of the future. But because I have endured both ends of the spectrum, the difference I have found is that with physical pain, we can usually diagnosis its source, name it, treat it, and have a course of action to heal it. Because physical pain is usually more apparent, it is easier for people to visibly see, show compassion, and offer help. People are usually more comfortable talking about and addressing visible things: the outward manifestation of an ailment. I know I was at one time. If I could get a definitive diagnosis of my physical pain, I felt I had some knowledge of and control over it, a choice of what to do about it, and understanding of how I could learn to live with it.

On the other hand, when pain generates from deep within, its source unseen, unclear, and unknown, it can make people uncomfortable, unsympathetic, or unbelieving. The person suffering with this invisible foreign mass growing inside of them and spreading into every fiber of their being, yet without a known cause, diagnosis, or name for it, becomes very isolated in their private pain. A light has been cast on what once perplexed me: Mental and/or emotional pain is greater and runs deeper than physical pain that is more tangible, even if evident only to ourselves. This is one of the main reasons I am writing this book, pouring out my heart, and re-experiencing my invisible and silent pain—to shed light upon, speak truth about, and bestow understanding into the reality and evil darkness of narcissism—to be a voice in the silence!

JOURNAL ENTRY — August 28, 2013

Imprisoned by bars the world cannot see,

Yet despite my confinement I find myself most free,

For the world claims no space in which

My Lord cannot be.

JOURNAL ENTRY — May 2016

He has brought way more tears and pain than he ever made me laugh. I think you need an upright soul to make someone laugh; his soul is not in the light but in darkness. Silence the whole ride home. I thought, "I could never even endure many more days in this forced silence; I would go mad!" Lord, help me to know what Your plan is so I can have peace here. I trust in Your plan I can't see yet.

JOURNAL ENTRY — November 28, 2016

Dear Father,

When I exalt myself and my needs and wants over Your will, may the Spirit bring me back to the place I must stand or fall at Your feet of grace. If it be Your will that my walk be a trail of pain and tears in silent injustice at the hands of man; then give me the portion of courage, grace, and love necessary every day, every hour, every minute to do so for Your glory. He who vindicates me is near!

JOURNAL ENTRY — December 9, 2016

I had a dream. It was a dream of frustration which brought back the memories of trying to talk to my husband and get a response. I saw a large, round, gray stone with a simple face painted on it. Talking to my spouse was like talking to that stone: cold, emotionless eyes and firmly sealed lips...silence. Sometimes I would provoke him to anger just to hear him say something. It was in those moments of angry abandon when he actually spoke some truth. I would get glimpses of the deep feelings of his judgments against me and others, his hatred of people and things he despised doing, his warped sense of feeling "overwhelmed" with his long "to do" list he never had—glimpses of his cold soul. He would realize afterward that he had given away glimpses of his inner self which shone a very unfavorable picture of the real man, and he hated that because it flew in the face of his perfectly formed fantasy image; the one he tried so hard to project upon the world! Over the years he became very controlled so as to not open himself up to self-incrimination. Our communication shriveled up to a trickle as more and more of his life was swallowed up in fantasy so that the reality of "real" life became distasteful and overwhelming to his numb senses. I shared less and less of my life, too; for two reasons: because he really didn't care so speaking about anything was salt in the wound and him knowing what I needed, wanted, and what hurt my heart actually became weapons in his arsenal that he could and would use in his warped attacks against me.

JOURNAL ENTRY — August 31, 2017

That I do not have to question my worth by the negative reactions of others—their own insecurities pushed back upon me—and that I no longer need to accept, live within, nor fear the voice of silence is such a place of personal victory! I had not really been aware...until just in this moment...that in certain realms of personal relationships I had begun to be anxious and fear the punishment of silence. You rescued me from that pit of hell, and I no longer need ever crawl back into it again nor fear it! Because You rescued me from silent desperation and have "opened my mouth" to speak with quiet strength against the abuse of forced silence, I need to guard against any constraints that would try to draw me back into the pit of low self-esteem, shame, isolation, and loneliness that tries to plague my mind and break my heart once again. Those who would purposely try to hurt me in that way are not my friends but my enemies...although I still love them and pray for them. Thank You that I do not have to fear the silence anymore!

> ...all who swear by God will glory in Him,
> while the mouths of liars will be silenced.
> (Ps. 63:11)

16
Origin of Our Deepest Desires to Be Seen, Heard, Known…to Be Loved

"You will be ever hearing but never understanding; you will be ever seeing but not perceiving."
(Matt. 13:14)

The Yearning

WHY? WHY DIDN'T you desire to see me? Why couldn't you look beyond the surface and into the depth of my pleading eyes and see my deep need to just be loved back through your eyes with passion, basic human kindness, understanding, and devotion? Why? Why couldn't you hear my cries? Why were your ears deaf to me? Why didn't you want to hear my thoughts, my dreams, my desires, my joys, my fears, or just about the simple parts of my day and that of your children? Why? Why didn't you want to know me? Why did you want me if you couldn't encourage me to be all that I could be, but instead try to diminish me? Why didn't you long to explore the depth of what was yours to know intimately within the covenant relationship of oneness?

Why did you marry me if you didn't desire to see, hear, know, or love me? Why would you bind me to yourself only to reject me and push me away, leaving me in loneliness and silent desperation? Why would you think it was your right to take a person's one lifetime here on earth and consider it expendable only for your personal gain? Why, when I asked so very little from you, could you not share a scrap from your table, as even a crumb would have been better than nothing? Why did you let me slowly die of starvation while you made yourself fat on your secret life and selfish pleasures? Why could you not comfort me when I sobbed for us, our daughters, and other loved ones. Why would you never come and look for me when I wandered off in pain? Why did you leave me yearning in the desert wilderness all alone, wounded, and in silence? Why? Why would you not let yourself be seen, heard, known, and loved deeply by me? I asked these questions of you for almost 25 years, yet I never received a single truthful answer—often none at all. The silence, the deep cavern of unanswered whys swallowed me up like an obscure and worthless object, an expendable piece of "damaged goods"!

Anyone who has walked in these shoes knows the endless questions and the empty answers to the whys. In the wake of these unanswered questions, we often feel disjointed and not completely assembled because of missing parts; we lack wholeness.

> **But for Adam there was found no helper fit for him. So the LORD God caused a deep sleep to fall upon the man, and while he slept took one of his ribs and closed up its place with flesh. And the rib that the LORD God had taken from the man he made into a woman and brought her to the man. Then the man said, "This at last is bone of my bones and flesh of my flesh; she shall be called Woman, because she was taken out of Man." Therefore a man shall leave his father and mother and hold fast to his wife, and they shall become one flesh.** (Gen. 2:20-24)

But what do we do when the other half of the whole refuses to become one with us? How does this happen and why? Why do we have this innate universal yearning to be seen, heard, known, and loved? Why can't we get rid of it, reject it, or ignore it? Why does it span every continent, nation, tribe, race, and religion like an infectious disease? As a woman of faith, I believe that it was placed within us—inside our human DNA, so to speak—as an integral part of our very being (self). Like air, food, and water that sustain the physical body to keep it working at optimal health, so these crucial elements of the heart and soul need to be met to fully feel well, balanced, and whole.

Of course, speaking from a biblical view, all of our needs can be met by God in Jesus; I can testify that He truly can be our "all in all" and make us complete (Col. 3:11 and 2 Pet. 1:3). But from the beginning of time, our Father God made us for human relationships as well. We were created in His image and are a blueprint of the intimate relationship shared and enjoyed in the mystery of the Trinity: Father, Son, and Holy Spirit, who are three yet one.

> **Then God said, "Let us make man in our own image, after our own likeness. So God created man in His image, in the image of God He created him; male and female He created them."** (Gen. 1:26-27)

I believe this was an act of unifying the created to the Creator as our Father God's heart would always long to see, hear, and know His beloved children—and so that the children of God would always yearn to see, hear, know, and love their Father: a divine weaving of our hearts together in harmonious relationship and mutual love. This unity of love would then circle down into the design for marriage and families. The husband and wife were to desire to see, hear, know, and love one another in beautiful intimacy and mutual respect, and parents were to see, hear, know, and love their children as individual and unique creations. The cycle would pass on throughout all generations like the timeless ripple of a stone cast upon the water.

So what happened? How did this unified train fall off the tracks? Well, let's just say that it didn't get very far in the first place; it derailed before the first couple even started their family in what is known by those of the faith as "the Fall." In this one act of pride and disobedience, the whole perfect, beautiful, and harmonious design in the give and take of mutual *selfless* love and respect became distorted and marred. Where once reigned an unabashed and unhindered exchange of body, heart, and soul…there entered in shame, deceit, lies, blame, and pain of every sort imaginable. There has been a succession of mini train wrecks, derailments, and wrong turns ever since. But because the yearning to be seen, heard, known, and loved

185

was woven into the very fabric of our being, it remains, though often a bittersweet remnant of what it once was. Like a distant memory that haunts our spirits, it is something we desperately long to remember and experience in our reality as a part of who we are, yet it eludes us and seems always just out of our reach. This makes me think of a beautiful butterfly that flits about on a summer day. We long for it to alight upon us so that we can examine up close its delicate and unique beauty, but just when we think it will land, it suddenly moves off into another direction, leaving us yearning for its touch.

JOURNAL ENTRY — September 21, 2015

You declare through Paul in Romans 8:31, "If God is for us, who can be against us?" I have had people that I have deeply loved, helped, and cared about turn against me. Rejection, emotional abuse, coldness of heart, manipulation...it hurt then and it still hurts now. Those who have not been "for me" but against me; although I dedicated my time, energy, prayers, and love toward them. Constant rejection makes you always question yourself and ask, "Why can't anyone love me? What did I do wrong? How can I change to be accepted? Why am I not worthy? Will no one ever just love me for me? Will I ever know what true acceptance feels like? Will I always have to perform to be seen, known, heard, cared about, and acknowledged?" But God tells me that He is for me and always has been. He will go before me and fight my battles and win. I am so grateful for Your love, strength, comfort, and peace for without them I would be lost and wandering, looking for a way to fill the empty holes in my vain life.

> **Show me a sign of Your favor,**
> **that those who hate me may see and be put to shame**
> **because You, LORD, have helped me and comforted me.**
> (Ps. 86:17)

Although the manifestations of harm and subsequent injuries incurred are generated by a variety of differing circumstances, I believe the core factors that blind the narcissist (or anyone who feels superior to others) from being able to acknowledge others as worthy of being seen, heard, known, and loved, are rooted in pride and disobedience. What is pride? It is an elevated sense of self-importance that stimulates selfish behaviors. At the core of Narcissistic Personality Disorder lies the misguided and distorted view wherein a person believes they are autonomous or self-governing, existing and functioning independently. When you separate yourself from others by self-induced notions of your own superiority, which is rooted in pride, entitlement, and an unrealistic view of who you really are, in a nutshell, you become your own "god" who rules over your own little universe that you created. You become answerable to no one (although everyone must be answerable to you), which would explain all of the unanswered whys. This is a pretty incompatible place to be in when locked into a marriage relationship with another person who is now supposed to be *one* with you!

A narcissist doesn't feel that they have to answer our whys for they see themselves as being above our insignificant questions. They don't desire to *see us* because they are too busy looking at and admiring themselves. After all, don't a narcissist's spouse and the other people in their lives only exist to be a reflection of themselves, like a shiny toaster or polished mirror? And if the toaster becomes tarnished or the mirror cracked, thereby reflecting poorly, is it worth anything now but the rubbish heap? And why should a "god" have to listen to or *hear* the cries of their servants? Shouldn't all good servants just do their work with diligence, commitment, gratitude, and happy faces because they have been "chosen," thereby having the privilege of being in the presence of such a "god." An autonomous person should not have to listen to the whiny complaints of the hired help and their need for attention, acceptance, kindness, and love.

This "hired help" mentality may strike a chord with many readers. My spouse would often proclaim (to my shock), "What do you want from me? Don't I bring home a paycheck?" To which I would respond, "I didn't marry a paycheck; I didn't need your paycheck. I married and needed a husband and father for our children." A classic derailment indeed! Now, in all honesty, some people do marry others for the paycheck or prestige that may go along with it. But most people sincerely marry for love, relationship, family, a future together, and to have a person by their side with whom they can be *known* in all ways and *loved* regardless. These proclamations from my husband were not only a shocking true revelation of his heart and mind, but a deeply sad view of the warped consciousness of his inner self and his detachment from all other people: the exchange of an inanimate object (money) for the purchase and use of another inanimate object (spouse/servant). And, of course, if we are only seen as an object—especially a malfunctioning object—we become very expendable!

> **For the LORD has called you like a wife deserted and grieved in spirit, like a wife of youth when she is cast off, says your God.** (Isa. 54:6)

As for being *known*, what a ridiculous notion for a narcissist to consider. Why would a "god" need to know anything about their servant other than, "What can you do for me? How can you help me? What can you do for my reputation, my household, my success, and my projected image to the world?" This is why a narcissist chooses what they deem to be a trophy wife or husband. A "god" would need someone who they feel is worthy to stand by their side because they are, after all, just a reflection of themselves. If after years of silent, verbal, and/or physical abuse, neglect, and the withholding of love, we (as the lucky trophy) are growing dull or full of dents, making the reflection not as clear or as shiny as it once was, then, by all means, we must be gotten rid of! Some narcissists keep replacing their trophies, but some may decide that they are more trouble than they are worth. This causes them to revert farther into their fantasy world where they can always reign supreme as a "god" over their forever-willing subjects.

> **Whoever isolates himself seeks his own desire;**
> **he breaks out against all sound judgment.**
> **A fool takes no pleasure in understanding,**
> **but only in expressing his opinion.** (Prov. 18:1-2)

Some narcissists will begin to believe after many years with one "object," who is (unbeknownst to them) training and feeding their spouse's enormous ego-appetites, in conjunction with their daily doses of affirming fantasy, that they have absorbed and assimilated the object's character qualities and unique personality. This comes with the false belief that they can now survive on their own—seeing, hearing, knowing, and loving only themselves. But just as a parasite cannot live without a healthy host, neither can a narcissist survive well without a new "host" or "object." For they discover relatively quickly, to their frustration and chagrin, that they truly are *not* a self-sustaining organism in need of no one, but rather a needy child who requires daily provided care and attention. What a tragedy it is that one who has been created for unity within relationships with the innate yearning to be seen, heard, known, and loved by others becomes detached from these core needs! I will summarize both this portion of the chapter and the last 25 years of my life with this statement of truth: *While I was silently desperate to be seen, heard, known, and loved, my husband was silently and just as equally desperate to* not *be seen, heard, known, and loved (in truth and reality) by me—and so the silent battle raged on.*

"For everyone who exalts himself will be humbled, and he who humbles himself will be exalted." (Luke 14:11)

JOURNAL ENTRY — August 2013

His confusion must be great! He desires to be detached, uncommitted, and able to move about freely—not to have to answer to anyone or be held accountable; free from duty and responsibility…at a distance but still in view. And yet he desperately needs me and those close to him to know who he is; to give him an identity and a purpose. Trying desperately to remain attached to something of depth yet without being connected by feelings and emotions; manipulating to try and achieve both identities and finding traps of his own making. It is a dangerous game where no one wins but much is lost!

I am going to revert back to the very beginning of this chapter and the repeated questions of "why" addressed to my spouse. Even though I was not consciously aware of it at the time, what the depth of my heart was truly saying through my tears was "why" to God: *Why are You letting this happen in my life?* As my faith deepened during those lonely wilderness days in the barren desert, I came to more fully understand that, as a child of God, nothing can touch our lives that He does not allow. Now, let me clarify here. *No forms* of abuse, injustice, neglect, or various elements of pain and suffering were a component of God's *original* design and perfect plan. These situations entered onto center stage at the time of "the Fall" when man exercised his gift of free will to exalt himself above God's commands. This subsequently ushered in sin, disease, dysfunction, abuse, violence, death, etc. And because God lovingly gave us *free will* so that we could be free agents over our lives and not puppets on a string, He must also allow the *consequences* of this free-will gift even if misused against ourselves and others.

This knowledge of truth would be almost unbearable if God left us alone in our fallen mess, pain, and suffering, but He does not. To those who choose to follow His Son, Jesus, He makes an irrefutable promise to never leave us nor forsake us (Hebrews 13:5). Our Father empowers us to be restored to our former status as sons and daughters, which was established before the Fall, by transforming us from within through the power of the Holy Spirit. **"But we have this treasure in jars of clay to show that this all-surpassing power is from God and not from us"** (2 Cor. 4:7 NIV). And because He works all things together for good (Rom. 8:28), because He *is* good, then we can always be assured that whatever touches our lives during the deepest lows has the potential to bring about a *good purpose* if we allow it. This leads us from the negative question "why" to the positive questions of "what" and "how":

*   What are You doing *in me*, Lord, during this trial?
*   What are You trying to *show me*?
*   How can this *change me* for the better?
*   How can *I use* this season of pain and suffering to grow and touch others' lives?
*   How can this *spur me* to see, hear, know, and love You more, as well as myself and my neighbors?
*   In what ways are You *allowing me* to see and experience more of Your love, power, healing, comforts, mercy, grace, wisdom, and knowledge?

The list is endless when dealing with an infinite God!

"In the world you will have tribulation (great misery, distress, trouble). But take heart; I have overcome the world."
(John 16:33)

I have learned that God rarely answers our "why" questions directly. He didn't for King David, Elijah, Jeremiah, Job, etc. Our "whys" often keep us looking backward at our past, which is really irrelevant now, as it cannot be changed or reversed. If we stay stuck there, we will marinate in our pain, loss, bitterness, and regrets, which will only cripple and destroy what God has planned for our "now" and our future. God is always in forward motion and working in the present moment. He just wants us to trust in His goodness, all-sufficiency, and power to make all things new.

"Remember not the former things, nor consider the things of old. Behold I am doing a new thing; now it springs forth, do you not perceive it?" (Isa. 43:18-19)

I mourned a great deal for all of the years I felt were lost and stolen from me in the haze of pain, confusion, and sorrow: years of my life that I couldn't get back or that could have been happier—if only. And I believe it is healthier to face our pain, disappointments, fears, anger, loss, and grief head-on than to stuff it somewhere, only to have it grow into a toxic cancer that will eventually consume us. We often try to run from our past as if it is something outside our hearts, souls, and minds that enough time, distance, money, possessions, distractions, hard work, and change will erase or remedy. But for better or for worse, our past experiences are a part of the fabric of our being;

> "In order to love who you are, you cannot hate the experiences that shaped you."
>
> —Andrea Dykstra,
> *Biblical Accounts of Our Timeless Yearnings*

they mold and shape us into the people we become. I have learned (through much trial and error) to glean from the past that which is useful and empowering in the present and for my future, leaving the unprofitable remains behind like a shed snakeskin, as I no longer need to be bound within its lifeless covering. The choice then is simple: Are we going to allow our experiences to define us for better or for worse?

Are we going to rise above the ashes in freedom and victory, or settle into them in self-pity and defeat? This is also the blessing and curse of free will. Choose wisely!

> **Jesus said to him, "Have I been with you so long, and you still do not know Me, Philip?"** (John 14:9)

I believe most of us would agree that until a problem, situation, or conflict personally touches our lives or that of someone close to us, we truly do not know the extent to which it will affect us or others until it manifests and alters our life in some way. Surely we can sympathize and have compassion for others when our hearts are moved by their distress, plight, or grief. But, to make that deeper connection, we also need to have an intimate understanding, which only happens when we have been touched directly by it. For example, I can relate to many individuals' physical ailments because I have endured nearly twenty years of chronic pain and the various avenues of treatment and maintenance often necessary to function with daily symptoms. I have also suffered bouts of insomnia and the negative residual effects of long-term sleep deprivation; this allows me to connect with a fellow insomniac.

In addition to my personal experience with narcissistic abuse and all of the subsequent pain and loss that resulted (including the dissolution of our marriage), I have lived up-close-and-personal with cancer, depression, anxiety disorders, and eating disorders. I have also cared for orphaned and neglected children and have assisted with in-home care for the elderly. Through the physical and mental training and pressures associated with a 10-year military career, in conjunction with living in a chronically stressful and toxic home environment, I have suffered from many stress-related health issues and trauma. All of this has equipped me to offer a means of comfort and support to others in our shared experiences. This is one of the purposes in the pain: to intimately connect with a fellow traveler and be able to truly see, hear, know, and love them while listening to their stories, sharing their pain, and attending to their needs. This is why I am deeply moved as I read through the Scriptures. I am drawn to those—even from ancient days—who have walked the journey with companions named *pain, sorrow, and affliction*. These men and women have left behind their stories so that we can connect with them as well as learn from their personal encounters with our loving God. I would like to share a few that have reached through the pages of history and attached themselves to my heart and soul—kindred spirits yearning to be seen, heard, known, and loved.

The first woman I found a personal connection with was Hagar. Unless you are familiar with the Old Testament, you may not recognize this woman's name. If you find yourself reading this book because of your own yearnings, you may find wonderful sources of comfort, hope, and peace within the pages of Hagar's story. Hagar was an Egyptian servant to a woman named Sarah. Sarah was the wife of Abraham, a devoted man of God who would become known as the "father" of the nation of Israel. Having a son during this period in history to carry on the family name and heritage was very important, but Sarah was barren and could not conceive. It was a custom of that time for a barren wife to offer her maidservant to her husband in hopes of conceiving a male child. So Abraham had "relations" with Hagar and, low and behold, she bore him a son named Ishmael. (The Bible is certainly *not* boring, nor are the life issues from the past very different from today!)

The part that is meaningful to me personally (and perhaps you as well) is this: After Hagar had done what her mistress had asked her to do and became pregnant, Sarah became extremely jealous of Hagar and began to treat her very poorly. Now Hagar, who probably never imagined she would have the privilege of bearing the firstborn son of such an honorable man, became a little "full of herself," which only infuriated Sarah all the more. She became so harsh with her that Hagar fled. And where did she flee? She fled into the desert wilderness—a place I so often found myself (spiritually speaking) during the many years of silent abuse and oppression. While in that barren and lonely place, an angel of the Lord found Hagar and convinced her to go back to her mistress and serve her so that she could have the protection and provision she would need to care for herself and the unborn child.

> **And the angel of the LORD said to her, "Behold, you are pregnant and shall bear a son. You shall call his name Ishmael because the LORD has listened to your affliction."** (Gen. 16:11)

> **So she called the name of the LORD who spoke to her, "You are a God of seeing," for she said, "Truly here I have seen Him who looks after me."** (Gen. 16:13)

How beautiful is the tenderness of our Father God who sees our affliction, pain, rejection, injustices, fear, and loneliness. Hagar could run away from Sarah, but she could not run away from the eyes of a loving God—a Father who sees, hears, knows, and loves us so much that He comes and finds us in our silent desperation. God saw her confusion and knew her plight. Returning likely meant more abuse, harshness, and rejection—but fleeing was filled with uncertainty, fear, loneliness, and danger, especially in her pregnant condition and all on her own.

What terrible conflicts we, too, often find ourselves in— physically, emotionally, mentally, and spiritually. I have found myself embroiled in all four ways, and I certainly knew the temptation to flee, to get away from the constant oppression and breathe freely. But I (often after much internal wrestling) would relinquish my will in the end, knowing in my heart that I would come to regret—not being free from abuse— but rather what that freedom would cost me. You see, we always have to count the cost of the jump *before* we take the leap. Once we are free-falling, we may find that where we end up landing is right back into a similar situation as the one we just left, or, as often is the case without wisdom guiding our decisions, a worse place than we were in to begin with.

If God hadn't sent an angel to encourage Hagar to return to a place of provision and protection, where would she have ended up?

She very easily could have died in the desert from lack of food, water, or shelter, or she could have been killed by wild animals. And even if she would have found a way to survive the wilderness and navigate her way out, who would then want her? At this time in history and in their culture, it was very disgraceful to be unwed and pregnant. She would have had a hard time finding a man to be a husband to her and care for another man's child. Women in this time period rarely had a way to support themselves and would live a hard life of poverty on their own. So, even though God encouraged Hagar to return to a harsh place, He knew that this was the best choice for her and her unborn child. But God is just and faithful. After He asked her to surrender her will, yield to her mistress, and make the hard choice to return, He also blessed her with a promise that her son Ishmael would produce a multitude of offspring and become a great nation (Gen. 16:9-10). In time, Sarah bore Abraham a son in her old age, and Hagar was sent away into the wilderness. Although alone once more with her son in the physical elements of the desert, Hagar was never again alone with her son in the spiritual realm, for the Lord God was always with them, keeping His watchful and loving eyes upon them. He protected and provided for their needs every step of the way, and when the time was right, He fulfilled the promise made long ago to make a great nation from the descendants of Ishmael (Gen. 21:8-21).

My tears have flowed freely with Hagar's in our shared pain and sorrow: two women who simply longed to be seen, heard, known, and loved—not as women *owned* but *belonging*—as well as to raise our children with provision, security, peace, joy, and much love. Our common bond was desiring to be obedient to those placed in authority over us (my husband, her mistress). Like Hagar, I found that my willing obedience led to abuse, rejection, ridicule, injustice, loneliness, and silent desperation. Also like Hagar, I became expendable when my presence was no longer needed nor wanted. Yet we also share another common bond, and that is this: While we endured our respective wilderness experiences, God sought us and calmed our fears while encouraging us in our plight. He provided much-needed protection and provision, and spoke wisdom into the way that we should go that all might end well for us. He kept us from "jumping out of the frying pan and into the fire" in our confusion and scorn. If we were to choose outside of God's will, we would have to forfeit His promises. He not only took loving care of both of us but also our children, who needed a good, strong, and faithful Father. He promised us that if we would wait upon Him in the pain and be of good courage, He would strengthen our hearts and pave the way for an amazing future for ourselves and our child(ren)—if we kept moving forward with unshakable faith, trust, and patience for His perfect timing!

> **Wait for the LORD; be strong, and let your heart take courage; wait for the LORD!** (Ps. 27:14)

> **But God chose what is foolish in the world to shame the wise; God chose what is weak in the world to shame the strong; God chose what is low and despised in the world, even things that are not, to bring to nothing things that are, so that no human being might boast in the presence of God.** (1 Cor. 1:27-29)

The next person who moved my heart to compassion was a man who had been an invalid for 38 years. He spent his days lying beside what was considered a healing pool (called Bethesda) in the city of Jerusalem, hoping that someone would take pity on him and help him get into the waters of potential healing. Jesus *saw* the man lying there and *knew* that he had been there a long time without any relief. I found this man's response very interesting when Jesus asked him, "Do you want to be healed?" Instead of a resounding "yes" as I would anticipate, the man instead expressed his sorrow and desperate plight with Jesus that no one would take the time, show him empathy, or help lower him into the nearby pool. He also shared with Jesus, a patient and compassionate listener, that whenever he did attempt to get himself into the awaiting waters, someone would step down in front of him *as if he didn't exist or wasn't worthy enough to deserve a chance at being healed and made whole.*

I sat with this man's story and reaction to Jesus's question for a long time. My heart ached with him as he was asking so very little, needing and wanting so small a favor—just a helping hand, a kind heart, and eyes of compassion. All this man wanted was for someone to just *see* his need, *hear* his pleas, and *respond* to his silent desperation by offering just a smidgen of tender, loving care and sympathetic understanding. A warm, comforting touch or a kind word from another human being could have alleviated some of his emotional pain even if the pool waters couldn't heal his physical body. Jesus, the epitome of loving-kindness, tender mercy, and limitless compassion, the One who performed countless miracles of healing, could have immediately alleviated this man's physical ailments. Yet, in the present moment, this man apparently *needed* to be seen, heard, known, and loved *more* than he desired outward healing; his soul needs were paramount.

This seems to confirm what my experience with both physical and emotional pain has taught me: The need for understanding and healing of our emotional pain can so often override our desire for physical relief. Maybe the weary man couldn't even muster the strength or courage to truly ask for help again, only to be ignored, unseen, or unheard. I know this feeling of repeated rejection in the wake of my pleas for help, understanding, and compassion—the cold eyes without sympathy or care. It's the pain of making ourselves vulnerable once again only to be left wanting, ashamed that we were so desperate, enough to plead one more time. But Jesus, the Healer, doesn't just give us the crumbs from His table; He always gives us the whole loaf! He didn't just see, hear, know, and show love to this man by filling his unmet internal yearnings of the heart, but He also gave him wholeness in his physical body. After He had patiently fulfilled his emotional needs, **"Jesus said to him, 'Get up, take up your bed, and walk'"** (John 5:8).

Despite the great joy experienced by this man who was once an invalid yet, after encountering Jesus, suddenly walked in health, strength, and freedom, a shadow still fell over his renewed lease on life. After almost 40 years in physical bondage because of his crippled body, and despite the miraculous newfound freedom he was given by Jesus, many people did not rejoice in his "rescue" and healing from the confinement of his unfortunate circumstances. Instead, they were more concerned that he had been healed on a Jewish Sabbath Day of rest, which was in keeping with man-made rules, laws that severely oppressed the people.

I had another personal experience that parallels this man's story. While I was indeed freed from the bondage of silent narcissistic abuse by the will of God given through the Holy Spirit saying to my spirit: "Pick up your things, go forth from this place of oppression and abuse, and be healed of your physical, emotional, and mental pain"—instead of rejoicing in what the Father had done for me, I was questioned, scrutinized, and met with unbelief. Because of a lack of understanding and *belief in me* regarding what was unseen, unheard, and unknown, many couldn't rejoice in my freedom. Some people even told me that I should return to my "gilded" cage of confinement —to stay lying beside the pool waters of healing without any chance of getting lowered in and receiving alleviation from my pain—a place I was slowly withering.

How often do we do this to others because we can't believe what we cannot see or fully understand, even going so far as to deny the truth because we don't want our own perception altered or our comfortable lives rocked by the waters of change? Often we don't want to acknowledge hard truth regarding a situation or about a person we trusted and *thought* we knew. Maybe we did see "something," detected a slight change in atmosphere or personality, but we didn't wish to examine or listen too keenly because a responsibility may be lurking close behind. Or perhaps, if we bent down over the water in the pool too closely to help another person in, we might catch a glimpse of our own reflection. We might see our own brokenness, confining cage, true character, heart, pair of rose-colored glasses, or silent desperation. Sometimes a person's pain, abuse, grief, or circumstances are just too close to our own (infirmities, marriages, relationships with our children, friends, ourselves), and we would rather ignore it and hope that it quietly goes away. If we can just push the freed bird back into her gilded cage, then she will remain perched with clipped wings like our own, for doesn't misery love company? Upon my release from the restraints that bound me, I felt the raw sting of these reactions. As with this elated man—once bound in his infirmity but set free—I experienced the pain felt when others do not support rescue and relief mercifully offered by a good God to those who suffer at the hands of others and life's unfortunate circumstances. But regardless, returning to the gilded cage was *never* an option for me. Therefore, I pressed on in the strength of the Lord, and was gratefully and humbly upheld by many who were faithful and true, those who rejoiced with me in my healing and freedom! (This story is located in John 5:1-17.)

> **May those who delight in my vindication shout for joy and gladness; may they always say, "The LORD be exalted, who delights in the well-being of His servant."** (Ps. 35:27 NIV)

I have one more encouraging story to share. (There are so many wonderful accounts of hope and healing, not only woven throughout the Scriptures, but truly—if we have eyes to see and ears to hear—everywhere within all of our personal spheres.) This touching story is recorded in both Matthew 8:1-4 and Luke 5:12-15. They are short and simple accounts of Jesus's healing or cleansing of a leper. Leprosy is an infectious skin disease that can cause deformity. We do not hear much about this disease in America, but it is still prevalent in other areas around the world. Because of its outward manifestations, many people are both afraid and repulsed by it. Ancient Jewish culture had strict guidelines to prevent the spread of this disease, banning those unfortunate enough to have contracted it to live outside the camps and cities. These poor people were placed in solitary confinement, their own flesh their cell. They were separated from family and friends and lost the ability to enjoy social gatherings or worship in the temple. What a lonely, isolated life they lived, feeling the effects of both physical and emotional pain! The world did not want to see them, and maybe they despised even seeing themselves—a twofold source of pain. While outside the gates, walls, doors, or bars separating humanity, who could hear their cries? If they couldn't be seen or heard, then how could they possibly be known and loved? I am sure they were greatly loved and missed by those who knew them before this fate, but love is an action word that can only truly be expressed by some type of relational connection and human contact. This sets the stage for the leper's encounter with Jesus.

Notice how in this narrative, as well as the one before it, we only know these two men as the "invalid" and the "leper," without mention of their names. I believe this is because names were recorded only if necessary to the overall content of the Bible as well as to connect people to particular tribes, lineage, heritage, etc. God only included exactly what was necessary to be profitable for our teaching, understanding, knowledge, and spiritual growth. I also believe names were often withheld because God didn't want us to just associate a particular story or lesson with that one person, but He purposely left blanks so we could more easily place ourselves or our particular need, situation, trial, affliction, sorrow, etc., into that place and make it personal to us. I can see this clearly by how these individuals' stories have touched my story in very profound and intimate ways.

Now it is recorded in the book of Matthew that when Jesus entered this particular region where the story takes place, He was surrounded by a great crowd of people. The leper came and knelt down before Jesus in faith, believing that He could heal him. How silently desperate do we imagine that this man was to not only break the law by coming inside the city area, but also to open himself up to the ridicule, rejection, and hard hearts of the multitude who were most likely shocked and disgusted that he dare show himself and expose them to his disease? What if Jesus turned him away? Imagine how ashamed he would feel in the midst of this crowd of onlookers. This I have learned for sure: When we get to the point where we are desperate, we can muster courage and determination to act upon and endure almost anything to find relief from our pain and suffering. This man had reached this point. I will relate the story from its perfect source.

> **While He was in one of the cities, there came a man full of leprosy. And when he saw Jesus, he fell on his face and begged Him, "Lord, if You will, You can make me clean." And Jesus stretched out His hand and touched him, saying, "I will; be clean." And immediately the leprosy left him.** (Luke 5:12-13)

How powerful and beautiful! Now, Jesus did not have to touch the man to heal him. He could have done what He did with the invalid and *spoke the words of healing* "you are clean" and received the same results. So why did He take the chance of touching him? I believe that it was simply because He knew the man's deepest need in the moment was not physical healing but to be *touched* and *seen* with love and compassion as the unique individual he was *before being defined* by his disease and circumstances. Jesus wanted the desperate man to know that He *heard* the cry of his heart, which had been silenced by forced isolation. The Lord desired for him to understand that He *knew* everything about his life hidden within the deepest recesses of his aching soul, and loved him unconditionally anyway. He wanted this lonely, hurting man to experience what should be unconditional truth—that no one is ever too "defiled" (in any definition of the word) *to be touched* with love and care. And, of course, Jesus the Master Teacher was exemplifying a beautiful lesson for all to see about *who He is* and *how we are to* truly love our neighbors as ourselves—without fear, judgment, rejection, condemnation, or disdain. This is the bridge-building love of Jesus Christ; there are no boundaries that a simple touch and genuine love cannot overcome!

I will fast-forward here to a modern-day story that I read in a daily devotional,[30] which fits in beautifully with our topic. It was about a young lady who accepted an opportunity to go on a medical

---

[30] *Our Daily Bread*, May 2, 2017.

missions trip in a remote area of East Africa. A woman from the region came into the clinic with a horribly deformed leg due to a disease. Though treatable, it initially repulsed this eager yet not professionally trained volunteer. Nevertheless, her heart of compassion kicked in as she was able to clean and bandage the injured leg despite her initial reaction. During the process, the patient began to cry, and she worried that she was hurting her. When inquiring if the woman's tears were caused from pain as she treated the wound, she replied, "No, it's the first time anyone has touched me in nine years." This woman's tearful response tore at my heartstrings. Nine years without the touch of another human being because of a disease she had no control over or treatment for! Nine years of loneliness, rejection, and isolation—as if her "problem" made her untouchable or unlovable!

How many people live in this great big world with similar stories and heartache? Often the source of fear, anxiety, bitterness, resentment, anger, self-pity, and depression—loneliness is a slow fade into feelings of unworthiness and obscurity. I know this pain of loneliness and lack of physical touch well as they had been constant invisible companions for most of my married life; they have been for many others reading this book as well. It doesn't take nine years to form these negative thoughts and feelings within a human heart, but the longer that loneliness, rejection, and isolation are a central element of our lives, the deeper they take hold of us and start to dismantle us into broken fragments of who we once were. They are like an eraser on a chalkboard, slowly smearing our identity and life story until we can't read enough of what is left to remember what it said, what it looked like, what it felt like, what it all meant—or even how to begin rewriting it again.

> **The LORD…He will respond to the prayer of the destitute; He will not despise their plea.**
> **He hears the groans of the prisoners, to set free those who were doomed to die…"** (Ps. 102:17,20, paraphrased)

JOURNAL ENTRY — September 6, 2015

I saw in my mind's eye how much I had changed. Somewhere buried deep within is the girl/woman I was; free with my heart, light, easy to laugh, to trust, to feel love and be loved, warm and affectionate. She is still there and emerges slightly when she feels safe. But mostly, especially in the current environment, she stays hidden in the dark recesses where she knows the narcissist can't really reach her. Oh, he tries to touch her, but he can't anymore. Christ's hand guards my heart and mind. The inner struggle is constant; the person I need to be now to survive and the woman who longs to be free to live and love.

The need for a human connection through *touch* begins with our first breath of life and only ends with our last breath before death; the need is there during every season of our life between the two. It is crucial to our growth, health, security, contentment, and happiness. A heart connection is made through our gestures of contact, whether in the brief handshake, high-five, pat on the back, or friendly hug, the close snuggling with a child, or the intimate embrace of a lover. The neglect or withholding of this gift of touch, that is truly so easy to give away, robs both the giver and receiver of great joy. Even so, there must be a genuineness in the exchange, or it doesn't sow the good seed nor reap the bountiful harvest. The receiver can perceive the reluctance, the fake attempt, the withholding of the whole self. This is extremely damaging in the parent/child relationship as well as the covenant relationship of marriage. Although nonverbal, it tells the child or spouse that there is something wrong with them, that they fall short somehow, that they are not worthy of receiving all the other person has to give and offer. It may even, at times, suggest that they are repulsive in some way.

Even if the hang-up is actually found within the parent or significant other, often it's the other person who feels responsible for the disconnect. I believe this can badly damage a person's ability to easily give affection away when they mature into adulthood, as it is hard to offer something we never truly received or experienced. Or, on a positive note, it may make a person even more generous with their gestures of affection because they do not want others to feel what they missed having on their own journey. And the longer *appropriate* physical touch and connection goes unfulfilled, the deeper the knife of neglect cuts and the greater the scarring that forms over the wounded and insecure heart. When there is intimate physical contact within the confines of marriage yet *without* a heart and soul connection flowing pure and deep, each partner having unequivocal knowledge that they are being touched by someone who truly sees, hears, knows, accepts, and loves them (speaking as a woman, here), she feels as if she were bought and used for a price rather than regarded as a beloved and worthy recipient of love. It is a beautiful gift and honor to see, hear, know, and love others. A heart connection with a lifelong friend or a passing stranger on the street adds flavor to life that we can't buy, bottle, or barter for. It is priceless because once it is given and/or received, it becomes a part of us— our life and story—no matter how long or brief. But an even more beautiful and priceless treasure is having that intimate heart connection with our Father God and Lord by way of the Holy Spirit.

> **O LORD**, You have searched me and known me!
> You know when I sit down and when I rise up;
> You discern my thoughts from afar.
> You search out my path and my lying down
> and are acquainted with all my ways. (Ps. 139:1-3)

Simple Gestures That Help People Feel Important and Loved

We humans act, react, and respond within our spheres of influence out of our own personal experiences and needs more often than we are aware of. In my latter years, while living in the country as mother and homeschool teacher of three, my sphere was pretty small. Because my husband was paid every two weeks, there was always a big grocery shopping day twice a month. Of course, at least one of my daughters had the privilege of tagging along and helping me; going out for lunch was always good incentive! It actually became special one-on-one time together as they grew older, and I miss those days, which we made not only tolerable but sheer fun! I found then, and still do, that grocery store checkout lines are a great yet simple place to share a moment of human connection with the spoken and unspoken message that says: "I see you, hear you, care about you, and desire to know you," if even for a few brief minutes. Although I didn't realize these things at the time, the Spirit has revealed to me a deeper understanding of how our daily actions and spontaneous reactions signify very meaningful truths about ourselves and are often a genuine reflection of our hearts (whether positive or negative) and unmet yearnings.

First, we need to be aware of other individuals around us. Because most people live and move at such a fast pace, we are frequently self-focused, distracted, and oblivious of our surroundings and the people sharing our space. But being aware of people lets them know that we see them as important individuals. Many people who just run into the store for a couple of items do not have a cart, so they are sometimes left standing in line with cold or heavy items with no place to set them. We can offer to let them ahead of us in line, or just to rest their load on the edge of our cart while they wait. We see mothers saddled with babies on their hips as they juggle purses, shopping lists, and awkward carts (often with malfunctioning wheels!). There are elderly or disabled men and women, and just the necessity of shopping can be challenging and exhausting. How many times do we hear the tired or hungry child crying or see the restless toddler squirming, yelling, or whining? Be proactive and consider simple ways in which you could be of assistance; just a peaceful presence can soothe another person's frustration and stress. Take notice of someone who appears to be running in to buy a few items on their lunch break, or hurrying home from work in order to whip up dinner and eat before rushing out again to evening activities, perhaps offering them your place in line. Most of us can relate to some or all of these scenarios, which gives us a foundation and the experience necessary to be able to see, hear, and care about what is happening around us, even with strangers.

What are we expressing to another person with our simple words, kind gestures, and sympathetic smiles? If we recognize and respond to a need, we are saying: "I see you as a person just like me." When we let someone go ahead of us in the checkout line, we are saying:

* *"You are important."*
* *"I respect you as an individual."*
* *"I care about helping you."*
* *"I understand your need in the moment."*
* *"I want to be kind to you."*

These humble acts of selflessness keep us mindful of another person's needs above our own. I don't ever recall a time when I acted out of genuine love for a neighbor that I did not receive a sincere "thank you" in return, usually given with a grateful smile. Now, I don't acknowledge people or extend acts of basic human kindness for the self-satisfaction of showing others what a great individual I think I am, nor in an effort to win a merit badge for being a "good" person. I so often taught and challenged our children to reflect upon not so much their actions but rather the underlying motivation *behind* their actions, responses, and gestures. The initiatives behind our actions are often a very revealing indicator of our true character. I do not think it is wrong to feel good in our heart after we extend kindness that helps and encourages another person or gives them a bit of extra time, relief, or comfort. But if the sole purpose of our gesture is for the building up of our own egos and feelings of self-righteousness, then I would say we have sorely missed the mark of what it means to love our neighbor as ourselves—unless, of course, we are narcissists.

Random acts of kindness, no matter how small, break down barriers that are often erected between strangers, usually providing an opening for a deeper exchange of communication. When another person knows that we are focused and truly listening to them, seeing them, or acknowledging their need, they become remarkably receptive and more open—vulnerable, really—to sharing a small piece of themselves. Making eye contact is very important, as much about a person and what they are feeling or needing is reflected in their eyes. We can perceive happiness, anxiousness, stress, fatigue, sadness, anger, physical pain, peacefulness, and even loneliness. I believe the eyes truly are a window to a person's soul as they reflect so much about the inner self. Along with that eye contact, a genuine smile always goes a long way too! A short yet sweet exchange between people in the midst of the masses where we can often find ourselves feeling kind of lost, disconnected, easily unseen, unheard, and unknown—well, it truly is a beautiful thing!

Be kind to one another, tenderhearted, forgiving one another, as God in Christ forgave you. (Eph. 4:32)

When my daughters first began accompanying me on these shopping adventures, they would often ask me as we were walking away from the cash register, "Who was that? How do you know that person?" And I would laugh and say, "I don't know them personally." With puzzled looks they would inquire, "But they talked to you like they knew you." I'd just smile because during those brief moments of exchange, we did *know* each other. It was a great opportunity to exemplify for our children how effortless it really is to open the door and communicate acceptance and brotherly love.

I am amazed sometimes at the rather personal stories an individual will share when they perceive we are genuine and truly listening. But it also reveals an underlying sad truth: With all of our technology and ways of communicating with one another, we really are *not connecting* with each other at the depth needed to truly feel bonded and known. When someone so openly shares personal information because a fellow traveler is willing to listen, it confirms to me that, no matter how great our technological advances may be, there is *no substitute* for face-to-face communication, where the genuineness of our exchanges are deeper, more meaningful, and more heartfelt. For Christians, open and honest communication is a beautiful way to "be Jesus" to others in our hurried, harassed, distracted, cold, and lonely world. This practice can reach into every aspect of our lives: with family members, friends, coworkers, church family, waitresses, bank tellers, neighbors, the mailman, etc. There are endless opportunities to see, hear, know, and love the people in our world!

We are all yearning for genuine love.

Let love be genuine.
(Rom. 12:9)

17
Purpose in the Pain:
How I Finally Found Joy in the Pursuit of Happiness

"Lost time is when we learn nothing from the experiences of life."
—Charles Ringma, author and professor, Regent College

I LONGED FOR joy in my life, but it was this vague and elusive entity that I couldn't seem to grasp. I didn't even truly know why I longed for it, as joyfulness wasn't a common word used in my upbringing; happiness was always the goal. Even in our U.S. Constitution we are given the inalienable right to life, liberty, and the pursuit of happiness. I had presumed that joy and happiness were pretty equal in definition and measure, so they had seemed interchangeable in my pursuit of them. Finding myself in an ever-deepening state of silent desperation, though, didn't seem to afford the opportunity or hope of ever grasping either one. But as is often the case when we don't have full understanding in the moment, we are prone to disregard the avenues in which to receive the many blessings that are only unearthed in the deep recesses of difficulty, pain, and sorrow. These are the best surprises and gifts—the ones received unexpectedly in the most unlikely of places and during our lowest seasons.

But on this journey that I didn't sign up for but was taking the trip regardless, I learned that happiness, although it certainly can be pursued, is just a *feeling*, like love and hate, peace and anxiety, depression and elation, tired and rested. Feelings are transient and constantly changing based on our character, temperament, mood swings, attitudes, current atmosphere, weather, season, hunger, or a good or bad "hair day." We can go from feeling happy to sad or mad 20 times a day. Feeling happy is as unique as the person experiencing or not experiencing it. Some people are happy when it is cold and snowy, while others are very unhappy unless it is warm and sunny. Some people (like me) are so happy when they can get outside and go for a long, brisk walk. For someone else, the word "walk" is a four-letter word that brings unhappy thoughts and feelings. Point made. This is why I couldn't truly find joy because what I was really looking for were *feelings of happiness*. Because I lived with someone whose main goal in life was to make me "feel" unhappy in an attempt to diminish, punish, and alienate me, thinking happy thoughts and feeling happy were as hard to grasp as a fluttering butterfly.

Of course, I had wonderful and precious moments of feeling happy while raising our daughters: during celebrations with family and special time with friends; vacations by the ocean while soaking in captivating sunrises, warm sand, and crashing waves; digging in the dirt amid flowers and vegetables; lazy summer days and campfire nights; long walks without destination—these were all simple pleasures that made me feel most happy. But the Happiness Thief was never far away, always hovering on the fringes to strike at an opportune time when no one was watching or understood the ways that my secret avenues to happiness, which I had whispered to my husband in love and trust, were being attacked and abused.

But, oddly, it was when I was in the midst of trying to adapt to a whole new environment (after my rescue from the pit of silent desperation where all hope of ever retaining this elusive state of happiness kept dissipating like vapor in the wind), that I began to experience this strange, yet warm (fleeting at first), alien feeling begin to bubble up from deep within my heart and soul. It didn't burst forth in fits of laughter but rather spread out with this wonderful sensation of *deep peace*. Peace...what a glorious new word to be able to add to my vocabulary! I first felt it in the midst of the transformation process, as I was being spun into a cocoon of drastic change while stepping into a different form of isolation. I eagerly began to pay attention to this amazing calm in the midst of my transition. It was like entering into the eye of a storm: The circumstances and force of power within the storm hadn't really changed, yet I found myself cocooned in this air pocket of gentle peace that transcended all understanding to the natural senses.

As this new sensation pushed ever toward the surface of my conscious mind like boiling lava from an underground cavern, I didn't know its name yet, but I perceived that it was going to be a most welcome guest. When the appointed day came that we were finally introduced, I found out its name was Joy! I was to learn (the hard way) that joy doesn't enter through the front door, nor is it something that comes from an outside source that stimulates our feelings of happiness. Joy is the result of an *inside job*, as it is generated from *within us*. It is a gift given when we make room for it in our hearts. How do we make room to welcome it? What is the criteria to receive this precious gift? What is the price to own it? Well, I can't speak for all people. I am sure it comes in a variety of ways, packages, and circumstances, but mine came at the price of great pain.

I had to go through the desert wilderness first and be broken-down, stripped of both self-effort and reliance, purged, taught, tested, tried, re-taught, tested, tried…repeat…until I was cleansed of all my old ways, wants, ideals, dreams, and dross that needed to be cast into the refining fire. **"Behold, I have refined you, but not as silver; I have tried you in the furnace of affliction"** (Isa. 48:10). I had to stop striving for the transient desire of happiness. It was only after I was patiently and lovingly convinced to give up my caterpillar mindset that I was ready to be cocooned, placed in isolation, and begin the transformation process to receive my wings.

In the midst of dissolving the natural, worldly things that had been a part of my life for many years, I began to be infused with more and more elements of the Christian faith and the supernatural. I believe this is where we begin to really experience joy. You see, *true joy* can't be found in the natural world because it is a spiritual gift. **"The joy of the**

Lord is your strength" (Neh. 8:10). Joy comes from our heavenly Father through the Lord Jesus. **"May the God of hope *fill you with all joy and peace* in believing, so that by the power of the Holy Spirit you may abound in hope"** (Rom. 15:13, italics added). I believe joy is implanted within our hearts in its truest and purest form when we are transformed by the renewing of our hearts and minds by faith. It is when we stop seeking and desiring our modern culture's definition of happiness and begin to embrace the higher state of internally generated joy that we finally experience the fullness of it! And because joy is generated inside ourselves—our circumstances,

> *True joy* can't be found in the natural world because it is a spiritual gift.

afflictions, sorrows, pain, grief, hardships, abuse, rejection, loneliness, isolation, and abandonment —things that touch us from the outside natural world can't encroach upon that which rests securely within. Outside sources can still steal and dispel our moments of happiness, but they have no power to steal our joy unless we *allow* them to.

"Joy" is by definition: *a very happy feeling; happiness; delight.* To "delight" means: *to be highly pleased, to rejoice.*[31] Scripture tells us to **"delight yourself in the LORD, and He will give you the desires of your heart"** (Ps. 37:4). Joy is a feeling like happiness, but it is *not controlled* by how we feel. It takes its proper place within our hearts and remains steady even in the most violent of storms. With it comes deep and lasting peace (harmony and serenity). It is a gift from God given by the Spirit through Jesus Christ. I finally found my joy: a pearl of great price, which was unearthed unexpectedly in my pain. **"...And no one will take your joy from you"** (John 16:22).

> "Find a place inside where there's joy, and the joy will burn out the pain."
> —Joseph Campbell, author

---

[31] Agnes, *Webster's New World Dictionary.*

JOURNAL ENTRY – May 17, 2016

Thank You for the blessing of my daughters! They are joy upon joy and fuel for my tank, which is often running on empty in this parched marriage. You always find a way to bring living, refreshing water into the barren desert! Amen.

JOURNAL ENTRY – February 25, 2014

Heavenly Father, help me to see beyond the veil of the natural world and peek into the supernatural workings of an Almighty God of purpose. Help me to see how my suffering extends beyond the grooming of myself to what You are doing with it in people around me. Help me to see how my pain may encourage others, soften hearts, develop compassion, perseverance, and character. However You use it, help me to be open to the personal sacrifice for the greater good of Your purposes. Amen.[32]

> Count it all joy, my brothers and sisters, when you meet trials of various kinds, for you know that the testing of your faith produces perseverance. And let perseverance have its full effect, that you may be perfect and complete, lacking in nothing. (James 1:2-4)

JOURNAL ENTRY – August 3, 2014

I know, Lord, that nothing is without divine purpose or a part of Your divine plan and will. I need You to drive this truth home to my weary and willful spirit so I can accept with joy the injustice I feel—accept the lies, deceit, and immoral behavior and know that somehow and some way it fits into Your plan for my life. Help me to have eyes to see the impossible and a heart to give love that is not always felt.

Humbled by Grace: To Receive What Is Given

As long as I can remember, even as a young girl, one of my greatest pleasures was giving gifts to others. I clearly recall the first time I had earned enough allowance (which, back in the day, was in coins and not dollar bills) to go to the local drugstore/gift shop and buy each person in my family a little gift for Christmas, which I

---

[32] These words were written over two years before my rescue from abuse on June 15, 2016, and three years before any inkling of ever being called to write a book about my silent pain would become a reality.

picked out all by myself! I waited with anticipation for them to open what I had carefully purchased. Although my gifts were nothing very grand by today's standards, they graciously seemed pleased by my efforts in picking out something uniquely special for each one of them.

To this day, I still find my greatest pleasure in giving rather than in receiving: the simple joy of causing surprise and happiness in a person's heart when they know that their delight was utmost in your mind when choosing their gift. When we give a gift tailored to an individual's personality and likes, the recipient perceives that we have taken the time to see, hear, and know them, and that we desire to show love to them in our giving. It is just as obvious to a person if we do not care to relay the aforementioned. I have had many gifts given to me over the past two decades in which the latter was the case: a very sad truth in the midst of what should have been an enjoyable exchange between a husband and wife. My giving was not limited to purchased gifts wrapped in pretty paper and tied with ribbons. I created handmade cards and presents, baked goods, home-cooked meals, offering my time and energy, my love wrapped in a listening ear, an encouraging word, a hug, a smile, a compassionate heart, a prayer, and shared tears of both joy and sorrow. These can often be the most precious gifts of all because they are sacrificial in nature and cannot be bought with a price. There is something almost sacred about a genuine gift from the heart poured out in loving sacrifice for another.

Each one must give as he has decided in his heart, not reluctantly or under compulsion, for God loves a cheerful giver. (2 Cor. 9:7)

I worked hard over the years to make our "nest" a comfortable, safe, and peaceful place—a labor of love to transform an ordinary house into a warm and welcoming home. This was never a chore for me but rather a delight to my heart. To show hospitality, even if meager during lean times, to whomever stepped over our threshold was a priority to me. God placed the call on my life to open our home to others for extended periods of time and for various reasons. There was never a shortage of physical, emotional, and spiritual giving to go around—in the strength of the Lord, of course! It had to have come from the Lord because my "natural resources" were constantly being drained by the narcissist faster than they could be refilled by outside sources. **"For this I toil, struggling with all *His energy* that He powerfully works within me"** (Col. 1:29, italics mine). I would come to understand, though, that just as much as those who came into our home, family unit, and hearts were recipients of all God gave us to offer them, what our family gained through these experiences were far greater gifts to us than we could ever have imagined! Our heavenly Father knew that I needed to be a vessel almost constantly pouring outward into others, so that I would not become consumed with my inner pain and be swallowed up by it. By keeping me outwardly focused on the immediate needs of others, I didn't have time or energy to spend on self-pity, self-absorption, or selfishness. By His grace, He knew how easily it would have been for me to be engulfed by any or all of the above, to be crushed under the weight of my insane reality. **"For He satisfies the longing soul, and the hungry soul He fills with good things"** (Ps. 107:9).

But as life would have it, all things must come to an end—at least for a season. In the wake of a terrible tragedy that touched our family very personally in 2008, the combination of heightened stress; increased demands on my physical, mental, and emotional being; and subsequent chronic fatigue would eventually take a serious toll on my physical health, which would hit rock-bottom by the summer of the following year. My physical strength, which I had leaned upon to push me through and above many of life's obstacles and private pain throughout the years during and since my military days (when I had fully embraced the "no pain, no gain" philosophy), came to a grinding halt. So many of my body systems crashed, one by one, until I was literally almost bedridden with fatigue and acute body pain. I could muster the strength to keep the household running, the bills paid, clean clothes in the drawers, and dinner on the table—but nothing more than was necessary. Thankfully, our girls were at an age when they were able to bless me with help, assisting in the daily toil of housekeeping. When homeschooling started up in the fall of 2009, often the girls would have to bring their schoolwork into the bedroom where I would instruct them and listen to their reading, etc., while propped in bed, as just being upright for long periods would tire me. Walking, which had been my passion and stress reliever for years, was not even an option. As the beautiful summer days of 2010 rolled by, and I could hear the kids outside playing in the yard yet could not often join them, I struggled, asking God to show me the meaning of what seemed so very senseless to me in my deep desire to be strong and healthy again. There was much silence as I sought understanding and purpose in the pain.

You know those days when something significant happens that you can recall exactly where you were, what you were doing, and how you felt when it occurred that it seems like only yesterday? Well, I had one of those moments while sitting in my favorite old rocker in our yard on a lovely afternoon. I was reading a mailing about a new homeschool group curriculum when I read a Scripture verse included in its contents. It said,

> **Trust in the LORD with all of your heart, and do not lean on your own understanding. In all your ways acknowledge Him, and He will make straight your paths. Be not wise in your own eyes; fear (revere) the LORD, and turn away from evil. It will be healing to your flesh and refreshment/medicine to your bones.** (Prov. 3:5-8)

Although I had read and even quoted this Scripture many times over the years, on this particular day, the Holy Spirit spoke it into my personal struggle in a deeper and more profound way. The truth hit me and my ego/self-sufficiency hard! Although I told myself that I was *trusting* in the Lord for my health and healing, I was at the same time trying to *understand* the source of my chronic pain and fatigue by searching for answers and a diagnosis within the realm of the natural world. I wanted to *know* what was plaguing my body and health, which is our human nature; however, people who are claiming a life of faith are asked to relinquish their desire to *know and understand*, to often walk in the dark by faith while trusting in the Lord's goodness, grace, and ways with us—especially when we don't understand. As I took to heart this revelation of my double-minded thoughts and actions, a great peace flood over my troubled soul. I needed to truly yield and hand over the reins of my health if I wanted my actions to match up with my proclamations of faith and in Whom I declared my trust.

I would love to say that this surrender came easily and without much wrestling, but that would be a lie. Being raised in a household that taught self-sufficiency, self-effort, and self-responsibility (which are not bad concepts in and of themselves, but can surely become a stumbling block for a person of faith), the ingrained principles had deep roots. Also, my 10-year training as a soldier, for whom words like "weakness" and "surrender" are nonexistent, only served to deepen and fortify the mindset of these principles and code of honor. In time I would uncover another deep root that compelled my desire to be able to label and clarify my physical suffering; this need to know and understand became a mask for underlying fear. The unanswered questions I fervently sought solutions for were laced with doubt, fearfulness, and anxiety, which my mind relentlessly chewed on day and night:

* *What is wrong with me?*
* *Do I have an undiagnosed disease?*
* *Am I dying?*
* *Who will raise and educate our daughters?*
* *Will I live like this for the rest of my life?*

Fear is such a powerful emotion. I believe it is the root of almost every other emotion. This fear was equaled by another powerful truth I had to face: my pride. The funny thing was that I never thought of myself as a prideful person. I never lorded over people what I would reckon to be my strengths; I always had a passion to use them only as a means of helping others discover their own strengths. I make a great partner but a lousy competitor, as I would rather see another person win or succeed more than worrying about me losing. However, the Holy Spirit would reveal to me that I had developed such a self-sufficient nature because I could not fully trust or count on my life partner; therefore, I had learned to trust in my own sufficiency and self-effort to keep our family strong, thriving, progressing, and secure as a default mechanism in my endeavor to stabilize our broken marriage. But when God speaks into a matter, He requires our trust and obedience regardless of our circumstances, for He is far above them and our personal strengths or weaknesses. He actually does His best work in the bleakest and darkest of situations where His power and all-sufficiency can be clearly seen, and His grace and compassion are evident beyond human limitations and reasoning. **"My grace is sufficient for you, for My power is made perfect in weakness"** (2 Cor. 12:9). And so began my journey into this new and unfamiliar realm of true humility under the covering of God's all-sufficient power and grace.

JOURNAL ENTRY – March 8, 2016

Broken and empty I come to You so You can mold me into Your chosen vessel and fill me with Your Spirit that I may humbly—yet with passion and purpose—be Your polished arrow (Isaiah 49:2) to call out "Arise, shine, for your light has come, and the glory of the LORD has risen upon you" (Isaiah 60:1).

> "In order to teach the necessity of having God's power or the scriptural dynamic for the 'outliving' of this new life, He has to let one fail sometimes when one tries to live the Christ life in the energy of the natural or human strength. This is only to bring the soul in touch with the third member of the Trinity, the Holy Spirit, Who is the strength of the new experience and life."
> —John Wright Follette, *Pressed Juice from Living Fruit* [33]

[33] John Wright Follette, *Pressed Juice from Living Fruit* (Hampton, TN: Harvey & Tait, 1994).

Upon truly being able to relinquish the *knowing* and the *understanding*, health and healing began to slowly return to my broken body systems, and the acute physical pain dissipated to days wherein I didn't even think about it at all. This surely didn't happen overnight, and I still occasionally deal with the remnants of them, gratefully on much smaller scales. I was tested in moments of weakness in which I would fall back into my old ways of doubt, anxiety, and fear when faced

> "The trouble with always trying to preserve the health of the body is that it is so difficult to do without destroying the health of the mind."
> —G. K. Chesterton

with a new manifestation of pain or odd sensations. Turning to prayer and God's promises was my source of peace and power to both embrace and persevere through this stretching of my "faith muscles." I must have looked pretty bad at one time, as years later, people would still ask me how I was doing and comment on how good I looked *now*; I guess it was a compliment! There is so much more I could write about that transpired during this part of my journey. The humbling grace, yielding, and the subsequent healing not only drastically improved my quality of life but were also used in many ways to help and encourage others in their struggles with physical and emotional pain. But I want to fast-forward to the present time wherein these initial lessons would need to be exercised in a new and deeper way than I had ever experienced before, revealing yet another layer of my abject poverty when I was finally rescued and called out from the familiar covering of my home and all I knew there…whether good or bad.

Shortly before my departure from our marriage, the Lord began to paint a picture using only a small portion of the empty canvas that would eventually depict my new life outside the confines of our home, which, except for the joy of our daughters and the natural beauty that surrounded the perimeters of my "gilded cage," had become blurry with tears and delusion. God had revealed very little of what the final portrait would look like, and I still cannot see much of anything beyond what is directly before me in the present moment. I am still too close to the canvas to catch a real view of what might be to come. I am sure this was also God's grace, as I had more than enough to handle during this drastic change from the familiar to the foreign, from caterpillar to butterfly.

When the Lord said "Go," I left with what clothes I could bring, toiletries, my journals and books, a little savings, and pictures of those near and dear to my heart. I moved from a house surrounded by both woods and wide-open spaces to a small spare bedroom at a friend's apartment in the middle of the city with a tiny backyard and neighbors in very close quarters on all sides. I was very grateful nonetheless. You find that, when push comes to shove, you need very little when freedom calls you out of a place of silent desperation. The confines of this new form of isolation, as well as the personal loss of the material, were more than a sufficient price to pay for the ability to breathe freely once out from under the dense oppression and stifling quarters—and for inner peace within my soul. But I soon realized that I was also underneath a whole new covering that I hadn't even really considered in the midst of the preeminent matter of separating myself from my abuser. I was now fully under the grace and provision of God and those who I would be relying on to help support me (physically, emotionally, and spiritually) through this transition phase of singleness in my marriage.

> **It is the LORD who goes before you. He will be with you; He will not leave you or forsake you. Do not fear or be dismayed.** (Deut. 31:8)

JOURNAL ENTRY — December 18, 2015

You needed to get me to a place of absolute dependence on You in which to let the Holy Spirit give me my marching orders without intrusion of the flesh and heart; to be stripped of the connections to people, places, and things that bind a soul from wanting to leave the comforts and familiar for the unknown and often harsh walk with Jesus. I feel like I am standing on the edge, trying not to look back or down so that fear will not overtake me—but only looking forward and up at Your face and holding Your faithful hand while stepping off of the cliff and into the unknown adventure with You. I do not trust myself with my fears, insecurity, weakness, desires, or free will. Lead me in the way everlasting. Amen!

In this way, I embarked on this new season of dependence upon my Lord, who graciously supplied all of my needs through the generosity, support, kindnesses, mercy, grace, and love of welcoming friends and sisters in Christ. I must admit that it felt terribly strange and uncomfortable to accept so much from others without having anything to really give in exchange for their gracious and generous hospitality. I had spent most of my life on the giving end, so turning the tables was both awkward and humbling, to say the least. The friend with whom I was staying in the city was in need of care because of health-related issues, so I at least felt I could give back something for all of the sweet kindness shown to me during the initial estrangement from my husband. And although I was very grateful for the opportunity to serve and contribute something by caring for the household, cooking meals, grocery shopping, doing laundry and yard work, etc., despite my lack of funds to help carry the bulk of the expenses, it was in the situations where I had really nothing to offer that God did the most work in stripping away pride and self-sufficiency while teaching humility in the wake of undeserved grace. Almost every weekend I made the trek back out to the country to see my daughters and friends. Though often tiring both physically and emotionally, it was so necessary for my heart and soul to see my children and love on them (even though they were young adults now) and to have fellowship with my friends during this time of great change and challenge in my life. It was refreshment to my lonely heart and hurting soul to be amidst the loved and familiar, if even for 24 hours at a time. These precious spans of time were priceless during my adjustment period, which brought me to the end of myself in every way imaginable.

> It was in the situations where I had really nothing to offer that God did the most work in stripping away pride and self-sufficiency while teaching humility in the wake of undeserved grace.

"I will refresh the weary and satisfy the faint." (Jer. 31:25)

Because I had been living on adrenaline and the ingrained routine and momentum of daily responsibilities while also transitioning our youngest daughter from homeschooling to preparing for college, I truly didn't anticipate how deeply exhausted I had become—physically, mentally, and emotionally. Although I was delivered from an increasingly difficult home life, becoming my friend's caretaker often required around-the-clock vigilance that was draining in a different way. I also continued to be a mostly single parent, but now from afar, which created additional pressures to navigate. I never questioned God's call upon my life to "move," but I certainly questioned my ability to "keep moving," as I was pretty tapped-out in every sense of the word. It wasn't until I was able to start letting down my constant guard and began to relax a bit that I felt the depth of my true state of being.

By the time I packed for my weekly visits to see my daughters and friends, made the long trek from city to country, and hauled my belongings inside the extended haven of hospitality for the weekend, I was pretty vacant. In the beginning, I always felt badly that I arrived without anything to offer. Quite honestly, though, just the thought of having to *think* about preparing something was too tiring, much less the actual strength and concentration it would take to bring it to fruition. The energy it would have taken to even conceive the pretense of pride, much less to actually conjure up the feeling of it, was by now a ridiculous notion. Although I was a person who by nature delighted in being a generous and joyful *giver* and was not very comfortable finding myself on the receiving end of such abundant grace, the Holy Spirit was teaching me how to be a gracious *recipient* of God's good gifts extended through the hands and hearts of others. My daughters and friends received me with nothing short of extravagant love, comforts, generosity, and joy at my presence despite my empty hands. They never made me feel ashamed that I had been reduced to this place at a pivotal point in my life when the children were all grown and I should have been entering a new season with my husband (instead of ending one) after 25 years.

I came to understand that eating "humble pie" was quite wonderful when shared with people whom you dearly love and who love you and accept you right where you are, just as you are, empty and all. This experience of great poverty from within, even more so than my physical state of being, has taught me many deep and meaningful purposes in the pain. I have learned to trust in these extended kindnesses from my Father through others who love me without cost or "stealing" from me in exchange for their kind words or gracious gestures. I have been taught many hard lessons about humbly and graciously accepting my heavenly Father's freely offered grace upon grace. These undeserved gifts granted me the strength to love and forgive others when basic human kindness and selfless love were withheld from my life and heart.

JOURNAL ENTRY — No date recorded

Despite all of Jesus' sufferings, especially on the cross, He never saw Himself as a victim of His oppression and injustice, but as a powerful liberator and victor over the evil and darkness of the world. Let us never look upon our own suffering as trials to just be endured, but with hope and great joy that through and by our suffering we are being liberated and made victorious as we ascend from glory to glory in Christ!

JOURNAL ENTRY — August 4, 2013

I will be victorious and break free from the shackles of pain—both physical and emotional—as my spirit and soul merge into Christ's glory and promise of true freedom.

Many people think that faith is for the weak, but it is for the strong…in Jesus Christ. Faith gives us the *power* to be humble and honest, and to admit mistakes and accept blame. Faith enables us to forgive those who wrong and hurt us, and to overcome pain and suffering. Faith grants us the ability to give something when we feel we have nothing, to be thankful when we are unhappy and empty, to have hope when life looks and feels hopeless. Faith sees the possible in the impossible because *nothing* is impossible with God. What in the world gives us this power to overcome? What relationship, friendship, drug, drink, food, entertainment, material possession, passion, or escape can truly give us hope and joy *despite* our circumstances? I have tasted some of them and have come away more empty. My faith has:

* given me peace when I could find none
* infused me with the courage to endure my physical and emotional pain
* assured me that I am safe even when I know I am not
* offered me unconditional love when the world often charges a heavy price
* filled my loneliness with peaceful solitude
* given me supernatural energy when I am exhausted
* renewed hope in each new day

Now, that is power! Although I enjoy the material offerings and experiences of this earthly life and am very grateful for the people who share them with me, I no longer depend on them for joy and fulfillment; my Lord and God fill me with all that I need. It is so freeing to not be dependent on the things of this world, which come and go, ebb and flow, live and die, make us laugh and cry. Whether my wings are clipped or I can be free to fly, I have found the secret to contentment of heart, mind, body, and soul. It is a free gift to all who will believe and put their faith in Jesus. I offer that gift to you; it is all I have to give of any value—it is the pearl of great price (Matt. 13:45-46)! As life is uncertain, you do not have forever to accept it and make it your own. What are you waiting for? It is true freedom and the truest of love!

JOURNAL ENTRY — April 17, 2015

Heavenly Father, in Jesus' name I call upon You and look to You for help and strength in this ever-shifting world. Each day has new blessings and trials, but I know now they are both from Your hand. If I had only blessings I would become stagnant, selfish, and lack sympathy for the hurting world. It is in my physical pain and emotional struggles that compassion grows into service. I do not always do this with as much grace as I would like, but You cover my shortfall with Your tender mercies. I praise You that I have been brought so low, that You can raise me up again—Hallelujah! Blessings and trials; the course of this life. Continue, dear Lord, to give me a new heart and yielded spirit; I cannot do it on my own strength—You alone transform us in all ways. Amen.

Humble yourselves therefore under the mighty hand of God that He may exalt you in due time. (1 Pet. 5:6)

Prayer Warriors: The Best Kind of Friend Is a Praying Friend

A friend loves at all times. (Prov. 17:17)

I would be remiss here if I did not pay tribute to the circle of faithful friends and sisters in Christ who had surrounded me like a mighty fortress during the most difficult and challenging season of my life. In the Father's great mercy and provision, He placed a tribe and army of women around me who became my fervent prayer warriors. There were times—too numerous to mention—when I just couldn't pray for myself, our family, anybody, or anything. Although my desire was great and my heart sincere, so often I tried and failed because of deep fatigue and lack of concentration due to physical, mental, and emotional burnout. I just couldn't hold a thought within the grip of my numb and weary mind; it would evaporate and disappear before I could even lift it up to the throne room of grace. Thankfully, it was through this very grace and tender mercy that I could find comfort in the weakness and failings of my flesh in exchange for God's all-sufficiency. These women stood in the gap for me and prayed in my mental and emotional absence. They were deep in the trenches beside me, still returning fire when I was wounded in the battle.

I felt like the paralyzed man who needed healing but couldn't walk to the One who could heal him; he needed the help and compassion of his friends. Therefore, his faithful friends carried him to the place where Jesus was teaching. There was a very large crowd gathered around Jesus so that they could not get near Him. They could have been discouraged and simply left, but they were determined to help their helpless friend. So, **"they went up on the roof and let him down with his bed through the tiles into the midst before Jesus"** (Luke 5:19). The Bible says, **"And when He**

225

saw their faith…" (Luke 5:20). Jesus saw the faith of this man's devoted friends and their determination to see someone they cared for and loved be touched by Him and healed. This healing would include not only the man's physical body but all his needs: spiritual, emotional, and mental. This is what my dear, faithful friends did for me during those challenging days. When I couldn't "walk" on my own, they were empowered by the Holy Spirit to carry me in prayer and lay me gently down—in my brokenness—at the feet of Jesus for healing.

> **Bring me out of prison, that I may give thanks to Your name! The righteous will surround me, for You will deal bountifully with me.** (Ps. 142:7)

An *Our Daily Bread* devotional touched on a very interesting topic that I felt fitting for this portion of the book regarding the importance of good and faithful friends. It addressed the results of a study done by researchers at the University of Virginia on what makes pain more bearable. The study used three different scenarios and recorded the outcomes based on dozens of tests, which consistently had the same results. The main purpose of the testing was:

> …to see how the brain reacted to the prospect of pain, and whether it behaved differently if a person faced the threat of pain alone, holding a stranger's hand, or holding the hand of a close friend. When a person was alone or holding a stranger's hand while anticipating a shock, the regions of the brain that process danger lit up. But when holding the hand of a trusted person, the brain relaxed. The comfort of a friend's presence made the pain seem more bearable.[34]

Although the results of this study were interesting and newsworthy to read, I was not at all surprised by the confirmed outcome, as I know firsthand the peace, warmth, and comfort that is found in the presence of dear friends who love you and are committed to your well-being.

---

[34] Amy Peterson, *Our Daily Bread*, April 13, 2017.

> "We do not so much need the help of our friends as the confidence of their help in need." —Epicurus, Greek philosopher

When you get to a point in your life when you are just so desperate, yet just as equally empty, you reach a whole new and deeper level of humility that shatters the very last remnant of your pride. This is a very hard, yet perfect, place to be if you desire both true healing and freedom. *This is the purpose in the pain.* When you have fallen and can't get up, you have two choices: You can roll over onto your stomach and bury your head in the sand, thereby sinking into darkness, bitterness, depression, and hopelessness (easy enough to do), *or* you can roll over onto your back and—even with squinting eyes filled with tears—look up into the face of the Son, to be infused with light, warmth, hope, and the Father's waiting love. The latter is what I did in my state of utter weakness and isolation with the ongoing support of a devout army of warrior friends encamped around me. I fully encourage anyone who is facing a foe or personal struggle (of any kind) while in a place of desperation and absolute exhaustion, battling to stay on the side of victory—to lean *on* and *into* the friends and people around you that have been placed there in your life **"for such a time as this"** (Esther 4:14). These faithful prayer warriors not only prayed me through, but they also upheld our family daily in the midst of this new, uncharted frontier in all of our lives. I am forever indebted to these women warriors who didn't leave me wounded on the battlefield, but carried me until I was able to get my feet back on solid ground—made free and whole again!

> **I will rejoice, for I know that *through your prayers* and the help of the Spirit of Jesus Christ this will turn out for my deliverance, as it is my eager expectation and hope that I will not be at all ashamed, but that with full courage now as always Christ will be honored in my body....If I am to live in the flesh, that means fruitful labor for me.**
> (Phil. 1:18-20, 22, italics added)

JOURNAL ENTRY – November 26, 2016

"And He (Jesus) saw that they were making headway painfully..." (Mark 6:48). This is me, making headway painfully, each step slow and with great effort. But every step, no matter how tiny, is progress forward!

JOURNAL ENTRY – December 11, 2015

I heard a more specific call that wherever You lead me—it will be to show and lead people to wholeness in You. Hasn't that been my journey and struggle—the whole struggle and longing of humanity—to be made whole and to feel worthy of wholeness? Jesus, that was Your mission here—to bring people to wholeness and holiness by offering the complete healing of their bodies, hearts, minds, souls, and spirits! This must be my mission, too. I understand the broken condition of all these areas of the human body; the turmoil of it all in the soul. As You heal me from the inside out, I believe You will empower me to lead others to this wholeness in You. Thank You for this awesome revelation and more definite purpose. Amen.[35]

JOURNAL ENTRY – April 4, 2016

I pondered in awe this morning while still in bed how You
use us broken vessels for Your work and Your glory
how only the broken can truly touch brokenness;
the lonely...others loneliness;
the abused...those abused;
the imprisoned...fellow prisoners.
The cycle of the broken helping to heal the broken;
the ripples of life.
Beauty from ashes,
Amazing grace,
Eternal love!

The Higher Purpose in the Pain

For He will complete what He appoints for me, and many such things are in His mind. (Job 23:14)

Some people have asked this question, "If you put your *real*

---

[35] Though silently desperate to be free from both physical and emotional bondage, at this point in time I still had no concrete knowledge of the plan that would eventually release me six months later, nor a conscious understanding of how God would one day use my pain for His purposes and glory. I was just trying to survive one day at a time in His promises, power, and grace...my spirit always ahead of my flesh and the present moment.

name on the book, couldn't that ruin your ex-husband's reputation? Your families? Yours?" Well, yes, it could. Honestly, though, I would wager that my reputation would be the greatest target of all based on my experience of speaking truth thus far. But, as a woman of faith, my life is no longer my own. God has placed this work upon my life for a greater purpose than my temporary earthly reputation. Besides, with what I have endured in those 25 years, what else can anyone really do to me? Reject me? Ridicule me? Call me a liar? Accuse me of being a bad wife and mother who abandoned her husband and family? Shame me? Judge me or my words and try to silence me? Leave me in isolation? Diminish me? Threaten me? Try to squelch my vitality? It's all been done to me—and then some! I will not live in fear: **"The LORD is on my side; I will not fear. What can man do to me?"** (Ps. 118:6).[36] I guess God really wanted to get this message across to those who stand up for truth and justice!

While writing these words, the Holy Spirit brought a picture to my mind's eye that I used as an illustration many years ago while teaching a young adult Sunday School class. I had read that if we are ever caught in the midst of a raging wildfire with no safe haven available and no open avenue or body of water to flee to, one of the safest places to go was a location that had already been consumed by the fire. Because a fire needs combustible material like trees, brush, and tall grass to burn, if we can find a spot that has already been destroyed by the fire, we have a much better chance of surviving if it passes through again. It is a safe zone, like the eye of a storm: a calm place in the center of the forces coming against us. This adequately depicts how I feel in the event of any backlash coming against me in the wake of the raw truth about narcissism and any other truth that people do not want to believe or receive. I realize that some of the content of this book may make some individuals or people groups unintentionally angry. After 25 years of being "burned" repeatedly and ravaged by a narcissist, I find myself in a safe zone with my

---

[36] See also Ps. 56:4, 11; Heb. 13:6.

heavenly Father, who has encircled me with His love, care, power, and protection. I have survived the abuse of this mental illness—physically, mentally, emotionally, and spiritually—because of God's merciful deliverance from the flames that threatened to consume me. I now stand within the center of His grace, continued protection, and provision. How true are the words written in the book of James regarding the tongue:

> So also the tongue is a small member, yet it boasts of great things. How great a forest is set ablaze by such a small fire! And the tongue is a fire, a world of unrighteousness. The tongue is set among our members, staining the whole body, setting on fire the entire course of life, and set on fire by hell…a restless evil, full of poison. With it we bless our Lord and Father, and with it we curse people who are made in the likeness of God. (James 3:5-9)

Yet despite the possible spark of the untamed tongue, I still stand firm on God's promise in Isaiah 43:2" **"When you walk through fire you shall not be burned, and the flames shall not consume you."** Perhaps you, too, will draw this same strength from an area of personal pain where you can speak out against injustice and abuse.

And our daughters? They are just the innocents who played no part in it all, other than to be my sweetest joy and source of constant motivation to fight for our marriage, to seek truth, and to be well in body, soul, mind, and spirit. And my ex-husband? *Nothing* that I wrote in this entire book would be a surprise to him (*if* he were to be honest with himself), as I told him every word countless times for over two and a half decades. He chose not to hear, receive, acknowledge, or be moved by my words, and that was his choice. Truthfully, my greatest desire would be that any exposure from the truth would finally change his current unchangeable reality. That he would be freed to live a "real," genuine life and to love fully as he is fully loved. That he would be, once and for all, released from the bondage of this terribly lonely void of selfish self-love that has consumed his heart, mind, body, and soul, before it is too late! I pray that in light of what is true and real—the masks can finally fall off, the web of lies be torn down, the game pieces put away, and the unfair rules shred and tossed out—and that the final curtain on this tragic show could now close for good, with no ovation!

But, ultimately, this book and the truth it contains are *so much more* than about our small family and what we have endured through this experience with a Narcissistic Personality Disorder—a higher purpose in the pain. As I have written, I believe there is *always* a greater purpose to our pain if we are willing to seek it. What we learn through difficult trials is not meant to be kept to ourselves, but rather, is intended to be shared with others so that we can connect with each other at our deepest levels of need. Knowledge gleaned from our painful experiences can be powerful tools used for the greater good when we see them as opportunities for new growth and depth within us. This, in turn, builds character and hones our individual gifts, talents, self-worth, and sensitivities.

Pain and sorrow give us occasion to connect with all of humanity, and should stir within us sympathy and love for our fellow travelers *without distinction or restriction.* Shared pain is not meant to cause more pain, injury, or injustice but rather to help alleviate it. This spirit of unity keeps us striving for solutions as well as fuels our passion and commitment to quench the evil that perpetuates human suffering. In its raw vulnerability, pain allows us to see others with eyes of empathy, mercy, and love as we acknowledge the reality of our own broken, empty, and seeking selves, also desirous to be seen, heard, and known by those sharing life's journey with us. A beautiful outpouring of compassion and basic human kindness can flow through the conduit of shared life in all of its joy and sorrow. This mindset makes us *comrades* on the battlefield instead of *enemies*, helping each other as partners and not competitors to make it to the finish line with hope, grace, courage, and shared victory.

We all have a responsibility to help untie each other's ropes: the ones that bind us to every kind of sin, dark and hopeless place,

231

fear, pain, abuse, and injustice, as well as to share the keys that unlock each other's cages. Let's work together and set one another free to fly in quiet strength on wings like eagles. It is then that we can *all* rise above our current circumstances and the storm clouds that block our vision—and soar toward the sun!

May it be so. Amen.

> "I am only one, but still I am one.
> I cannot do everything but still I can do something;
> and because I cannot do everything I will not refuse
> to do something that I can do."
> —Edward Everett Hale, American author and clergyman

18

My Deep Well of Loneliness

I am like a lonely sparrow on the housetop.
(Ps. 102:7)

JOURNAL ENTRY – November 2012

The sparrow sings its song yet no one hears, and it returns void.

> "If home is no longer the place of intimacy and sharing,
> where in the world do we then go?"
> —Charles Ringma, author and professor, Regent College

I SAW A counselor by myself once, hoping that my husband would also join me one day. I spoke to her about how lonely my marriage was. I said, "It is easier for me when he leaves me alone and goes somewhere." She looked at me with eyes that said, "Well, no wonder you have marriage problems when you don't even want your husband around!"

As my eyes blurred with tears, I then added, "It is so much easier to feel lonely all of the time when I am actually alone than to feel so terribly lonely when my husband is with me." If you have been in my uncomfortable shoes, you know that pain so well:

*   Driving in the car, sitting across the dinner table, attending a social gathering, watching a movie, lying in bed—together, yet always feeling alone
*   Wanting to reach out but knowing there is nothing to hold onto
*   Longing to share your day, talk about the kids, exchange the latest family news, describe the sunrise that morning or what is growing in the garden, discuss an interesting thing you heard or read, reveal how you are feeling or what you are thinking…but having no one who really listens or cares

It is easier not to have ears that *could* hear than to have ones that simply *won't*. Easier not to have eyes that *could* see than ones that don't care to look at or see you. Easier not to have hands that *could* help or comfort than to have ones that refuse to do either. Easier not to have arms that *could* draw you in than ones that choose to push you away—this is loneliness. To hear breathing beside you, but there is no life together—this is loneliness. To bring children into the world yet not be joined heart-to-heart in the miracle, joy, memories, challenges, and rewards while raising, teaching, and caring for them—this is loneliness. To talk about the future when there is nothing binding or being built in the present—this is loneliness. When you soak your pillow with silent tears almost nightly as you pray for a miracle while your spouse lies in peaceful, undisturbed slumber—this is loneliness.

JOURNAL ENTRY – February 18, 2015

Dear Father, in the name of Jesus, I pray. My heart aches for the homeless and those without adequate daily bread. My heart just aches; it is a tangible thing. My pillow You gave me for comfort is wet with tears. Forgive me, Father, my failures and weakness. Keep telling me that I am not alone. Amen.

Author Max Lucado writes, "Loneliness—It's a cry. A moan; a wail. It's a gasp whose origin is in the recesses of our souls."[37] To be able to write those poignant words, one has to have experienced the deep well of loneliness. It is a pit of silent desperation. It is the lonely heart's lament, reverberating around the world, that cries out, screams, demands, pleads, whispers…"Please, somebody—see me, hear me, know me, love me!" Loneliness is a constant ache in the human heart. My heart ached so chronically that I would catch myself throughout the day gently rubbing my chest, holding it as if I could stop it from breaking somehow. Oh, we can try to stifle the cry by filling the void with activity, noise, entertainment, social engagements, fellowship within the church or outside the office, food, drink, drugs,

---

[37] Max Lucado, *No Wonder They Call Him the Savior Experiencing the Truth of the Cross* (Thomas Nelson Inc, 2011).

sex, books, movies, exercise, travel, money—all of the treasures and experiences out there—until our distraction of choice stops, leaves, wears off, runs out, closes, ends.

Then, in the tiniest thought, word, song, name, picture, memory, or quiet moment, that loneliness resurfaces and wells up in the heart with a force and ache so powerful that we think it just might burst through the skin and consume us. Loneliness comes like waves of grief, washing over us until we can barely stand, let alone breathe. It seems to live in its own chamber somewhere within the depth of our hearts. For each individual, the key that unlocks that chamber door is different. For some, it may be a small reminder of what could have been, would have been, should have been in their marriage or other relationships gone awry...*if only*. For others, it could be the loss of a beloved spouse. For many, it is the untimely death of a dear child or a lost prodigal son or daughter. For still others, it is the loss of health that keeps them isolated or the loneliness that often accompanies old age. It could come in the wake of lost souls to addictions in every form. Countless people are lost in selfless sacrifice while defending freedom, establishing peace, and upholding justice. It comes in every shape, size, and circumstance, but when it comes—it always comes with pain.

JOURNAL ENTRY – December 12, 2014

Oh, how I wish I hadn't shared some of my inner pain with others. Like being lonely is so much easier when you are alone, pain is so much easier to bear when you carry it alone —how much more it hurts when you share your pain and no one cares. You see my pain; You know personally every one of my scars. You love me anyway. You have carried me so many times; I would be no more without You near. Help me, my Savior. Deliver me. I knock hard on the door. Open it unto me so I can come in and find rest for my soul. Amen.

Most people don't talk about the pain of loneliness. Loneliness makes us feel vulnerable and appear weak. Sometimes it comes with an unwarranted feeling of shame, as though we did something to deserve this badge of dishonor or lot in life. Many people might not even know the name of this unwelcome "friend" who shows up without prior notice; they just know when it arrives and knocks at the door of their tender hearts. I personally know the keys that unlock that dreaded chamber door; I just don't always know when or from whom the key will slip into the lock and spring it open. As with all undesirable pills we swallow, loneliness can make us bitter or better. Although it is human nature to become bitter, especially when loneliness is forced upon us, harboring bitterness is like sipping poison: If it is allowed to take root, grow, and fester, it will slowly kill us.

I have walked the loneliness road a very long time and have experienced just about every side street, pothole, roadblock, detour, and dead end. I have wallowed for a time in the mire of bitterness and self-pity; it is messy, it stinks, and you only sink deeper into loneliness because now *no one* wants to be around you! So to save you the trouble, when you get to the crossroads marked *bitter* or *better,* I definitely recommend the *better* road! It is the high road that will take you away from loneliness and lead you to a beautiful new place called solitude.

JOURNAL ENTRY — September 27, 2014

It is harder than anything I know to be lonely when you are not alone, and to be still and wait in your desperation for the Lord to fill those empty places.

JOURNAL ENTRY — September 14, 2013

You, and only You alone, know my deepest pain. My sorrow is beyond words, and I am grateful I don't have to speak them to You. You are enough to fill the hole, yet I still ache; a perpetual grieving of loss I have no control over. My chronic pain is just an outward manifestation of my broken heart and dead dreams. Keep writing my story, Lord— maybe it will still have a happy ending here. Amen.

Loneliness to Solitude

JOURNAL ENTRY – August 4, 2014

You have groomed me to be peaceful in the desert, to know the joy of solitude in place of the pain of loneliness.

I would love to say I found the road to solitude all by myself. But, since anyone who knows me also knows I have a terrible sense of direction (unless I am using a GPS), they wouldn't believe me anyway! A dear friend of mine introduced me to a wonderful book called *Reaching Out: The Three Movements of the Spiritual Life* written by Henri Nouwen, which pointed the way and laid the groundwork for my journey. This pilgrimage began in the pit of silent desperation and loneliness yet brought me closer and closer to the place where I would find longed-for freedom, quiet strength, and peace in solitude. I shared some of this journey in a monthly newsletter I wrote for the church I was attending. You might be thinking, "Aren't loneliness and solitude the same?" I initially didn't clearly understand the difference either until I actually *experienced* the variance between the two in my life. One clue, though, is that feeling lonely, or loneliness, is by definition, "unhappy at being alone."[38] The essence of solitude is finding joy and contentment in your loneliness.

JOURNAL ENTRY – March 2014

Walking the road of loneliness has helped pave the way to the secret path of solitude. This blissfully peaceful place is hidden behind the walls of a desperate world lost within their need of constant words and reassurances. Thank You, Lord, for leading me to the gate, which opened upon the mystery and timeless beauty in the garden of solitude—I have found You waiting there.

---

[38] Agnes, *Webster's New World Dictionary.*

"Therefore go out from their midst, and be separate from them," says the Lord.
(2 Cor. 6:17)

When God called me into the desert wilderness, I have to admit that I did not like those first experiences at all. It was too quiet, barren, unpredictable, and very lonely. Stripped of noise, busyness, and the distractions of life, I felt uncomfortable and vulnerable in this strange place. But God kept wooing me there and gradually replaced my trepidation and loneliness with peaceful solitude.

Practicing silence in solitude is an essential and blessed discipline for life in the Spirit. It is our fallen nature that desires fulfillment in, and depends upon, the constant interaction with other people to feel connected and alive in the physical world. Yet, only in solitude can we truly connect with our spirit and grow in spiritual maturity, thereby deepening our love relationship with our Spirit God. Earthly solitary confinement is meant to break a man's will for the world's purposes, to conform a human spirit to the laws of man. Solitary time in the "desert" with God is meant to transform a man's heart so that he voluntarily and joyfully surrenders his will for the purposes and pleasure of his loving Creator.

Our modern world often sees solitude as a weakness: one who needs to withdraw from the world because they cannot take the pressure of our fast-paced and often-troubled times. But the ability to withdraw from our daily routines and human support systems (and today, our almost constant electronic companions) is an indication of someone with great inner strength and self-possession, a person who knows who they are in Christ and leaves earthly distractions, time restraints, and comforts to voluntarily seek closer and deeper communion with their Maker. A person who is not afraid of their own thoughts nor deterred from searching the depth of their heart can uncover a treasure trove of eternal love, wisdom, understanding, and peace, which God is just waiting to bestow upon His beloved. Was not our Savior the prime example of the benefits and power gained in times of solitude? God says in Isaiah 30:15, **"...in quietness and in trust shall be your strength."**

When we learn to sit quietly in silence, we begin to improve our hearing. We suddenly hear the beautiful song of the cardinal, the cooing of the mourning doves, or the hammering of the woodpecker off in the distance; the rustling of the leaves in the wind; the steady tick of the clock—the background noises of our world can come to the foreground and be heard and enjoyed. We can hear ourselves think and know what our hearts are really saying.

In solitude, we can come to know ourselves, not in a self-centered way but in a way that enhances our love-relationship with God, our families, and our neighbors. We become tuned in to His voice, His will, and His unique call on our lives. Solitude allows us to gain self-control over our tongues so when harsh and hurtful words come at us, we have time to "chew" on our crisp retorts and swallow them before they escape. I have come to believe that one of the strongest testimonies of a Christian, or anyone who desires to exchange their negative feelings of loneliness for the joy of solitude, is the ability to embrace moments of silence and to be good listeners. The desert can truly be a beautiful place to transform something painful into something wonderful!

—*Excerpt from a newsletter I wrote in December 2013*

JOURNAL ENTRY — March 14, 2015

I am home alone. You seem to be offering me up more of these quiet times of solitude. I am coming to see how different I feel when I am alone or out; the internal stress is so much less and I feel like "myself." She resurfaces in the moments when there is no oppression. I need this place to come alive and heal. It is sad but true. I need truth. I am hoping in You—hope is the expectation that You are going to do something! Amen.

JOURNAL ENTRY — December 17, 2015

I feel different, lighter; my mind and heart are more at peace. The endless weeping has mostly dried up, and I feel restored balance and clarity returning. The circumstances have not changed, but the Spirit is changing me.

> "Facing the emptiness inside of you is simply the prelude
> to being filled with My fullness."
> — from Sarah Young, *Jesus Calling*

We were not created to be alone but to be in relationship. After God had created all of the animals and made each with its mate, He then said, **"It is not good for man to be alone; I will make him a helper fit for him"** (Gen. 2:18). A helpmate, by definition, is "a helpful companion; specifically a wife or a husband."[39] So God made Adam a wife, Eve, and gave her to him as his intimate companion. She was to help him to become the man God created him to be and to do the work God gave him to do. Adam was to care for, provide for, and protect her. They were to love one another exclusively and bring forth children into the world. This beautiful "order of things" is still meant to be the blueprint for our marriages today, but, as is very evident throughout the world, we have fallen very far from this original desire of God's heart. Pain and suffering are evident in all of the brokenness found in every corner of the world. We were created to be loved, wanted, needed, and cherished, and then to return those gifts outwardly, and *not* inwardly upon

---

[39] Ibid.

ourselves. Even Jesus, except when He went off to pray alone, lived in almost constant companionship with His friends and disciples.

There are very negative consequences of prolonged loneliness to the physical, emotional, and mental wholeness of the human body, as proven through medical research at the University of Chicago. I discovered some of its findings in a daily devotional entitled *God's Promises to a Woman's Heart*:

> Being chronically lonely can cause as many health problems as high blood pressure, obesity, lack of exercise, or smoking. Loneliness causes our bodies to release stress hormones. It interferes with the body's immune function. It impedes cardiovascular efficiency. Lonely adults tend to sleep less efficiently, eat foods higher in fat, and age prematurely. In truth, loneliness acts a lot like a disease![40]

After reading that, I felt even more grateful that I was not only released from the bondage of forced loneliness but that I also am experiencing the degree of health that I have today!

JOURNAL ENTRY – March 26, 2016

We (humanity) were intended to live and relate in relationships and community, not isolation. I have lived a lonely life of isolation from the heart and mind of my spouse; no real intimacy or friendship, communication, or soul-bond. That is why it so often felt like I was in prison and not a loving home—he banished and condemned me to solitary confinement; to live a lonely life under the guise of a loving marriage. This has been the hardest; living my reality of dysfunction under the false shell of normalcy. I did aid in the facade for the stability and security of our girls in hope that it would someday change and I would be set free!

As I wrote in the excerpt from my newsletter, though, there are times when God needs to bring us to a place of isolation and set us apart from the world (with its noise and distractions) so that He can prepare us for a special mission. We see this pattern time and again in the Bible with people such as Moses, David, John the Baptist, and Paul; even Jesus was sent into the wilderness before entering into

---

[40] Jane L. Fryar, *God's Promises to a Woman's Heart: 25 Daily Devotions* (Fenton, MO: CTA, Inc., 2011).

His public ministry. Many men and women throughout recorded history have also received profound enlightenment and empowerment that greatly impacted the world after their times of solitude in the "wilderness" with God. At times these wilderness wanderings can make us feel abandoned, rejected, isolated, lost, parched, weary, and broken. These solo sojourns are not meant so much to break us as they are to chisel down, round off, and soften our sharp edges so that we can be molded to reflect the character of Jesus.

Several years ago I was given an amazing book written by a man named Jamie Buckingham: *A Way Through The Wilderness— Following the Footsteps of Moses to Find the Way Through Your Personal Wilderness*. This author has journeyed many times through the wilderness of the Sinai. These excursions have equipped him with a deeper understanding of Moses's travels with the Israelites and the culture and traditions of desert nomads (Bedouins). They have revealed the amazing beauty to be found within this unique yet harsh environment as well as the dangers that can prove fatal if not taken heed of. Jamie reminds us of what God did with that first group of desert pilgrims and what He still does with all pilgrims who find themselves in the wilderness today; that is, God uses this place of isolation (literal and/or spiritual) to reveal the depth of His divine nature and the depth of our humanness. For it is only in the quiet of this place where we can truly see, hear, know, and love our Father God. It is also the place where we realize how intimately He sees, hears, knows, and loves us.

When we are alone with God in the desert, there is no pretense: no noise, no busy work, no distractions, no glitz or glamour. Our family name, fame, fortune, titles, labels, success, prestige, trophies, fancy clothes, cars, phones, jewels, etc., are worth nothing in the desert. There is no one to impress (we can't impress God with the material or achievements), or schmooze, or spitefully use, abuse, manipulate, oppress, put down, lie to, or put a mask on for (I don't think we can impress the Bedouins either!). It is just us, the sand, the wind, the heat, the cold, the mountains, the valleys, and God. No matter how many layers we wear, actually or figuratively, we stand before our Maker empty-handed and naked (probably not literally, but who knows—I am sure stranger things have happened!).

And no creature is hidden from His sight, but all are naked and exposed to the eyes of Him to whom we must give an account. (Heb. 4:13)

But it is not our outer flesh He desires to see or know; it is our heart, soul, mind, and spirit that are exposed to the awesomeness of God. This is what He looks into the depth of. Although the thought seems daunting, maybe even embarrassing and overwhelming, we should not be afraid. It may be a place of conviction, but it is not a place of condemnation. It may be a place of hard truth, but it is also a place of cleansing. It might feel like a sentence of solitary confinement for a time, but it takes you to a place of the most blessed freedom. No more feigning, little white lies, half-truths, worthless striving, meaningless words, false promises, broken commitments, neglected responsibilities, fake smiles, dishonest handshakes, empty prayers, forced laughter, or hidden tears. I can tell you from personal experience that, no matter how strong you think you are or big in your own eyes, you will feel very small.

> But it is not our outer flesh He desires to see or know; it is our heart, soul, mind, and spirit that are exposed to the awesomeness of God.

But it was in this place of smallness that I finally knew what it meant to be a child of God: a daughter held in the sovereign, strong, and yet exceedingly gentle hands of my Father. It was only in a place where everything that once defined me was stripped away—when I was removed from the familiar and comfortable and found myself completely dependent on the protection, provision, and care of Someone so much bigger than me and my circumstances—that I was clearly able to see who I was in comparison to who God is and how very much I needed Him. It was in my poverty and emptiness that I could finally understand and experience the fullness and all-sufficiency of God.

I believe this is His one true desire: not to take all *from* us, but to finally be able to give His all *to* us. We are unable to take this from His outstretched hands because ours are already too full of our own "stuff." We are so busy trying to fill up our lives, time, minds, hearts, dreams, plans, visions, etc., that we leave no room for what He has for us, which I can attest is *so much greater* than we could ever give ourselves! He longs to see and know the man or woman He created and breathed life into *before* we were enmeshed in and tainted by the world around us.

> **Or do you suppose it is to no purpose that the Scripture says, "He yearns jealously over the spirit that He made to dwell in us!"** (James 4:5)

I believe that this is what our heavenly Father searches for when He calls us out into the desert wilderness with Him: the people He envisioned before we were even knitted together in our mother's womb. The people who He had plans for before we took our first breath. The people He desires to watch and help accomplish the work He specifically gave us to do using the unique experiences, gifts, talents, creativity, and passions He gave us. Most of us feel so empty and unfulfilled because we are doing our own thing and *not* the very "thing" God has purposed for us to do. So we try to glam up our lives and fill them with transient offerings and possessions to make up for the lack of joy, fulfillment, and feelings of completeness in our routines of life. This only leaves us more empty, lonely, longing, endlessly searching, in debt, in chains, in bitterness and hopeless that there is nothing in this world for us but to **"eat, drink, and be merry for tomorrow we die"** (Isa. 22:13).

But Jesus came to give us an abundant life! **"I came that they may have life and have it abundantly"** (John 10:10). The beauty is that we don't have to search for this promised abundant life. We can't Google it or look it up on Pinterest. It isn't going to be found on Facebook, in chat rooms, or on dating sites. We can't locate it with our GPS, or scour the earth for it like buried treasure. But we often have to do one of the hardest things in the world to do: We have to WAIT for it! Ah, the waiting. This is what we spend most of our time doing while on our pilgrimage in the desert wilderness. How *we hate waiting*, especially in our modern-day, drive-through, instant-gratification world! It is excruciating at times. I know this place very well; it is my familiar friend—we are on a first-name basis. "Wait" is truly a four-letter word we tend to despise and would probably do away with it in the English language if we could! But it is the most crucial ingredient in transforming the distasteful bread of affliction often found in loneliness into the sweet bread of new life discovered in solitude (Isa. 30:20).

Although we can discover much beauty in the wilderness as we make our pilgrimage from loneliness to solitude, there are also many dangers. I will only touch upon two of them, which I believe are the most important pitfalls to be mindful of. First, I know there were a few brief moments during my desert sojourning that could have become a devastating snare to me if I had allowed the desire to take root; this trap was becoming inwardly focused instead of outwardly focused. When we are already suffering from any type of abuse, pain, feelings of abandonment, isolation, rejection, or loneliness, to be sent into the wilderness solo can feel like the ultimate casting away to our raw, hurting souls. It would be easy to lie down, curl into a ball, close our weary eyes, and turn our thoughts and hearts inward—to become consumed with our new set of changes and challenges and decide that the outcome and promise on the other side couldn't possibly be worth more trials and tears. I like the words Jamie Buckingham uses regarding this temptation:

> This is not a static process. It always involves change and progress from one stage to another. It can be done only on the move. The wilderness is a passage through trouble, but not a place to stop and wallow in our adversity...we pass through trouble, adversity, grief, pain, and hardships—all are wilderness experiences. But these deserts are not designed to choke the life out of us; rather, they are

designed to mold us and shape us into the image of Christ. We are not ever to allow ourselves to become desert settlers like the hermits of old, or even the Bedouin of today.[41]

It is crucial to see *purpose* in our desert experience to maintain the strength, perseverance, motivation, and vision needed to make it through to the other side and to enter into our "promised land." When we lose our forward motion as the mountains become steeper and the valleys drop deeper, it is a real temptation to look back and ask the most dangerous question: "Was it *really that bad?*" In our fatigue, foggy minds, and aching hearts, the fear of the unknown begins to creep up and call us back to what is known and familiar— **"Would it not be better for us to go back to Egypt?"** (Num. 14:3)—even when in our heart of hearts we know going back should *never* be an option. We fled or were freed for a reason and we have to keep that reason before us while taking one tentative, weak, wobbly, tear-stained step at a time into the unknown future, knowing that we are *never truly alone.*

Unless we personally come to the distinct knowledge that we fled without just cause or moved outside the will and purposes of God, we must continue on in faith that all will be well. This Scripture became a staple in my wilderness diet; it was a constant reminder that we do not always know where we are going but can always trust in the One leading us, even in the dark. **"Let him (her) who walks in darkness and has no light trust in the name of the LORD and rely on his (her) God"** (Isa. 50:10, parentheses added). If we could always see the entire plan or map perfectly and clearly laid out before us, we would have no need for faith or the Lord to show us the way! The desert is the place to grow and deepen our faith, trust, and belief in God—a training field wherein we attain a higher knowledge of God as well as a greater understanding of who we were created to be. If there is no struggle, no temptation to overcome, no testing or

---

[41] Jamie Buckingham, *A Way Through the Wilderness* (Old Tappan, NJ: Fleming H. Revell Co., 1986).

pruning, then how could we mature and grow?

In all honesty, I experienced this temptation during the initial weeks of my second and markedly harder wilderness journey following my exodus. While feeling so weary, sorrowful, and overwhelmed by the new environment I was placed into, I simply longed for the familiar and to be with my family and friends. It didn't take me long, however, to replay just a snippet of my former life with my narcissistic husband, recalling just a fraction of the abuse, pain, tears, endless silence, loneliness, and absence of love, to shake me out of my reverie and get my eyes back into focus as I pressed on toward my goal: to be free from silent desperation and to embrace new life leading me toward quiet strength!

Because You are my help, I sing in the shadow of Your wings. (Ps. 63:7)

JOURNAL ENTRY — September 6, 2015

How I did, You know...for us I cried buckets; it seemed it would never stop flowing. But then one day the stream of tears just dried up. The oasis in the desert was parched and barren with no fresh spring or new life. I still care; human kindness and love still exist. I do not curse or wish ill-will upon the narcissist; just no more tears right now—they won't come, though I try.

The second important snare to be aware of is the knowledge that a wilderness journey is not meant to last a lifetime; it is always for a specific purpose and a season. If we never get out of the desert, then we have probably either lost our way (having taken our eyes and ears off the Guide), or we have become complacent in the ways of the wilderness and lost our vision and motivation to get out. During my years of loneliness while solo sojourning, the isolation often felt like a harsh punishment for someone who desires companionship, communication, and loves to be around people in general. But I slowly came to understand that in this period of quarantine, I was actually being protected from those who were trying to use and harm me.

Thus, the wilderness seasons can be used to protect us, as

well as to purge us (to empty, cleanse of sins), to purify us, and to prepare us—or a combination of all—but they are never meant to become a permanent address. We should never be walking with our eyes looking down or behind us but, rather, always ahead toward that "something new" that the Lord is doing in our lives. After all, as it was with the Israelites following their time of exodus from Egypt, the desert journey is meant to ultimately prepare us to enter the Promised Land! **"Behold, I am doing a new thing: now it springs forth, do you not perceive it?"** (Isa. 43:19).

> "Solitude is thus the place of purification and transformation, the place of struggle and encounter. It is the place where God remodels us in His own image and frees us from the images of self we all bring with us when we enter the wilderness." —Jamie Buckingham, *A Way Through the Wilderness*[42]

Don't misunderstand me. I still experience loneliness, and it still hurts sometimes. The key still gets slipped in the chamber door, and I feel the waves wash over me, yet I am no longer consumed (Isaiah 43:2). The defining difference is a beautiful truth that I have come to understand only by journeying alone with God in the wilderness. I have found that I would rather be alone and feel the pain of loneliness than to ever again forfeit true peace and inner harmony to be in a relationship where there is neither. This, to me, is the joy and essence of solitude. I may still be a lone eagle, but the spirit of inner peace, contentment in solitude, and the joy of the Lord are the wind of quiet strength beneath my soaring wings!

> The wilderness seasons can be used to protect us, as well as to purge us, to purify us, and to prepare us, but they are never meant to become a permanent address.

My beloved speaks and says to me: "Arise, my love, my beautiful one, and come away…." (Song of Sol. 2:10)

---

[42] Buckingham, *A Way Through the Wilderness*.

For everything there is a season and a time for every matter under heaven. (Eccles. 3:1)

A desert is called that because it is dry and barren most of the time. Grasses, flowering plants, and scrub trees go dormant during a time of drought and often appear dead, but they are only waiting patiently for the life-giving rainy season. It may be a long time, even years, before they taste the first drops of desert rain, but when it comes, lush new life springs forth and what once seemed dead bursts open with stunning beauty. Our eyes, hearts, and souls rejoice at its breathtaking lushness, and we should! All seasons and cycles of life are truly a miracle, but we tend to love the vibrant season of sunlight, warmth, color, and scent much more than the dark and often dreary seasons of cold, barrenness, and gray. Maybe this is because the latter reflects too closely how we feel much of the time. I have some thoughts to share on this often-dreaded season of dormancy, which can lead us into a "blue funk" (as one of my old friends used to say) during the long winter months in the North. I believe it fits in with this topic of loneliness to solitude, offering a new perspective as we encounter the transformation that takes place during our own desert wilderness journeys.

This is an analogy that came into my heart and mind while looking out the second-story window of a downtown mansion for women, which I am currently living in while separated from my abusive, narcissistic husband. There is a large tree that stands at the edge of the busy city street. Its gray, barren branches stand motionless as if they are frozen in place like children pretend when playing "freeze dance"—arms outstretched at all angles just waiting for the music to start their movement again. This tree is waiting too: for the spring rains, the sunshine, and the warmth that will bring it back to life again—new leaves to dance and sway in the breeze.

But I also realize that because the tree is barren during this winter season, I have a clear view of what is on the other side of the street. There is another beautiful brick mansion adorned with huge white pillars that span the width of the porch. Next to it, separated by a parking lot, is another large building, which houses many apartments. Much activity goes on in the city—a faster pace and an interesting change for this country girl! Throughout the day, people come in and out of the apartment complex to walk their dogs. I enjoy watching them run and play: all different breeds, shapes, sizes, and colors. Along the sidewalk there are people coming or going to work, parents pushing strollers, people running to catch the bus, joggers, bikers, and electric wheelchairs. Neighbors carry grocery bags from their trip to the local store while others rifle through the garbage cans looking for recyclable items and other treasures. This is the life flow of humanity. Although I anxiously await spring and the joy of watching the now-dormant tree bring forth new life, I also know that it will eventually block my view of other life, which, though still happening, I won't be able to see anymore, and I will miss it.

The analogy here—as the Spirit has taught me this early April morn—is that we need to fully embrace what we are being offered in the present moment, hour, day, and season where we are, even if we don't always like what we see or how it makes us feel. With every new gain there is a loss, and even though we may be *very* ready for the rainy season, we need to glean the hidden treasures offered during the drought. This becomes a matter of the heart, the mind, and our attitude—seasoned with humility, gratitude, and grace. We need to humbly accept what is placed before us and make it a feast even if it looks like dry crumbs. It may be unappetizing to our flesh but could be just the right food for our souls. Often, it is only during our seasons of barrenness that we are even open to seeing what we would otherwise never be able to behold if our view was always satisfying and plentiful. If we were never thirsty, how could we truly appreciate and enjoy an oasis?

O God, You are my God; earnestly I seek You; my soul thirsts for You, in a dry and weary land where there is no water. (Ps. 63:1)[43]

---

[43] This is a Psalm of David, when he was in the wilderness of Judah.

Every good and perfect gift is from above, coming down from the Father of the heavenly lights, who does not change like shifting shadows. (James 1:17)

Life is always moving, changing, and cycling from season to season. We need to learn to flow with the rhythm of it. Sometimes the beat is more steady, with familiar steps, like during the seasons of raising babies and establishing roots, responsibilities, boundaries, etc. Our children *need* stable environments during seasons of growth and maturity. But too often we become stagnant where we are planted, and then, when it is time to fly or is a new season of planting on fresh ground for better growth, we resist the change and miss all of the wonder and joy it can bring. I write these words only after many years of hard lessons steeped in resistance, fear, and the painful pruning needed to cut away the old and now unfruitful to make room for new growth. Each step played out the same: resistance, a fierce battle, frustration, tears, prayers, surrender.

Sometimes we are called to take up arms and fight. Our nature is to fight against change, and often what we don't understand at the time is really a beautiful gift from God. It is hard sometimes to recognize the gift because it isn't always wrapped in pretty paper with a big shiny bow and colorful ribbons; it is often wrapped in a rough and drab covering. If we are never forced to dig deeper, we will usually choose to stay on top near the surface. We tend to like it there because it is safe, easy, light, comfortable, and familiar. Unfortunately, though, if everything is given to us easily, we will never be able to envision what new life awaits us *after* we have had to walk through a dry, dormant, and often dark season in our lives.

Underneath the guise of deadness, I promise you that there lies hope for a new season filled with joy and abundant life. It is a wonderful journey from painful loneliness to sweet solitude!

"I will make a way in the wilderness and rivers in the desert."
(Isa. 43:19)

**He (she) is like a tree planted by streams of water that yields its fruit in its season, and its leaf does not wither.
In all that he (she) does, he (she) prospers.**
(Ps. 1:3, parentheses added)

19
Transformation

Therefore, if anyone is in Christ, he is a new creation.
The old has passed away, the new has come.
(2 Cor. 5:17)

THE PROCESS OF transformation is nothing short of a miracle, both in the natural and the spiritual realms. I wish to portray a person's spiritual transformation by using as an analogy the incredible metamorphosis that occurs in the natural realm of a caterpillar changing into a beautiful butterfly. I'm astounded by the instinctive nature that God gave His many creatures to create the most intricate and intriguing masterpieces for protecting, sustaining, and developing new life. Have you ever studied a spider web, a hornet's nest or beehive, an ant hill, a bird's nest? They are the most amazing creations brought into existence by the lowest created order, and even man—with all of our ingenuity and technology—could never produce something their equal. This same unfathomable instinct prompts a caterpillar to form a cocoon, to be ready for change. Leif Hetland explained this so well: "Once inside it is trapped. It can't leave. It can't move. It can't do anything. All it can do is lie there and wait."[44]

There are many situations that can make us feel as if we are also living inside of our own little cocoon. I cannot relate to all of the various ways individuals find themselves living in these restrictive places of bondage in the *natural* realm. I can only write from the perspective of my cocoon, spun by the skillful hands of a narcissistic spouse. Since my deliverance from this oppressive relationship, though, I have also experienced the cocooning process necessary to

---

[44] Leif Hetland, *Seeing through Heaven's Eyes: A World View That Will Transform Your Life* (Shippensburg, PA: Destiny Image, 2011).

be truly transformed within the *spiritual* realm. There is confinement, darkness, isolation, loneliness, and pain within both realms, although with significantly different end results: the natural leading to hopeless desperation and the spiritual leading to flight and freedom! Both the caterpillar and I lie within our respective cocoons in the deep darkness, bound by confining conditions that render us helpless to undo what has already encased us. "We are not the ones acting; we are being acted upon" by an outside force.[45] We must wait in the dark and lonely place "until it is time, our time, our appointed time to emerge and reveal to a watching world the soaring beauty of what we were created to be."[46] But for now, we wait. As believers, we have to wait and fully trust in God when we are in total darkness without knowledge of what is to come, with no concrete thoughts as to what we will be or what we will do in the aftermath of the impending change. Though we cannot see what God is doing with our natural eyes, I believe that if we lie quiet and still long enough, we may begin to have an inkling…while peering into the unseen realm with spiritual eyes that see through the heart.

> "Do not fear change; when you cling to old ways and sameness, you resist My work within you. I want you to embrace all that I am doing in your life; find your security in Me alone."
> —from Sarah Young, *Jesus Calling*[47]

Unfortunately, we sometimes become too complacent within the comforts of our caterpillar state and decide that we want to remain a caterpillar. Although this state of being becomes terribly ill-fitting and restrictive, it is what we know. We are creatures who like to remain in comfy places that we are familiar with; they make us feel safe. We like our routines, daily habits, behavior patterns, and the comfort zones we so carefully stake out with posted signs that read "No Trespassing." We carve out our mental boundaries and

---

[45] Hetland, *Seeing through Heaven's Eyes.*
[46] Ibid.
[47] Sarah Young, *Jesus Calling: Enjoying Peace in His Presence* (Nashville, TN: Thomas Nelson, 2004).

conservatively stay within a foot of them, just to be on the safe side. We err on the side of caution and try not to talk to too many strangers. We have our circle of favorite family members and the friends who know us and still like us anyway. Many people head off daily to a job they despise (or maybe it is just the people there), but it is a job; it pays the bills with a little "mad money" leftover! We may not really know (much less love) our neighbors, but we do know what kind of cars they drive, their favorite pizza delivery place, and if they have a German Shepherd or Schnauzer. We avoid eye contact as often as possible, and try to pretend we don't see "Mrs. Smith" from church, who we know is going to ask us again about volunteering for the bake sale or nursery school. We caterpillars are funny creatures. We really dislike the confines of the now tight and scratchy wool sweater. We may be truly bored with the outdated style that is no longer flattering or colorful, but we have been wearing it for years and so we tolerate its drab irritation; it is what we have always worn and what we know.

These are perhaps silly scenarios, but I believe they convey a real problem in many of our lives: We have stopped, or never really started, desiring to be transformed by the renewing of our minds. We have become too comfortable in our daily lives as well as in our walk of faith. We gather knowledge both in the greater world as well as in Sunday School classes, Bible studies, workshops, retreats, and our small groups. But what are we doing with it all? Is it *transforming* us? Is it transforming our lives? Is it transforming our family dynamics and personal relationships? Are we being renewed to the point that people notice a difference within and outside ourselves? Have we stopped desiring to soar to new heights within the confines of our marriage, family, circle of friends, career, ministry work, and spheres of influence? These questions are not meant to make you feel badly, guilty, ashamed, or angry. These questions are for me as well. But they *are meant* to provoke thought, though, with an open heart and mind seeking truth about the state of our being. Are you still in the

255

caterpillar stage, are you cocooned, are you on the verge of emerging, or have you already been fully transformed into a new creation?

JOURNAL ENTRY – December 15, 2015

Mold and groom my "self," Lord Jesus, by Your Spirit so I can finally emerge from my cocoon and be a butterfly and fly wherever You would have me go!

It would be so good if God could extract us from our comfort zones more easily and place us into the cocoon He has ready and waiting, thereby beginning this wonderful transformation more quickly. But most of us resist it with every fiber of our being. We want to just sprout wings and fly off into glory-land, but we can't fly until God gives us our wings through this terribly wonderful process of renewal. We go into the cocoon kicking and screaming—at least I know I did—because we do not understand that this is what needs to happen *first* before we can reach the butterfly stage of life. Or, maybe it is because we have too keen an idea of what is about to happen to us, and we shrink from the prospect of the pain we must endure to achieve the desired outcome. As I mentioned above, author Leif Hetland so poignantly describes this Christian rite of passage:

> What God does that seems so terrible is that He starts to dissolve the caterpillar; everything turns to liquid. Halfway through the process, the caterpillar becomes a gooey mess. Out of this mess comes the miracle. Out of most messes comes the miracle. Both your messes and my messes. Out of this shapeless mass of goo, God causes the cells to reorganize and build a butterfly, a being that is totally beyond the caterpillar's wildest imagination....One thing I have found out about the Father's love. Though He loves us as we are, He loves us too much to let us *remain* as we are.[48]

The "as we are" is that which has become comfortable and complacent. When we fear change, we cling to our familiar ways and life becomes a monotony of daily tasks without variety or excitement. We have to ask ourselves the hard question: Do we want to stop at

---

[48] Ibid (paraphrased).

just the crawling stage and continue to chew on plain green leaves, or do we want to exchange our legs that keep us grounded for a new set of beautiful wings that will allow us to fly free and drink in the sweet nectar of new life?

JOURNAL ENTRY – April 14, 2015

I see the reflection of this time of new life in my own heart. The slow peeling away of the past and the beautiful unveiling of the new life in me as You transform me into a new creation.

"Pain is part of the process of transformation. Perhaps it *is* the process"[49]—acute and sometimes chronic pain endured without the relief of distractions, drugs, alcohol, or other numbing agents.

> To see other people through heaven's eyes means you have to lose your earthly eyes. This happens through a process of isolation, transformation, and emergence. God sets you apart by cocooning you; then one day you emerge from the restrictive, dark, pain-filled cocoon, and He releases you into the world to fly! In the terrifying middle of the process, though, He dissolves you. The old you, that is. The lost you. The orphan you. The anxious you. The you that believes your true identity is still a caterpillar. Understand that the process of transformation, of getting new eyes in which to see and new wings with which to fly, is a painful one. But what emerges from the transformation is worth the pain.[50]

There is no other way around it; one must just bite the bullet and go through it! My life is a living testimony to this truth. "What emerges is your truest self, your most beautiful self, the self that the world is needing to see, longing to see, aching to see."[51]

JOURNAL ENTRY – December 28, 2015

I feel somehow detached from my emotions, and I do not like it. I was reminded today that You are both protecting and preparing me for what lies ahead. During this season, I "saw" myself as in a protective cocoon like a caterpillar; safe from the dangers of the world until ready to fully emerge to new life. You are protecting me from unnecessary pain and emotional

---

[49] Ibid.
[50] Ibid.
[51] Ibid.

trauma as You groom and heal me from the inside out. The lack of emotional swings are a way of keeping me steady as I travel the shifting desert sands; not an indication of my love and compassion toward others. The Spirit doesn't want me to be guided by my passions and emotions but only by His voice and leading. He is lovingly buffering the pains that would so readily overtake me and hinder my progress forward; leading me farther away from the familiar and comfortable and slowly cutting the ties that bind so I can step out beyond the limits of self into the spiritual realm of freedom in Christ.

Several years ago, while eating a meal at a Greek restaurant, a woman (accompanied by her somewhat embarrassed husband) came up to our table and introduced herself as a fellow Christian, as she had seen us praying over our meal before we ate. She said, "I have never done this before in my life (to which her husband quickly affirmed), but as I was sitting at our table, the Lord gave me a message to give to you." As she had never had this happen to her before, she thought maybe it was just a strange imagining. But as she sat there a while longer, the exact same message was given again with the clear mandate that it was meant for me. She delivered the message, what I would call a (prophetic) "word of knowledge" from God. After a few more brief moments of exchange, I thanked her so much for having the courage to give me this obviously important word from the Lord.

It wasn't as specific as I would have liked, and I felt perplexed by it, as it could have referenced several situations in my life at the time. I had wondered why God would have it be somewhat vague, but I believe now that the reason was twofold: a hidden message that He didn't want the other party at the table to understand as well as His desire that I fervently seek Him to receive the answer. I did seek and receive an answer, yet only in part at that time. Although I knew what He had spoken, it didn't fully make sense to my finite understanding and even seemed somewhat adverse to what *I would think* the Lord would instruct me to do. Maybe that is why He used a stranger in a restaurant to give it to me, so that I would accept it as His word and not *my* imaginings.

I am sharing this certain puzzle piece of my life for two specific reasons. First, we certainly do not fully understand the thoughts and ways of God (Isa. 55:8-9). When *we think* we have achieved such a complete state of knowledge and wisdom, then, I dare say, we are on dangerous ground. It is so hard for us to fathom sometimes what God asks us to do, or the ways in which He leads us to accomplish His purposes in and through our lives. Secondly, as I began to receive revelation of this message, in all honesty, I resisted the truth of it. It seemed contrary to God and to my character. I wrestled with the Lord and myself for several years over this internal spiritual conflict. But the ensuing battle was not fought in vain, for as we tumbled and He began to wear me out, I finally stopped fighting and truly began listening.

During the intervening years between the receipt of that word of knowledge and the actual fruition of it, the Lord God had done a huge transformation work in me. This could not have been achieved any other way except for that restrictive, dark, isolated, and lonely cocooning period. There had to be both a complete yielding to my lack of understanding (to lead me to a place of absolute trust through faith), as well as a complete surrendering to everything outside my comfort zone in order for me to submit to the cocooning stage necessary for transformation and renewed life.

We must not become impatient with God, even when He gives us a specific vision or implants a passion within our hearts. He is both the God of time and timelessness; He works His will and ways within both spheres. For me, it was a word of what was to come. More time was needed for me to be taught and to learn, to finish current calls upon my life, and to lead me to a deeper place of silent desperation so that I would not resist when the marching orders came for me to leave the familiar in exchange for the great unknown. All the while, God was preparing, setting in motion, and orchestrating all of the people, places, and little details required for when this weary and battle-worn

> He is both the God of time and timelessness.

caterpillar—now in the middle stage of transformation—was called out of the place that had become so unbearable.

When finally rescued from my abusive marriage, stating that it was God's will and divine plan that paved the way for my departure (because it seemed like such a contrary thing that God would do), many people questioned the validity of my words with a spirit of unbelief.[52] They judged my honorable departure with their natural eyes and not with spiritual vision. Although I understood their quandary, it hurt my tender, already grieving heart. Several years pre-exodus, a Christian "sister" offered more words of clarity pertaining to the message from God delivered by the stranger: That "I needed to stop trying to be the *perfect wife* in order to lift my spouse up to *look like* the *perfect husband*…as well as the other parts he played."

Better is the end of a thing than its beginning, and the patient in spirit is better than the proud in spirit. (Eccles. 7:8)

JOURNAL ENTRY – November 22, 2015

But…I find myself in a new place this morning; a new state of mind and heart. This has come at a great price with much wrestling, tears, and letting go of precious dreams. "The project you are working on, you need to **abort**." It has taken me so long to abort my plans, my dreams, my hopes, my future, my way which in my eyes was best for all. But I see now that my "best" is not making anything better; just more painful. This new direction doesn't seem like God's ways at all—to let it all go and watch it fall. But to build a new building or start a new "project," you have to tear down or abandon the old. I can't go back to how it was. The past is gone; I can't cling to empty dreams and love lost. I move forward with no regrets; I poured myself out as a drink offering. I did my best.

JOURNAL ENTRY – February 27, 2016

Lord Jesus, during my devotion time I reread a familiar verse…Romans 12:2 "but be transformed by the renewal of your mind." I wrote this down and thought of my husband, but it was also very much for me. Although I can look back and see so many places and times You have renewed my heart and mind and "switched" roads of thought to the ways of God; I have still a deep rut in my reactions to the narcissistic assaults on my heart and

---

[52] This was discussed in greater detail in a previous chapter.

mind. Precious Jesus, strong and mighty Lord to which all things are subject, please continue the work of transforming my heart and mind for what my mind thinks, so my heart feels. I need You to fill-in the well-worn paths which lead to strife and start paving a new road which leads to peace, light, and life! I can't do this work for my spouse; that is between You and him, but I can abandon myself to You to do this needful work in me. Please give me the needed portion of grace to be transformed in this critical place of healing and renewal. I trust in You to do this work in me. Amen and amen!

The Isolation Period: Out of Body, Out of Mind

Isolation—the very word produces a sad feeling, doesn't it? Especially in light of the fact that we were created for relationships, family units, community, and citizenship. There are certain times, though, when isolation is necessary. Isolation is imposed as a means of quarantine to stop the spread of contagious diseases.[53] Sometimes individuals opt to isolate themselves if they are on a spiritual retreat or working on a book or project that necessitates a quiet and distraction-free environment. Solitary confinement imposed in both civilian and military prisons is a forced isolation from others as a form of punishment for bad and dangerous behavior and/or to break a person's spirit. It is so effective because being isolated from other people (especially by force and against a person's will) is withering to a human's heart, soul, mind, and spirit. It goes against our created nature; it is unnatural and foreign to our being, which longs to be seen, heard, known, and loved.

As I write these words describing isolation, even the times when it is necessary, tears stream down my face. It is one of those "keys" that slips into the chamber of my heart and unlocks the memories of my years in isolation. In many ways I still am isolated as I write this book and continue to heal, though not nearly to the extent I once was while trapped within my silent desperation. This period of isolation is meant for good and not for evil, to build up and heal and

---

[53] Unbeknownst to me at the time of this writing, COVID-19 would soon affect the entire world in its own form of isolation.

not to break down and destroy. And although I have come to love my days of precious solitude, there are moments when the deep pain of loneliness and isolation floods my heart chamber and stirs up embers still smoldering. When we are isolated and left lonely for extended periods of time, we tend to become detached from concrete things and feel porous as holes are punched through all that we once knew, who we once were, where we have been, and where we are going. Life becomes surreal at times. Fear strikes our hearts with panic that we are floating away and do not know how to put our feet back on the ground and our minds back in the game. At this point, I will share words already penned by my hand that express what I was feeling during one period of forced isolation from my husband's cold heart.

JOURNAL ENTRY — No date recorded

My slow stripping away began long ago while in our house in the country. The surreal moments when I was in the same place, with the same circle of people, doing many routine things, even enjoying it still on one level—the solid and familiar level—yet at the same time feeling oddly detached from it all. The only way to describe the sensation would be to think of it as an out-of-body experience where your mind knows who you are, where you are, what you are doing, saying, hearing, feeling, etc. but at the same time there is another part of you somehow detached; like looking down upon yourself while perched on an elevated shelf and seeing life as it has always been yet not fully a part of it anymore. Like I was slowly drifting away but by an unknown force; intriguing yet unsettling at the same time. Knowing something significant is happening in the unseen realm, something spiritual, yet there are no human words to fully describe it. One word that parallels this experience is isolation; an awareness that you are a part of what is happening yet at the same time feeling left or forced out.

JOURNAL ENTRY — November 26, 2014

I cannot see beyond the mountains that block my way, but I know He will somehow make a straight path. He will make me to forget the former things, which have diminished me and crushed my spirit and broken my heart. He is doing a new thing in me, and it will refresh my wounded and thirsty soul. I lay in bed this morning, feeling so tired and as if all I can do is breathe—breathing and existing with occasional bursts of energy to keep going. I feel I can't dive too deep right now or I may not make it back up to the top. I lean heavily on my Lord for help and support. I float alone in the natural world. I am tired and drained from the struggle. I have slowly faded from being filled with passion, energy, and a robust life to a colorless life of daily routines, commitments, and responsibilities. Letting go of the former things can be so scary. You are a patient and loving Teacher. Amen.

My flesh and my heart may fail, but God is the strength of my heart and my portion forever. (Ps. 73:26)

Those raw words, penned during my forced isolation, in the wake of narcissism at its best, come from a place I wouldn't wish on anyone. But I believe there is a time when isolation during a spiritual cocooning period is necessary (even crucial) to allow what I will refer to as "adaptation." We need this pivotal time to adapt to our new "self," a newly created being. We can't just go from crawling all our life and chewing on leaves to flying weightlessly and enjoying the sweet life of freedom without a span of preparation time. How much you were attached to the ways of a caterpillar will determine how much time it will take to adapt to your new life with only six legs and two wings. The caterpillar life keeps you pretty close to home base. I mean, how far can you really walk in a day with those little legs? How much do you desire to wander from your comfort zone of the familiar trees you enjoy nibbling and resting upon?

God lovingly and slowly prepares us at the pace He knows we can handle, as He isn't looking to put us into culture shock. He wants us thoroughly ready to fly once we emerge—with grace and peace—as our new life begins. There is the adaptation of the heart (cutting and detaching from close ties that bind) as well as physical adaptation (separation); we need to be trained in both realms. Both physical and mental/emotional adaptation are necessary for us to fully emerge without dragging around a carry-on bag every time we fly. To take flight, we have to fly light with as few hindrances from the past or even present "old" life as possible. Jesus said that to follow Him would include a (often weighty) sacrifice in leaving behind the old to receive the new life He offers (Matt. 10:37-39).

Too often, we try to mesh the two realms by keeping some remnants from the past, attempting to keep our two back caterpillar

263

legs on the earth while trying to lift off the ground and fly. We can't do both. An airplane can't keep its wheels on the runway and lift off at the same time. The tires don't hang out of the bottom of the airplane while in flight but, rather, are drawn up into the plane; they are no longer needed when flying. They would cause unnecessary drag and slow down the momentum. So, too, we need to fully relinquish our many caterpillar "legs" during the isolated cocooning stage of metamorphoses to emerge fully transformed and adapted to our new wings!

JOURNAL ENTRY — July 17, 2014

I have been chiseled much by those whom I share daily life with. I pray they are doing their good work in making me the person You desire to emerge someday; like a delicate but strong butterfly—full of grace and beauty. May my heart always bless and praise Your holy name no matter where I find myself; on the mountain top or in the pit. Amen.

Though the loss will appear great at times in both the physical as well as the emotional realms of the familiar, we have to *believe* in our heart and spirit that the gains resulting from seasons of isolation, transformation, and adaptation are far greater than the losses. Most people do not truly appreciate life at its greatest depth until they know they are dying. I had to reach a place of silent desperation, to the acute knowledge that I could make myself stay and *just exist* until I took my last breath (which felt closer every day), or I could choose the new life being offered me and *really live*—not just for myself but for the sake of my daughters. This newly transformed life would also be my testimony. It was only in my dying to the old caterpillar life that I am now able to truly live. It has not been without much pain, loss, and sorrow.

I couldn't have endured the pain if I didn't believe there was purpose in it. There *always* needs to be a higher purpose woven into the fabric of our pain, trials, suffering, and grief; otherwise we cannot endure it—at least with any hope and grace. It is my hope, as Leif Hetland experienced, to emerge as a lover—a lover of *all* people and a messenger of hope and new life to those who are unjustly isolated, oppressed, and abused, living within the restrictive covering of silent desperation. May my life's story encourage you to yield to the cocooning and isolation process, which is the precursor to total transformation, so that you may emerge and fly forth in quiet strength into the amazingly beautiful new life just waiting for you!

> **Now faith is the assurance of things hoped for, the conviction of things not seen.** (Heb. 11:1)

JOURNAL ENTRY — March 10, 2016

I realize that I have already done so much of my grieving for years and years. Grieving for lost dreams, trust, security, a godly husband and father, a partner, confidant, lover of body and soul; what we could have had if he wanted it—wanted me. Loss of peace and health because of stress and burden; loss of our future. Jesus, You lifted me up and brushed away my tears. In the midst of this crisis—the end of something which is sacred to me—You are breathing new life into my heart, soul, body, mind, and spirit. The chains of pain, loss, shame, and confusion are falling off of me link by link. I am feeling so close to some newness of life flowing in and through me. I feel the stirring of a beautiful new experience with You. I feel a sense of self-worth and passion for living in exchange for the deadness in me and in my marriage. The narcissist was burying me alive—and he may have succeeded—if You hadn't dug me out, lifted me up, and set my eyes on You and Your precious love for me. I feel safe only when I know You are near. Lead me out of the valley of the shadow of death and into the new life You have waiting for me.

20

True Freedom

It is for freedom that Christ has set us free. Stand firm, then, and do not let yourselves be burdened again by a yoke of slavery.
(Gal. 5:1)

To BE VERY honest, when I felt led to write this book, I had no forethought about sharing the depth and rawness of my pain and sorrow, to make myself so vulnerable after already feeling so unprotected under the deceitful administrations of my narcissistic husband. I had no intention of baring so much of my soul by including excerpts from my private journals, which held the secrets of my silent desperation and the range of deep and sometimes dark emotions that churned within me. The penned words were between God and me. But as a woman of faith, I have honored the Scripture that says, **"My thoughts are not your thoughts"** (Isa. 55:8). The Lord's ways and thoughts are always for a higher purpose than our finite minds can conceive. The one thing I do know is that during the summer of 2016 while on my regular morning walk after my "exodus" (departure) to Buffalo, I began to feel an unusually heavy burden to pray for others who were held in some form of abuse, bondage, or incarceration. Tears began to come as I took in the magnitude of it all. This was only intensified by my faith, as I knew the Lord Jesus Christ had come to earth from heaven, died a terrible death of crucifixion on a cross, and was resurrected for the very purpose of *setting us all free* from captivity (Luke 4:18, John 8:36).

I became even more troubled and experienced feelings of guilt that my Father God had set me free when so many other people, in much more terrible bondage than I had been, were still imprisoned—whether in body, soul, mind, or spirit. I asked, "Why,

Lord, why me?" And He spoke by the Spirit into my conflicted heart, "Because I am going to use you as My instrument of truth to shine light into the darkness of narcissism and other forms of abuse and bondage. I am going to use your words to be a voice in the silence, bringing understanding and My hope to the hopeless—whether a believer or nonbeliever—because of My deep love for them and the grace I offer to all." That revelation would initiate my new journey as I offered up my renewed life, my hands, my time, my experiences, my private thoughts and words…and I said, "Give me Your words, and I will write them as You wish."

> **But I trust in You, O LORD; I say, "You are my God." My times are in Your hand; rescue me from the hand of my enemies and from my persecutors! Make Your face shine on Your servant; save me in Your steadfast love!** (Ps. 31:14-16)

> "Let us be lovers of the truth and let it do its powerful and magnificent work of disentangling our hearts from anything and everything which needs to be cleansed away, or from which we need to be freed."
> —John Wright Follette, *Pressed Juice From Living Fruit* [54]

After living in a cloud of deception for almost 25 years, I have become an ardent lover of truth! I seek it diligently, even when the truth hurts. Wrought through my experiences, I have perceived and embraced with understanding that we cannot "get real" with ourselves unless we are able to *see ourselves as we are*—broken, needy, vulnerable, full of fears and insecurities, all covered up by protective shells of our own making. In our fear of failure and insufficiency, we pile on layers of masks to protect our hearts and our image, trying to deceive the world yet only deceiving ourselves. The process of taking off the masks is difficult because each layer, now in its removal, is going to strip away all that once defined us. Yet, until we get to the bottom layer in all honesty and humility, we cannot truly be free to live as the unique and wonderfully created people we were meant to be.

---

[54] Follette, *Pressed Juice From Living Fruit.*

In some ways, I think I arrived at this point a bit easier because I didn't have to strip off all of my layers; I had much of the work done for me. I didn't have to work as hard at being humble, as I was humbled by constant reminders that I was unworthy of love and was rejected by the man who promised to care for and honor me for the rest of my life. It is easier to get to the end of ourselves when someone systematically steals our identity and leaves us in shreds. It is a shortcut to understanding our own helplessness and poverty when we are already lying in the bottom of the pit with no way out unless someone comes to rescue us and carry us to freedom.

While I waited there in the cold and lonely darkness, I allowed myself to be taught many things. This is a choice: to fight against one's truth and reality, or to yield to it and eventually embrace it as a source of power and precious life. Oh, I didn't go down into the pit easily; I fought against truth for years and still bear the scars. But in the end, I surrendered to my circumstances and desired to know what wisdom and treasure I could glean from the wreckage of our fragmented marriage and the Refiner's fire. *And when the Lord's work was done*, He came—my Knight in shining armor. He lovingly carried me up from the pit of silent desperation and out into the light of freedom. Then He breathed into me new life, restored my strength, and taught me how to fly with renewed purpose and passion.

JOURNAL ENTRY — April 14, 2015

Saturate yourself with freedom
which Jesus bought and secured for you
with His precious blood!
Thank You, Lord, for the gift of new life, hope, and freedom.
Under the wings of Your power and love, we can soar.

That is why I am writing this book...how could I not? I knew I had the choice to run off, lick my wounds, and go into hiding so that no one could ever hurt me again, but that would have been such a selfish way to use my freedom. So I write and pray that the experiences of my life—my pain and loneliness in silent, solitary confinement and my ultimate rescue—offer new hope, strength, and courage in seeking freedom to a world of fellow travelers desperate to be seen, heard, known, and loved. This is a *labor of love* because *you* are loved! **"Return to your fortress, you prisoners of hope; even now I will announce that I will restore twice as much to you"** (Zech. 9:12). What a beautiful promise—a double portion returned to us for our pain in captivity if we hold onto our hope in God!

> **The word of the LORD tested him (her) and he (she) was released—a slave in fetters and iron collar around his (her) neck.** (Ps. 105:18,19, paraphrased and parentheses added)

In a small yet potent book by Maya Angelou entitled *Wouldn't Take Nothing For My Journey Now*,[55] I recently read about a true story passed onto her from an extended family member referred to as "Aunt Tee." Aunt Tee was a live-in housekeeper and at one time worked for a very rich couple who lived in a 14-room ranch house in Bel Air, California. This couple had everything that money could buy yet they were dying a slow death in lonely silence without any joy, laughter, peace, and love that are often found in the simplest pleasures of life. They started to live vicariously through their housekeeper and her friends, who gathered together in her room and ate simple home-cooked meals, played games, told jokes, laughed, danced, and sang together with great delight. The couple, grown old beyond their years, hearing their laughter and happiness, would watch them through the slightly ajar door. They didn't want or ask to participate, just to watch and yearn for that joy. Perhaps they were too afraid, set in their ways, or felt too sophisticated to associate with the housekeeper's social group (the reason wasn't given).

I have seen this dynamic firsthand in my personal sphere. I saw it clearly in my (now) ex-husband. We hear or read about it every day in the news or magazines. People having an endless array of material wealth, often living selfish, self-centered lives yet without any

---

[55] Maya Angelou, "Living Well. Living Good," *Wouldn't Take Nothing for My Journey Now* (New York: Random House, 1993), pp. 61-66.

real pleasure or enjoyment in their "stuff." They know no peace, no joy, no heartfelt laughter, no real life—only existing. Many of these people have the means to live way beyond that of the three-quarters of population of the world living in or are just above poverty level, yet they are bound by invisible cords of self-induced bondage instead of *really living* in the beautiful blessing of freedom they have been given to enjoy a fulfilling and grateful life.

These words bring a visual to my mind's eye of the character Scrooge from the book *A Christmas Carol* by Charles Dickens. Scrooge was notorious for being stingy with others while hoarding all of his wealth for himself. Our "wealth," by the way, does not have to be monetary, but rather is anything that we cling to out of fear as we try to control some aspect of our life or identity—without which we feel vulnerable, lost, empty, unsuccessful, unimportant, or unloved. Mr. Scrooge was both a *miser* and *miserable*! It was only after he had been given a stark reality check that he realized *genuine* richness was not found in the keeping but, rather, true treasure comes in *the freedom* we have to let go and give fearlessly and joyfully! In his song, "This Is Not a Test,"[56] Christian song artist Toby Mac expresses that the "feeling of love" is in the complete emptying of ourselves toward others. I have found that at the lowest times in my life when I felt the most empty, impoverished, and as if I had nothing to offer—if I stepped out in faith and allowed the Lord to pour Himself out through my broken, barren vessel—I could give what I didn't have and yet come away *full*. I love God's version of economics!

One of the greatest sources of my courage to seek freedom was the deep and dire need to experience more of life during my short span of allotted time here on earth. I did not want to merely exist. I knew at times I was on the very edge of darkness, hopelessness, and joylessness. I was desperate not to fall in, as I didn't know if I would ever come out again. I longed to live…to live free and breathe in the goodness that can still be found at every turn from

---

[56] TobyMac, "This Is Not a Test," *This Is Not a Test*, ForeFront, 2015.

the hand of a good God who delights in the joy of His children. I needed to get back to the "land of the living"[57] with every fiber of my being. This need would be fueled daily by our daughters, who still needed a parent filled with the life, peace, joy, hope, laughter, and love that I had spoken, read, taught, sung, and prayed about.

In *Wouldn't Take Nothing For My Journey Now*, Maya Angelou writes about that yearning and joyless couple watching *real* life being lived out before them just steps away from a doorway, yet still remaining on the fringes as if an invisible, electric wire fence surrounded them like a prison courtyard constructed in their mind— experiencing life only vicariously through others.[58] I don't know what is more sad: not knowing the joy of truly living because you never had the example or tasted of its pleasures, or seeing it played out right before your very eyes and still choosing to watch from afar. It is like walking with intrigue around the outside of a swimming pool, afraid to jump in, and just hoping that you get splashed with a few drops of its refreshing water. This was and still is what I consider the unfortunate life of my ex-husband, as well as others among my acquaintances: taking nibbles off the crust of life instead of receiving the whole loaf that is offered. I kept inviting, coaxing, and pleading with my ex-husband to join us and enter into real life. But he would never move toward what was freely offered because of invisible barriers that none of us could see, yet my heart and soul could painfully perceive, just beyond the veil.

> For You have delivered my soul from death,
> my eyes from tears, my feet from stumbling;
> I will walk before the LORD in the land of the living.
> (Ps. 116:8-9)

In "Living Well. Living Good," Maya Angelou wrote:

> I realize that living well is an art which can be developed. Of course, you will need the basic talents to build upon: They are a

---

[57] Psalm 27:13 (NASB): I would have despaired unless I had believed that I would see the goodness of the LORD in the land of the living.
[58] Angelou, *Wouldn't Take Nothing for My Journey Now*, pp. 61-66.

love of life and the ability to take great pleasure from small offerings, an assurance that the world owes you nothing and that every gift is exactly that, a gift. That people who may differ from you…can be founts of fun, and if you are lucky, they can become even convivial comrades. Living life as art requires a readiness to forgive. I do not mean that you should suffer fools gladly, but rather remember your own shortcomings. Life seems to love the liver of it. Money and power can liberate only if they are used to do so. They can imprison and inhibit more finally than barred windows and iron chains.[59]

I recently found myself weeping once again as I thought about all that my husband had missed and lost with me and our family in what could have been a blessed life together. All that he wasted away on selfish abandon. His life has remained a waste since our divorce in a cycle of sleeping, eating, unhappy toil, watching television, and acquiring an abundance of inanimate things, all the while remaining behind his multilayered masks. These activities bring no real life; they are merely existing. He has the *pretense* of freedom from commitment and responsibility, yet the most profound bondage encapsulates his heart, soul, and mind, preventing him from living fully and freely. I longed to truly be able to see *him*, his true self; to hear *him*, his own thoughts and words; to know *him*, who he really was apart from the lies, deception, and masks; to be able to love *him* —all of him—with trust, truth, and open vulnerability. But because he never could or would allow himself the freedom, I therefore never truly did.

For you, my brothers and sisters, were called to be free. But do not use your freedom to indulge the flesh; rather, serve one another humbly in love. (Gal. 5:13)

On July 4, 2017, I read a devotional in *Our Daily Bread* entitled "Celebrate Freedom," which truly resonated with me. The author, Julie Ackerman Link, wrote about Olaf Wiig, a New Zealand news cameraman who was kidnapped and held hostage for 13 days. With a

---

[59] Angelou, *Wouldn't Take Nothing for My Journey Now*, pp. 61-66.

broad smile upon his release, he said, "I feel more alive now than I have my entire life." Julie then wrote, "For reasons difficult to understand, **being freed** is more exhilarating then *being free!*" (emphasis added).[60] For most people, this slight change in wording probably doesn't mean that much, but for me personally (and for many readers who have been set free from a narcissistic relationship or some other form of abuse and bondage), this statement isn't hard to understand at all! After 25 years of desperation while living in my prison of silence, manipulative abuse, and extreme loneliness as a hostage of narcissism, I, too, feel more alive than I have in the last half of my life!

I have not only been set free from the imposed chains of an oppressor, but also from the shackles I had placed upon my life with my own hands. There are so many distractions and duties that consume our time, money, and energy that God wants to release us from, but we won't let go! When we live as free people, born into freedom in the United States, for example, most of us do not truly appreciate this priceless gift or the high price that has been paid (and still is being paid) by so many to keep it. Thank you to our men and women in uniform. Your faithful service, courage, and selfless sacrifice are *so* appreciated! Truth is unchangeable, and **freedom is not free!** It is *always* bought and paid for by the shedding of precious blood. As a military veteran, a survivor of a long-term relationship with a narcissist, and a sinner saved by grace, I am grateful to my very core for both physical and spiritual freedom!

JOURNAL ENTRY — November 17, 2014

Lord, grant that wherever I may find myself, I make Your ministry of liberation, redemption, and justice my priority! Amen.

So we need to ask ourselves, "How are we going to live in this freedom we have been given? Are you, or am I, going to live in fear or in joy?" I have found that many people do not fully embrace

---

[60] Julie Ackerman Link, "Celebrate Freedom," *Our Daily Bread*, July 4, 2017.

freedom because they cannot *control it*. To truly live free, we have to be willing to release ourselves from self-imposed boundaries, limitations, self-sufficiency, and comforts, and to embrace change with joyful abandon. *The need to control is rooted in fear.* Multitudes of people live in fear of what they cannot or do not understand. That is why the Lord said, **"Trust in the LORD with all your heart and lean not on your own understanding"** (Prov. 3:5). Our Creator knew that humans, with our finite ability to understand and have full knowledge, would be constricted by or even paralyzed by fear and remain in bondage because of our own limited capabilities to comprehend and control every aspect of our lives.

"Fear not" is the most repeated command in the Bible. Take a few honest moments to think about all of the ways in which you have allowed, or currently are allowing, fear to rule your thoughts, emotions, and heart, as well as your past, present, and future decisions. How does that fear keep you in a constantly anxious state while you try to anticipate every possibility of what could go wrong—thereby believing you can somehow avoid all mistakes, heartache, sickness, suffering, loss, pain, and even death. Our Father desires not only to give us new life but also to have us enjoy it in all of its abundance. Yet, we cannot embrace this unless we are willing to *trust in God's goodness* rather than our own limited and controlled understanding. God has opened up the door of the gilded cage in my flesh life, is stirring up the eagle's nest in my spiritual life, and is asking, *"What are you going to do with your freedom?"*

He is asking you the same question.

Are you going to remain paralyzed with fear because you do not fully understand what He is doing and offering—or, are you going to trust Him with your new lease on life and freedom?

Spread your wings and fly!

275

> "My chains fell off, my heart was free,
> I rose, went forth, and followed Thee."
> —Charles Wesley[61]

JOURNAL ENTRY – April 12, 2017

I am "letting down my hair" in public (Luke 7:37-38) and making myself vulnerable in my raw pain to reveal truth and "be real" in humble grace. May this book be used to remove people's masks and let them see and know that to live free in our brokenness with You is what You bought and paid for on the cross of Calvary and in Your triumph over sin and death! May they see that to be broken can still be beautiful! Amen.

> "No one had ever asked me what it feel like to be me.
> Once I told the truth about that,
> I felt free."
> —From the movie *The Help*[62]

---

[61] Charles Wesley, "And Can It Be?" 1738 [Public Domain].
[62] *The Help*, directed by Tate Taylor (Walt Disney Studios, 2011), 2:26, DVD.
(Based on the The #1 New York Times bestseller by Kathryn Stockett.)

21
The Battlefield and Beyond:
Living in Enemy Territory

Have I then become your enemy by telling you the truth?
(Gal. 4:16)

JOURNAL ENTRY — September 6, 2013

Life has given me a bitter pill to swallow and it is going down hard! I know I need to live in harmony with the enemy, but it goes against every fiber of my character and beliefs. My soldier's spirit wants to fight for truth and what is right and noble, but has come to understand that my adversary knows neither. To continue to fight against it only makes me my own worst enemy, as my thwarted attempts at reconciliation only come back and stab my own heart. Only through God's constant dose of grace can I learn to be content in all circumstances. Lord, help me to swallow this pill; may You be the honey that coats its bitter aftertaste.

JOURNAL ENTRY — January 29, 2018

I never ran away from a fight. Even if I was the cause of its beginning—the sole goal was always aimed at communication, reconciliation, and the restoration of the relationship in the end...as I am a lover not a fighter—yet...I will always fight for the cause of love!

The Lord has asked me to do many hard tasks and to go many places I didn't really want to go. But this is where my military training was to my advantage...a good soldier never asks "Why?" They react instinctively to the order given by the commanding officer or sergeant without arguing. This prompt adherence to orders can mean the difference between life and death in a combat situation and most assuredly the difference between a continued military career or a dishonorable discharge! A good soldier "simply does their job, believing there is a purpose behind the order which they may not understand," Jamie Buckingham wrote in *A Way Through The*

Wilderness.[63] Likewise, a person of faith very often does not understand the requests of God, yet out of desired obedience and trusting confidence in Him as our Leader and Life Guide, we should "move out" without argument or questioning "Why?"

> **Be gracious to me, O God, for man tramples on me; all day long an attacker oppresses me; my enemies trample on me all day long, for many attack me proudly. When I am afraid, I put my trust in You. In God, whose Word I praise, in God I trust; I shall not be afraid. What can flesh (man) do to me?**
> (Ps. 56:1-4, parentheses added)

JOURNAL ENTRY — August 2014

The Lord desires and requires complete dependency on Him. I have nowhere else to turn, no more ideas, and nowhere to run or hide. The enemy closes in. Dear God, if You don't stand firm and strong for me, then all is lost and I have no hope. Only You can rescue me—my refuge and strong tower; the inner keep in the fortress.

Even though I didn't understand why the Lord had assigned me to this place and given me this mission, where I could not see the strategy that would finally win the war, I knew there had to be a purpose sufficient for the pain endured on this battlefield. My heart said, "I know You know exactly where I am, what I am doing, what I am dealing with, what I am feeling, what I am needing—I know in my soul that You see, hear, know, and love me." I asked God to not only help me to accept this place of "deployment" in a land (narcissism) very foreign to me, but to also embrace all that He had for me to learn and understand while in this desert wasteland of a marriage. And He did teach me, slowly, as I started to accept the truth of it all. Oh, there were many trying days of pouting, self-pity, tears, temptations, and wrestling. But I discovered over the years that the soldier in me surrendered much more quickly and easily in the midst of each fight because I came to understand so profoundly—during the heat of battle or while laying low in the trenches to avoid enemy fire—that God was *always* on my side, *always* my ally, and *always* had

---

[63] Buckingham, *A Way Through the Wilderness*.

my back. He also knew the battle plan and how to receive the victory every time. I realized that I was never the Commander-in-Chief but rather the beloved foot soldier who He would never leave wounded or behind on the field. In our hearts, every person wants and needs to know they are worth fighting for. Our Father God will *always* fight for you!

> **Out of my distress I called on the LORD; the LORD answered me and set me free. The LORD is on my side; I will not fear. What can man do to me? The LORD is on my side as my helper, I shall look in triumph on those who hate me.** (Ps. 118:5-7)

JOURNAL ENTRY – August 3, 2014

You have graciously shown me, Lord, that in the darkest and deepest pains in life—when I can feel no song or even desire to hum a melody—that if out of love and obedience to You I march out onto the battlefield with praise and worship to You; that You will then fight my battles for me and reign victorious!

When you are on the battlefield every day, your heart can become hard in the face of a constant enemy and the threat they pose. This Scripture became my motto: **"Be wise (smart, sharp, clever) as a serpent and meek (humble, patient, well-trained) as a dove"** (Matt. 10:16, parentheses added). I didn't want to grow callous like my spouse, who had become hardened inside and out. I knew if I lost my softness, I would lose myself. So what were my options? What could I do to preserve the very essence of my being from becoming permanently tainted by the hostile environment I had lived in for so long? There is only one real option for a person of faith, and I believe that the best safeguard for **all** people is *to surrender.*

Trust me...there was a prolonged time when I thought I was strong enough to keep marching and fighting; after all, I was a soldier who had trained in the Army for 10 years. I was physically, mentally, emotionally, and spiritually strong—a leader in both military and civilian life. I was in no way a quitter; surrender was not a word in my vocabulary...yet. But all those experiences were not enough to anchor me through more than 20 years of boxing matches in the ring and hand-to-hand combat, which I fought almost daily with a quiet yet deadly enemy. Toward the end, during the last few hellish years, I began experiencing symptoms I never had before. I was hypersensitive to sounds and more acutely aware of his mind games, which were almost constant at that point. Sleep became increasingly more difficult. My sensitivity to his movements around the girls became heightened, as I knew he was often using them as pawns unaware. Like a Momma bear with her cubs (you do *not* mess with *Momma's* cubs!), I had these games to contend with also.

When I sought help for chronic body pain, I was always told that the main source of it was excess tension caused by stress. My body didn't even know how to fully "relax" anymore, as it was always "on alert" for danger—not from a well-trained sniper or roadside bombs, but rather from the hidden attacks of the man who said "I do." I would be quite peaceful and calm during the day, but I noticed as the clock ticked closer to the time he would be arriving home from work, I began to feel anxious, and in his presence I would often involuntarily shake. I was having more difficulty looking at him in the eyes, which I never did before; I couldn't stand the cold indifference toward not only me but those close to him. He carried an air of smugness, which spoke volumes without any words: "I have everyone fooled, and there is nothing you can do about it." I finally realized that I was experiencing symptoms of Post-Traumatic Stress Disorder (PTSD). I was familiar with this sad and often debilitating by-product of war affecting too many of our soldiers returning from the battlefield. Yet, I never could have imagined that I would develop these symptoms while living in my own home.

> **I hear, and my body trembles; my lips quiver at the sound; rottenness enters into my bones; my legs tremble beneath me.** (Hab. 3:16a)

I fought the good fight and had led my "troops" safely through the minefields the best I could; which to the untrained eye may have looked controlling as opposed to leadership by default...but it was taking a serious toll on my body. I needed to get off the battlefield for a while and gain a new perspective of the battle plan.

One important lesson I learned was to sometimes just bear a burden in silence, as it doesn't give people ammunition to shoot you with when you are already wounded. We truly need wisdom and knowledge from the Lord to clearly discern what and who the enemy really is. **"Wisdom is better than weapons of war..."** (Eccles. 9:18). Too often, we cheer for, believe in, and support the wrong team, sitting on the wrong side of the field and upholding the enemy. The Word of God rightly says, **"Be sober-minded; be watchful. Your adversary the devil prowls around like a roaring lion, seeking someone to devour"** (1 Pet. 5:8). Trust in what and who you know, not just what you perceive or even desire to be true. Take time to truly see, hear, and know yourself. Then make it a priority to really see, hear, and know others. Look into someone's eyes, *really look*, and have compassion on them. We all carry some pain, sorrow, or old wounds. Be sensitive to those in silent desperation and, if possible, seek justice for them, show mercy, and walk humbly with them toward a place of quiet and peaceful strength.

My personal battles exhausted me. This verse was a continuous cry from my soul: **"Oh, that I had wings like a dove! I would fly away and be at rest; yes, I would wander far away..."** (Ps. 55:6). It wasn't until I was physically, emotionally, and mentally brought to my knees that I finally understood this battle was no longer mine to fight but the Lord's. God said, "Okay, soldier, now give me your gloves and lay down your weapons; surrender to Me and find rest. Let the God of justice fight this battle for you, and I will achieve a victory." So I relinquished our marriage into His faithful care. I had many other fields I was manning, and I needed to finish the race.

JOURNAL ENTRY — February 2016

Holy Spirit, yield my "soldier's spirit" that is trained in hand-to-hand combat...to face the enemy head-on...and allow me the courage to "be still" and know that You are God and are doing all of the fighting for me. Help me to see that this is Your way and will, as I do not wish to prolong the conflict but to move forward with You.

> "God may allow me to fall, but He'll never allow me to be defeated! Be ready to laugh with delight as He walks with you, in His power, to places you never thought you could reach! Amen."
> —David Jeremiah, *When Your World Falls Apart* [64]

JOURNAL ENTRY — July 2013

It says in Proverbs 13:12 that "Hope deferred makes the heart sick." My heart is sick and deeply entrenched in sadness too hard to describe. The careful and loving toil of this wife and mother's hands is unraveling before my eyes. The veil of dimness has fallen off, and I see all too clearly. The enemy is close at hand. Only God's strength and grace will allow me to remain so close to my foe. Lies drip so easily from the mouth; "Lying lips are an abomination to the LORD, but those who act faithfully are His delight" (Proverbs 12:22). Covered in the Lord's armor, I will walk with the wise for "...the tongue of the wise brings healing" (Proverbs 12:18); my heart needs healing. I will choose to "love my enemies" (keep your friends close and your enemies even closer), thereby heaping hot coals upon the head. I have fruitlessly tried to give wise advice, but "The way of a fool is right in his own eyes..." (Proverbs 12:15). Although my hope is deferred, it is not yet gone. As long as I have breath, I will have hope in my Lord. I have a strong desire in my heart for what is wrong to be made right. With God's tender mercy and steadfast love, I will endure the race for the prize set before me.

JOURNAL ENTRY — March 31, 2014

He came upon me, his strategy to divide and conquer; to place himself on the throne over the weaker vessel.

I submitted the body, which is not my own,
but not the spirit, which is the Lord's.

I lay captive in enemy territory, waiting patiently upon the Lord for my release, which I know will come.

Invisible bonds restrain me,

---

[64] David Jeremiah, *When Your World Falls Apart* (Nashville, TN: Thomas Nelson, 2004).

> but the power of the Spirit cannot be bound.
>
> So I hope with praise on silent lips;
>
> My Lord will come.

Surrendered

JOURNAL ENTRY — November 23, 2014

I forgave him today. I surrendered my pain and bitterness to embrace the fullness of my Lord and Savior who forgave me and the whole world in His once for all complete sacrifice on the cross.

Civilian and military life can often be at great odds with each other, as once you sign on the dotted line, your life as you once knew it is not your own! You eat, sleep, and move within a whole new set of rules, all geared toward taking a civilian and indoctrinating them into a new sphere—the sole goal being to train them as an American soldier ready to fight at a moment's notice and defend this great country. This is no easy feat considering the diversity of backgrounds, ethnic groups, geographical differences, etc., to contend with. Once you are in the military, no matter where you come from, to those training you, everyone is "green." There is something unique and wonderful about a group of people living together in close quarters with a shared agenda. In Basic Training, everyone starts out on the same playing field, level with one another. Teamwork and unity of mind, body, and spirit are key to a successful unit. The rigorous discipline is geared toward training soldiers to be strong physically and mentally, motivated, fast, mobile, adaptable, alert, wise, strategic, respectful, and self-controlled—ultimately to work as a team ready for action. You are trained to fight the opposition at all cost, even unto death, as (unless in extreme circumstances) *surrender* is not an option! If you take what you are there to do with the seriousness it deserves, this drill training becomes deeply ingrained in your heart, mind, and spirit. A battlefield is not the place for a casual or defiant attitude...nor is it for quitters.

JOURNAL ENTRY — March 30, 2014

Dear Lord: You tell me to be grateful, thankful, and to rejoice in all circumstances. You tell me to be meek and bear the image of my Savior. You have given me a life in which I am asked to be completely selfless; to give up all human desires to be loved as Jesus loves the Church. Oh, how I long to be loved that way—just once, with an understanding heart! But I love You more than myself. I can only live a loveless life here if You completely fill me with Your love. Come fill me then, Lord, or I will be no more. Help me to fully surrender to You. Empty me of my dreams and desires, and replace them with Yours. Be near, or I will not be able to bear this cross.

Just as there are many differences between a civilian and military lifestyle, there are also many contrary teachings between the life of a soldier and that of a Christian. Wherein a soldier is trained to fight without entertaining thoughts of surrender, a believer is asked to willingly surrender themselves and the battles they are embroiled in as they walk by faith and newfound life in Jesus Christ. This call to surrender is *not* a declaration of defeat or failure, but rather, it is the empowerment to relinquish the fight into the hands of God, who always has a new strategy toward assured victory!

I will not go into all of the theological doctrine regarding what it means to give your life to Christ as a new creation in Him, as there is much already written about saving grace and eternal life, which stems forth from the crucial decision each individual will inevitably make. The focal point of this book is to address the decision an individual has to make when faced with a different kind of enemy, especially when it is a member of your own household. The Bible speaks clearly into this reality as written in Matthew 10:36, **"And a person's enemies will be those of his own household."**

JOURNAL ENTRY — October 16, 2015

Because I am a soldier I have been taught and trained to be a leader, strong and efficient—an example. But as leaders under Christ, we need to be stripped of our self-sufficiency and rely completely on You for the source of our strength and direction. When I was empty, if others had "poured" into me, I would have run on that "fuel," but You took every source of "fuel" away so I could get to complete emptiness—nothing from the world. I still struggled against surrendering to my own weaknesses—a soldier doesn't surrender to the enemy. But this is the truth—I am looking at the wrong enemy to blame; I had to look inside myself and see I was attacking myself with doubt, fear, and judgment. The purpose of the battle was between God and I; to break my self-sufficiency and self-punishment for being weak. I need to glory in my weakness, for in that I am made strong in the Lord and His sufficiency. Lord, You have been working on me hard! Praise God for this time of serious spiritual training. I feel both tired and at peace but with a sense of growth and understanding. I know most of these things already; I guess I didn't fully let them take root and grow. My sense of fear, failure, and pain was too much to bear. But I am ready to leave the past behind—so much pain. I desire new life, new purpose, new vision, new love in Christ. Lead this old, weary soldier back onto the battlefield, renewed and surrendered to Christ alone. Use me for Your glory; win battles with my hands and feet and voice. Amen.

JOURNAL ENTRY — No date recorded

Surrendered, broken, yielded, empty of myself—
It was only when I stopped fighting, that I began to win;
When I surrendered, that I had victory;
When I emptied myself, that I was filled;
When I stopped being afraid, that I had courage;
When I stopped needing to be loved, that I found love;
When I stopped clinging to my wants, that I was given what I need;
When I submitted to the chains, that I became free.

Love Your Enemies

"You have heard that it was said, 'You shall love your neighbor and hate your enemy.' But I (Jesus) say to you, 'Love your enemies and pray for those who persecute you.'" (Matt. 5:43, parentheses added)

JOURNAL ENTRY — October 12, 2015

Dear gracious and patient God of Lights:

Today I was feeling weary and without direction. I saw myself in a deeper way, the places I have been hiding in to keep me safe from pain. But playing it safe, even in one area of our lives in order to prevent heartache, is never Your way. I know in the depth of my heart that You have been moving me to this place of surrender for quite some time, and I have made excuses of why I couldn't or shouldn't go there. But You, in Your love, broke down those walls and crushed those excuses by showing me truth, hard truth.

Love my enemy. The Scripture I heard clearly: "Love your enemies," for what gain is it to you to love those who love you? To love those who hate you is true gain, costly discipleship, and Christ-likeness. Your Spirit brought to my heart's eye Jesus loving those who hated Him, disappointed Him, denied Him, betrayed Him, tortured Him, and crucified Him. I saw myself standing before God on Judgment Day, and Him saying:

"You followed Me, loved My world, were not ashamed of Me, were obedient in the many different calls I placed on your life, served Me, and taught in My name; but this I have against you—you did not love your enemies. This is one of the hardest and highest callings; for a person can persevere through anything if they feel loved and see hope. You, Deborah, are being commanded to love where you see no hope nor feel loved, cared for, nurtured, or respected. Where there is no trust, no security, no mutual faith base. You offer up yourself with no safety net, no assurance of anything the eye can see—walk by faith alone and not sight. Find yourself in Me alone, I am all you will ever need."

God reached out for us while we were sinners, His enemies. Jesus died for us so we could be reconciled to our Father. Both God and Jesus Christ as One showed that loving our enemies is the ultimate sacrifice of true love and obedience. Help me, Holy Spirit, to walk blameless before the Lord and deny myself—my earthly desires for human love—and take up my cross and follow You alone into peace, blessing, and eternal life. Amen.

JOURNAL ENTRY — December 6, 2015

I re-read a journal entry about loving your enemies and feeling it is one of our most highest callings as disciples. Please help me to love that which cannot receive love nor give love in return. I await Your strength and deliverance.

JOURNAL ENTRY — December 8, 2015

I asked the Spirit to lead me to a word from the Lord. He led me to Scriptures (again) to love my enemies and those who hate me. I saw hate yesterday in the eyes of the narcissist. His eyes spoke hate, but his lips dryly spoke of love—I believe those two words overlap in his heart and mind. I have been led to pray for him each day for his protection and blessings and healing. This is the call of Christ. But the Word also promises that there will be no prosper for the evil man and that "Vengeance is Mine, I will repay, says the Lord." To the contrary, "...if your enemy is hungry, feed him; if he is thirsty, give him something to drink; for by so doing you will heap burning coals on his head. Do not be overcome by evil, but overcome evil with good" (Romans 12:19-21). So I am to be obedient and love my enemy, pray for him, feed him, give him my other cheek when he strikes me, for the Lord my God is He who goes with me, to fight for me against my enemies, to save me (Deuteronomy 20:4). I need only to be patient and wait upon the Lord. In the meantime, I need to be about the Father's business. Empower me, Holy Spirit, to not faint in daily toil and to honor God with my life. Thank You for healing my soul, spirit, heart, and body. Amen.

JOURNAL ENTRY – December 9, 2015

Heavenly Father, again You convicted my heart to love my enemy(s). There is so much cold detachment I feel I will die of exposure. My heart aches and my appetite has left me. After 24 plus years, how a person can still be so detached is beyond my human comprehension. Yet Your Spirit keeps saying, "love him; love your enemy." So I prayed for him through my tears and broken heart. Your peace settled over my soul and saved my heart from sinning. I keep my eyes fixed on Jesus, who washed the feet of His betrayer; who suffered the most at the hands of those He loved and came to save. As I die more each day in my physical marriage, let me die more each day in my spiritual union with You, Lord; help me to die to self. Father God, I pray it is Your will to clear the fog off my brain because of living with the narcissist. Guard my heart and mind in Christ. Amen.

JOURNAL ENTRY – February 2016

As I die to self and the flesh, help me to not focus on the death—but the life and resurrection to follow!

So how could I not only get off the battlefield, which had become the familiar territory where I would meet both my spouse and my adversary each day, but also defuse the hidden bombs that were constantly blowing up in my face as I walked gingerly through the minefield? The world offered many answers and avenues, but none of them had either worked or were options in light of my faith, which had become the cornerstone of my life and survival. As you can see by reading my journal entries, a reoccurring theme emerged that would not relent (even though I tried many times to tune it out), and that was the call *to love my enemy*, and not only that, but also *to pray for him*! But how could I pray? What would I say? How could I navigate around all of the negative, hurtful feelings I carried like a ball and chain around my tired ankles? It all came down to one crucial word, which is the essence of the Christian faith, the culmination of all that Jesus did on the cross—**forgiveness.**

Forgiveness

"Father, forgive them, for they know not what they do."
(Luke 23:34)

> "To forgive is to set a prisoner free and discover the prisoner was you."
> —Corrie ten Boom, *The Hiding Place* [65]

The remarkable thing about these 10 words spoken by Jesus, the Son of God, was that they emanated from His parched and bloody lips while His innocent hands and feet were being nailed to a Roman cross by those who hated Him and what He stood for; the "them" were His enemies. Forgiveness—it is the *only* true way to healing. It is the *only* real path to peace. It is the *only* complete avenue to wholeness. It seems impossible, and it truly is, without faith in Jesus Christ and the power of the Holy Spirit. The genuine act of forgiveness is not found in the spoken words, "I am sorry," but rather, it takes place in the deep and silent recesses of the heart. Like undergoing the transformation from caterpillar to butterfly, a type of complete metamorphosis takes place. It is the process of taking a heart hardened by abuse (in all of its forms), neglect, rejection, abandonment, disappointment, lack of love and tenderness—and turning it back to flesh (Ezek. 36:26), which is both soft and vulnerable.

This chapter on forgiveness is the most important chapter in this book. It is the culmination of every single tear shed and word that has been written thus far! Even if you are not a Christian believer yet are persevering through this book looking for answers, wisdom, knowledge, power, justice, hope, healing, and freedom, I strongly encourage you to press on just a little bit more, as it has even *been proven in the secular medical community that there is healing of the body and mind through the act of forgiveness.*

At this point, I am going to let the medical experts take over

---

[65] Corrie ten Boom, *The Hiding Place* (Peabody, MA: Hendrickson Publishers, 2015).

by quoting from an article written by Dr. Caroline Leaf entitled "Thinking Changes Our DNA—Part Two":

> Taking this to a deeper level, research shows that DNA actually changes shape according to our thoughts. Remember, what we think comes first; our feelings follow on the heels of our thoughts. As you think those negative thoughts about the future—the week ahead, what a person might say or do, even in the absence of the concrete stimulus—that toxic thinking will change your brain wiring in a negative direction and throw your mind and body into toxic stress.
>
> According to Dr. Herbert Benson, M.D., president of Harvard Medical School's Mind-Body Institute, negative thinking leads to toxic stress, which affects our bodies natural healing capacities. Toxic thinking wears down the brain and body.
>
> The Institute of HeartMath, an internationally recognized, nonprofit research organization that helps people reduce stress, discusses an experiment titled "Local and Non-local Effects of Coherent Heart Frequencies on Conformational Changes of DNA." This study showed that thinking and feeling anger, fear, and frustration caused DNA to change shape according to thoughts and feelings. The DNA responded by tightening up and becoming shorter, switching off many DNA codes, which reduced quality expression. So we feel shut down by negative emotions, and our body feels this too. But here's the great part: the negative shutdown or poor quality of the DNA codes can be reversed by feelings of love, joy, appreciation, and gratitude! The researchers also found that HIV-positive patients who had positive thoughts and feelings had 300,000 times more resistance to the disease than those without positive feelings. So the takeaway here is that when we operate in our normal love design—which is made in God's image (Genesis 1:26)—we are able to change the shape of our DNA for the better.
>
> So when we make a poor-quality decision...when we choose to engage toxic thoughts (for example—unforgiveness, bitterness, irritation, or feelings of not coping)—we change the DNA and subsequent genetic expressions, which then changes the shape of our brain wiring in a negative direction. This immediately puts the brain into protection mode, and the brain translates these poor-quality, toxic thoughts as stress. This stress then manifests in our bodies. But the most exciting part of this study was the hope it demonstrated because positive attitude, the good choice, rewired

everything back to the original healthy positive state. These scientists basically proved we can renew our minds.[66]

Isn't this amazing! The Word of God says, **"Do not conform any longer to the pattern of this world, but be transformed by the renewing of your mind"** (Rom. 12:2).

So, overall, what would you say is the "pattern of this world"? When you get together with family and friends, coworkers, or just sitting in a doctor's office overflowing with sick, suffering, and hurting people? What is the now "normal" pattern of this world we live in? What are the *thought patterns* of your own life? What *was* the pattern of mine, gauging by my years of journal entries and the words written within this book? Is it one of health, strength, energy, joy, relaxation, contentment, and peace? Or would you rate it as stress, frustration, fatigue, fear, anger, depression, discontentment, joylessness, illness and disease, and pain and suffering at the top of your list as the "norm"?

After reading this article and then comparing it to my own experiences over the last 25 years, I think it was a miracle that I had been able to function physically, emotionally, and mentally at all...but God! No wonder I have had severe chronic pain for the last 20 years with the degree of toxicity in my everyday environment compared with a battlefield! How would you rate your environments overall?

We are unhealthy and unhappy people because we have slowly conformed to the toxic conditions that have permeated our once perfectly created world after "the Fall." Our *thoughts* are consumed with negativity, which produces *feelings* of unforgiveness, bitterness, resentment, irritation, frustration, jealousy, fear, anxiety, stress, etc.—all of which are extremely toxic to our bodies and minds. We tolerate and medicate the best we can, but the offerings of this world are insufficient when compared to the scope of all of our

---

[66] Caroline Leaf, "Thinking Changes Our DNA—Part Two," SpiritMindBody Connection, accessed January 29, 2022, https://spiritmindbodyconnection.com/dr-caroline-leaf/.

suffering in body, soul, mind, and spirit. Here are a few sobering statistics for us to consider, ones that continue to escalate with each new generation:

* From 2015 through 2018, 13.2% of US adults aged 18 and over used antidepressant medications in the past 30 days. Use was higher among women (17.7%) than men (8.4%).[67]
* In 2019, 8.1% of US adults aged 18 and over had symptoms of anxiety disorder, 6.5% had symptoms of depressive disorder, and 10.8% had symptoms of anxiety disorder or depressive disorder.[68]
* An estimated 31.1% of US adults experience any anxiety disorder at some time in their lives.[69]
* According to the study from QuoteWizard, nearly 65 million Americans—1 in 5 people—are currently taking prescribed mental health medications.[70]

Not a very promising heritage to pass onto our children!

We desperately need something, Someone, beyond ourselves to even begin to touch the depth and root of illnesses that stem from negative thoughts because of the way others make (made) us feel and, thereby, how we feel about ourselves and others. If we are fed negative thoughts or abused in ways that make (made) us feel unworthy of being seen, heard, known, and loved—then the subsequent emotions that naturally substantiate how we are (were) treated or made to feel manifest themselves in the parallel negative thinking process, which

---

[67] Brody DJ, Gu Q. Antidepressant use among adults: United States, 2015–2018. NCHS Data Brief, no 377. Hyattsville, MD: National Center for Health Statistics. 2020. https://www.cdc.gov/nchs/products/databriefs/db377.htm.

[68] "Mental Health - Household Pulse Survey - Covid-19," Centers for Disease Control and Prevention (Centers for Disease Control and Prevention, January 19, 2022), https://www.cdc.gov/nchs/covid19/pulse/mental-health.htm.

[69] "Any Anxiety Disorder," National Institute of Mental Health (U.S. Department of Health and Human Services), accessed January 30, 2022, https://www.nimh.nih.gov/health/statistics/any-anxiety-disorder.

[70] Lauren Crawford and Nexstar Media Wire, "1 In 5 Americans on Prescribed Mental Health Meds amid Covid-19, Study Finds," WFXRtv (WFXRtv, April 14, 2021), https://www.wfxrtv.com/news/health/coronavirus/1-in-5-americans-on-prescribed-mental-health-meds-amid-covid-19-study-finds/.

starts a toxic cycle of thoughts and feelings that are killing us (emotionally, mentally, and physically) from the inside out. Take a narcissist, for example, who continually feeds negative and belittling thoughts to their victim. This is done in conjunction with physical, verbal, and/or manipulative abuse, such as forced silence and isolation, pathological lying, dismantled trust, and the withholding of love, empathy, and basic human kindness. These demeaning tactics, in turn, breed toxic thoughts that take hold in our minds, which then birth negative feelings that infiltrate our hurting hearts and souls where insidious emotional, mental, and physical "sicknesses" grow like cancer and spread to every part of our being. I can testify that it is a vicious cycle of pain and insanity, and I know—without a shadow of a doubt—that if it was not for my faith that was my anchor during all of those years of silent desperation, I would have been swallowed up in it all without a true and lasting source of hope or healing!

There is a book, written by Henry W. Wright, entitled *A More Excellent Way to Be in Health,* that has had a profound impact on my understanding of our physical well-being in connection with our emotional/spiritual well-being. He has been recognized for his accomplishments and achievements in the field of Religion and Health, Healing and Prevention, which warranted his inclusion in The Heritage Registry of Who's Who in the 2004-2009 Editions. He has also been widely recognized in the medical community for his research and work in the realm of physical, mental, emotional, and spiritual healing. For the purpose of the topic at hand, I will focus exclusively on his insights regarding how unforgiveness is an obstacle to our body's ability to achieve maximum healing: "The first block to healing is lack of forgiveness, and this is the *most important one.*"[71] This is the first block in a list of 33 blocks and is considered the most crucial one to deal with. Before Mr. Wright will work with someone for healing, when he feels there is a block preventing it, the first avenue he seeks is any issues with unforgiveness. He writes,

---

[71] Henry Wright, *A More Excellent Way to Be in Health* (New Kensington, PA: Whitaker House, 2009).

If we don't get this first block dealt with, *we are going no further in any dimension.* We are wasting our time with roots or the other possible blocks. We are wasting our time even talking to God on the subject.[72]

But why? Why is being forgiven for a wrong *we* have committed against someone, and forgiving another individual's wrongs against us, so important to both God and us in conjunction with our overall well-being? By the leading of the Spirit, I will attempt to explain in layman's terms the mystery and beauty of this powerful word "forgiveness."[73] "Forgiveness is an attitude of the heart toward others in love."[74] If you can earnestly think of a person and feel nothing but *agape* love (Greek word; selfless, unconditional) toward them, then you know you have made peace with them, yourself, and God; your soul can now be at rest. However, if thinking about the person still gives you some angst in your heart and a bitter taste in your mouth, then you still have some work to do. The sooner you forgive, the quicker you will feel the freeing power and healing that you so desperately long for!

> "We're changed by love, and at the center of love is forgiveness."
> —Holley Gerth, *What Your Heart Needs for the Hard Days*[75]

"I find more freedom every day, by God's grace, to do what is impossible in my flesh. I forgive you every day, at a new and deeper level, for your hatred of me and for how you spitefully used and abused me."

—Words I wrote in a letter to my husband on July 23, 2016.

Forgiveness is not a suggestion, one option of many, or a feeling; it is a command from God and has eternal consequences,

---

[72] Wright, *A More Excellent Way to Be in Health,* p. 308.

[73] Of course, it is not always possible to ask for or extend forgiveness with all people, as someone may have passed away, moved away, or refuses to interact with you about an issue from the past. If for whatever reason, you cannot make a wrong "right" personally between each individual you feel the need to make peace with—on either side of the fence, so to speak—then sincerely make it *right* with God concerning that person.

[74] Wright, *A More Excellent Way to Be in Health,* p. 311.

[75] Holley Gerth, *What Your Heart Needs for the Hard Days: 52 Encouraging Truths to Hold on To* (Grand Rapids: Revell, a division of Baker Publishing Group, 2014).

both good and bad.

> **"For if you forgive others their trespasses [sins], your
> heavenly Father will also forgive you, but if you do not forgive
> others their trespasses [sins], neither will your Father forgive
> your trespasses [sins]."**
> (Matt. 6:14-15, brackets added)

In Mark 11:25-26, it is written:

> **"And whenever you stand praying, forgive, if you have
> anything against anyone, *so* that your Father also who is in
> heaven may forgive your trespasses."**

Why is it important that we forgive others who harm us? Why
do the promises of forgiveness toward us hinge on our first forgiving
others? How can we possibly forgive our enemies? It may seem so
unnatural and absurd to forgive someone who has terribly abused you
or someone dear to you: a Hitler, a Stalin. It is indeed contrary to our
senses, minds, and fallen hearts. Almost everything that Jesus did and
taught during His time on earth flew in the face of what was natural
to our human senses, thoughts, reasoning, traditions, and emotions.
He turned the world upside-down in three short years of ministry—
and still does! So again, why does a loving Father God command that
we do it? Because, whether you are coming at it as a believer or a
nonbeliever, there is healing in body, soul, heart, mind, and spirit if
you do! The medical sciences, using modern-day technology, are only
now proving what the Scriptures taught thousands of years ago!
Forgiveness is a gift from God to His beloved children so that *they
may be well* in their bodies and souls, which *will* find rest and peace that
passes all understanding when we trust in His goodness and obey
what He asks us to do. The act of forgiveness is *not absolving the guilty
party*, but rather is the avenue that brings about true healing and
wholeness. The amazing thing is that we can release the offender
from our grip and place them into the faithful hands of our Father
(through the act of forgiveness), the only One who can bring about
perfect justice. When we do this, the offender often feels convicted in

their heart of the wrongdoing or crime against us or our loved one(s), and they are brought to a place of personal acknowledgment and true repentance. This can result in reconciliation and restoration for all parties.

We can more readily forgive when we can *separate* the sin from the sinner. To do so, we first have to *see ourselves as sinners* for we are *all* born with a sin nature. I believe this is evident in our human inclinations to be prideful, disobedient, impatient, natural-born liars, easily angered and vengeful, selfish, self-righteous, and self-centered. The only difference between my spouse and me is that I have been redeemed through faith in Jesus Christ. I am "made new," and in this newness, I am empowered by the Holy Spirit to now live a life *not consumed* by all that is sinful. Apart from the agape love of God, I would *not* have been equipped to extend this selfless love, grace, and forgiveness to the man who stole half my lifetime and filled it with endless pain. However, because I have come to understand that my husband was acting against me because of his own sin nature, my resentment and desire for vengeance has been altered to a heart of compassion, mercy, and grace—the very same compassion, mercy, and grace God has already extended to me. Again, this does *not* in any way absolve him or justify his actions, as he *will* be held accountable before God. This act of obedience *only freed me* from the self-induced bondage of guilt, bitterness, and unforgiveness—allowing me to heal and live free, having peace in my heart, mind, and soul.

> **...but God shows His love for us in that while we were still sinners, Christ died for us.** (Rom. 5:8)

> **"For the Son of Man came to seek and to save the lost."** (Luke 19:10)

> **...that Jesus Christ came into the world to save sinners, of whom I am the foremost.** (1 Tim. 1:15)

"Hate the sin, but love the sinner."
—Mahatma Gandhi

Hence, the crucial need for a heart "transplant"! The beauty is that we do not have to do this transformation in our own strength or willpower. Our part is to surrender our free will and yield our spirit, and our miracle-working God, through the power of the Holy Spirit, does it all for us.

> **"And I will give you a new heart, and a new spirit I will put within you. And I will remove the heart of stone from your flesh and give you a heart of flesh."** (Ezek. 36:26)

Another important element about forgiveness, which I didn't fully understand until I matured in my faith, was that I didn't have to "feel" forgiving toward someone who hurt me in some way *before* I could extend this act of grace and mercy toward them. It somehow seemed like I was uttering a "false" statement when I said, "I forgive you" if I didn't have the feelings to back it up, but in the words of Henry W. Wright:

> You don't forgive people who have wronged you because you feel like it; you to forgive them because you are obedient to Christ and His commandments. You don't do it from an intellectual standpoint. You don't do it because it is the law...it is not a ritual of performance. You need to do it because it is just the way you are. If you are just a lovebug who will forgive all manner of sin, then you are just like your Daddy, your Father in heaven.[76]

Jesus said in John 14:15, **"If you love Me, you will keep my commandments."**

JOURNAL ENTRY – November 23, 2014

When we forgive someone, we look more like Jesus than at any other time in our life.

JOURNAL ENTRY – November 22, 2015

Matthew 18:21-35—the recorded story of the king who canceled the enormous debt of his servant...that king, of course, represents Jesus who paid the enormous debt for our sin by His grace and the forgiveness found in His sacrifice. It is about forgiving the unforgivable—not in our power and strength—but in the power and love of God through Christ. I have been

---

[76] Wright, *A More Excellent Way to Be in Health*, p. 312.

forgiving my husband's debt to me over many years now. Just when I think I am done, the Spirit shines light on more. The other night when I felt this deep pain and resentment burst forth—I was surprised by the passion behind it. I didn't know I still had that stuffed down inside. It felt foreign; I didn't want to feel it or to have God see it. I grieved and poured it out in heart-racking sobs. I let it pour forth like a toxic river of disappointment, bitterness, loss, and waves of pain as the rejection of my person washed over me. In the end, I lay exhausted yet cleansed. The past is gone; I can't cling to empty dreams and lost love. I can only move forward with no regrets.

For You, O Lord, are good and forgiving, abounding in steadfast love to all who call upon You. (Ps. 86:5)

JOURNAL ENTRY – July 2016

Thank You, Holy Spirit, that You convict my spirit when I begin to walk in my flesh and not Christ-like. Yes, what I spoke to my husband was truth, but I didn't speak it in love. I realize with him, more than any other, how raw some wounds are still. As always, Your Word of truth spoke to me again this morning, both chastising and encouraging me, Your weak and weary servant. "Turn away from evil and do good; seek peace and pursue it" (Psalm 34:14). In this verse You are not denying evil, but the call to a higher place of seeking peace and pursuing it despite—and even because of—the evil, hate, and spite. "The Lord is near to the brokenhearted and saves the crushed in spirit" (Psalm 34:18). This is Your promise and encouragement to me for "You are the God who sees." I prayed again for Your forgiveness first and foremost, then my husband's, and then forgave myself for my weakness and letting myself get pulled once again into the manipulation of the NPD. In the words of C. S. Lewis in *Mere Christianity*— "He knows what a wretched machine you are trying to drive. One day He will fling it on the scrap heap and give you a new one." Amen.

Corrie ten Boom wrote:

I thank You, Jesus, that You brought into my heart God's love through the Holy Spirit. Thank You, Father, that Your love in me is stronger than my hatred. Forgiveness is the key that unlocks the door of resentment and the handcuffs of hatred. It is a power that breaks the chains of bitterness and the shackles of selfishness.[77]

The remarkable thing about these words is that they were penned in the wake of her horrific experience as a prisoner in a Nazi

---

[77] Corrie ten Boom, *The Hiding Place.*

concentration camp during World War II. Her beloved sister and father died, as well as many other people she knew and loved, behind the walls of these wretched places. They had been arrested for concealing Jews in their home in Holland during the Nazi occupation. Upon release, she would unexpectedly come face to face with one of the prison guards who had a hand in the inhuman extermination of multitudes of people—a man who now wanted to shake her hand in peace. Her personal struggle with the choice to extend or withhold forgiveness is so powerful that I will let her tell you in her own words.

In 1947, Corrie was delivering a message at a church in Munich, Germany, that God forgives. A man made his way up to the front of the church upon the conclusion. Though he did not recognize her, the face of one prisoner among thousands at Ravensbrück concentration camp, she remembered him immediately as a guard she had been forced to walk naked past with her frail sister ahead of her.

> And I who had talked so glibly of forgiveness, fumbled in my pocketbook rather than to take that hand he had thrust out. I was face-to-face with one of my captors and my blood seemed to freeze.
>
> "You mentioned Ravensbrück in your talk," he was saying, "I was a guard there. But since that time I have become a Christian. I know that God has forgiven me for the cruel things I did there, but I would like to hear it from your lips as well. Fräulein, will you forgive me?"
>
> And I stood there—I whose sin had again and again to be forgiven—and I could not forgive. Betsie had died in that place—could he erase her slow terrible death simply by asking? ...it seemed like hours as I wrestled with the most difficult thing I ever had to do. For I had to do it—I knew that. The message that God forgives has a prior condition; that we forgive those who injure us! I knew it not only as a commandment of God, but as a daily experience. Since the end of the war I had had a home in Holland for victims of Nazi brutality. Those who were able to forgive their former enemies were able also to return to the outside world and rebuild their lives, no matter what the physical scars. Those who nursed their bitterness remained invalids. It was as simple and horrible as

that. And still I stood there with the coldness clutching my heart. But forgiveness is not an emotion—I knew that too. Forgiveness is an act of the will, and the will can function regardless of the temperature of the heart.... "Help!" I prayed silently. "I can lift my hand. I can do that much. You supply the feeling!" And so woodenly, mechanically, I thrust my hand into the one stretched out to me. And as I did, an incredible thing took place. The current started in my shoulder, raced down my arm, sprang into our joined hands. And then this healing warmth seemed to flood my whole being, bringing tears to my eyes. "I forgive you, brother," I cried, "with all my heart!" For a long moment we grasped each other's hands, the former guard and the former prisoner. I had never known God's love so intensely, as I did then.[78]

I got the same shivers all over my body writing the above words as I did the first time I read this amazing act of forgiving grace. Unbeknownst to me at the time, I would need this example of grace to forgive my own "prison guard," the same choice to extend or to withhold forgiveness to my captor. Now, please do not get me wrong; I am not placing myself in the same shoes as someone in a Nazi concentration camp. But the same *act of obedience* is necessary to extend forgiveness to anyone who has harmed us or a loved one. No matter the magnitude, our pain is our pain—it is not minimized by the measure of our circumstances.

Although the details of this horrible time in world history are difficult to read and fathom, I highly recommend this book. Her experience with this man not only made me cry and lingered in my mind for days, but it also radically changed the way I viewed the act of forgiveness. It deepened my understanding of how the extension of forgiveness isn't based on human feelings but is a supernatural action empowered beyond our human capabilities; it's an extension of agape love, selfless love. This means it has absolutely no human "strings" attached to it or selfish motives behind it; it is pure and undefiled. It is a deep, enduring concern for others' welfare—an

---

[78] Corrie ten Boom, "Guideposts Classics: Corrie Ten Boom on Forgiveness," Guideposts, November 1972, https://www.guideposts.org/better-living/positive-living/guideposts-classics-corrie-ten-boom-forgiveness.

essential characteristic of God that comes only as a gift. It cannot be bought or earned and is never removed once given for any reason. To understand true forgiveness, it is really important to understand the difference between our very real yet limited power to love one another completely and selflessly and the agape love of God, which far surpasses our finite human ability and comprehension. Because it is no longer a part of our fallen nature, this gift of selfless love is given to a believer when they surrender their heart and life to God through Jesus; then it is bestowed as a free gift of grace from our merciful and gracious Father.

> **God's love has been poured into our hearts through the Holy Spirit who has been given to us.** (Rom. 5:5)

JOURNAL ENTRY — August 1, 2016

I awoke this morning asking the Spirit to please define this love I have for my husband now, which You revealed the other day. This is what was shown to me: This love is not a romantic love like I had when we were first married; he has systematically killed that long ago. And it is not a friendship love, for to have that kind of love you need to be able to connect to a person on some level—preferably a soul to soul connection—which he is incapable of by his own will. This love is generated apart from myself; it is the love God gives us through Jesus Christ and the Spirit to love our enemies and to love our neighbors as ourselves.

> **...and without the shedding of blood there is no forgiveness of sins.** (Heb. 9:22)

In *Beyond Ourselves*, Catherine Marshall shared how Pastor Harvey Smith offered good insight from personal experience when he said, "There is so much to learn *the hard way* about forgiveness."[79] Forgiveness is costly. It is not natural, and it is often not easy to extend when it is given in earnest. Jesus's work on the cross was motivated by agape love so that our sins could be forgiven; the power of His blood shed in sinless, selfless sacrifice is what empowers our ability to forgive ourselves and others. It was *very* costly. Forgiveness should cost us something as well. If it doesn't, then I would certainly

---

[79] Catherine Marshall, *Beyond Ourselves* (London: Hodder & Stoughton, 1998).

question whether or not it was given in all sincerity or just offered as a flippant platitude to get past an unpleasant situation or manipulative ploy, only to be used against another at a later date.

I have come to understand over the years that there is truly a big difference between an "I am sorry" and the words "I forgive you" or "Will you forgive me?" Just in daily living among other people we might utter the words "I'm sorry" countless times. We say, or should say, "I am sorry" when we accidentally bump into someone, step on a person's foot, forget to make that phone call, or are late for a lunch date. We miss birthdays and appointments, spill our milk, and burn dinner, which warrants both an "I'm sorry" and take-out! These words have become such a staple in our vocabulary that we often speak them without really thinking about why they are coming out of our mouth, like "God bless you" when someone sneezes or "thank you" when the waitress pours you more water or someone holds a door open for you. The definition of the word "sorry" is *full of sorrow or regret.*[80] Most of us are probably genuine in our sorrow, but too frequently our "I am sorry" statements come with the added word "but" after them. The "but" is often attached to an off-the-cuff remark or an elaborate story *but,* in the end, it is usually only an *excuse* for our behavior, insensitivity, thoughtlessness, etc. It is like a "half" sorrow or regret. To me, it greatly diminished or eradicated the genuineness of the spoken words stated before it. Unless there is personal ownership or acknowledgment for what we do or don't do, the person on the receiving end of it is left to feel that they are not worthy of the real apology, and that in truth, you really don't care enough to prevent it from happening again in the future. This is why there are repeat offenders because the "I am sorry" didn't cost them anything in order to change their behavior from the inside out.

My husband said, "I'm sorry" countless times for the exact same things that he kept doing over and over again. Of course, it would be many years before I would understand that he did this *on*

80 Agnes, *Webster's New World Dictionary.*

purpose to upset, hurt, punish, and diminish me. In a classic scenario and mind game after a hurtful or abusive gesture toward me, my spouse would say, "I'm sorry...I made a mistake. Can't *you* just forgive me?" Do you see how a manipulator works? They throw out an insincere apology, chalk it up as a mistake (repeated a hundred times), and then throw the curve ball at you—can't *you* just forgive me—making you feel as if *their* callous actions against you are now somehow *your fault* or *problem* to "fix," and the subsequent fallout is now blamed on your ungracious heart and inability to forgive. Always looking for a way to peace, I would either accept his shallow apology or swallow the blame in the hope that it would one day stop happening.

Because he was a repeat offender, I eventually began to wisely ask him, "Forgive you for what?" Always silence. You see, he couldn't name the offense that required forgiveness because to do so would be admitting he actually *did* something wrong, and narcissists *never* do (much less honestly confess) anything wrong! This is why a narcissist cannot or will not change, because to change a course of thought, behavior, or heart first requires admitting that there is a need to do so. Projecting their faults and guilt onto the victim is a great ploy for the narcissist who knows that their spouse or significant other is a Christian and takes the Word of God seriously with regard to forgiveness. But because my husband could never extend a sincere apology, there could never be any genuine reconciliation, closure, or lasting peace.

> Forgiveness is based on Christ's unconditional love, but reconciliation is based on repentance—an unconditional agreement that we have wronged others. Forgiveness only opens up the possibility of reconciliation, but depends on the husband's willingness to repent for breaking his wedding vows and owning up to a hidden truth.[81]

---

[81] Laurie Hall, *An Affair of the Mind* (Colorado Springs, CO: Focus on the Family Publishing, 1996).

Once again, what we need to get our hearts and minds around is that in our loving and wise Father's ways, we (the victims) who obey and do what He says, actually become the victors! Our extended forgiveness does not release the offender, but in reality releases us and makes *us* free. How so? Let's look at the following scenario as an example: Take a police officer who arrests someone who broke the law or committed an unjust act against another. They don't have the rightful authority to decide that person's fate or just punishment. They have only limited authorization to exercise justice. So they hand the offender over to the court system and now they are releasing that person into the custody of a higher authority, entrusting that they will uphold the law and seek justice for the victim(s) of said offense. With peace in their heart, the officer can walk away knowing that they are free from carrying the load of what that person has done, and now justice can be served for the offense(s) committed.

Admittedly, in our fallen world, this does not always happen as it should; however, the original justice system was established to be fair and equitable. But with a perfect, just, and unbiased Judge—the Most High God—the justice system always works perfectly! Following this scenario: We, the victims, are in the place of the police officer. We know that a "crime" has been committed against us or someone we love, but we don't have to (and shouldn't) seek justice for ourselves. Why? First, when we are innocent victims we carry no guilt or shame. But if we seek our own justice by harming another (with our words, deeds, or heart) or by breaking the law, then we are not free from guilt anymore and actually bring more harm and pain upon ourselves. The old saying that "two wrongs don't make a right" still stands as good counsel. Secondly, when we are already physically and/or emotionally wounded, by turning over our offender (abuser) to a Higher Authority (God) in the wake of offered forgiveness, this *releases us* so that we can begin the process of healing and finding peace. This positive action allows us to move forward in life without extending our "prison sentence" by seeking our own vengeance. The righteous Judge then takes over the responsibility of doling out perfect justice, and our hearts and minds can rest and be free from blame or a guilty conscience.

> **Beloved, never avenge yourselves, but leave it to the wrath of God, for it is written, "Vengeance is Mine, I will repay," says the Lord.** (Rom. 12:19)

I can testify to this truth; such deep peace and freedom comes in the wake of forgiveness on our part and allows God to seek justice on our behalf, which will be far more "just" than we could ever seek on our own. By following Jesus's perfect example, whether a believer or nonbeliever, we *all* benefit from the selfless act of forgiveness!

> **"And will not God give justice to His elect, who cry to Him day and night? Will He delay long over them? I tell you, He will give justice to them speedily."** (Luke 18:7-8)

JOURNAL ENTRY – August 2014

I believe that forgiveness comes in stages or phases; the third phase is the blessing. We need to, as we process the forgiving stages, start praying for and blessing the one who harmed us. In doing this our pain becomes promise, our hurt becomes healing, and our tears become joy. When we can pray for and bless willingly and joyfully our enemies, we have reached the final leg of the forgiveness journey—it is finished. What direction and comfort this all gives to me, as I struggle to "feel" the desire to forgive, when I understand that the process involves time for healing. What a great and loving Father!

The Consequences of Withheld Forgiveness

As I stated previously, forgiveness is costly, but the withholding of forgiveness can cost even more. The Lord recently gave me a revelation, which put a shiver in my bones and brought me to my knees with prayers of thankfulness on my lips for God's conviction and grace in empowering me to forgive my enemy. The following is my own story running parallel to that of several other women's personal stories I have sadly heard about or witnessed—having similar circumstances but very different outcomes. I will speak about only one, though my heart beats in unison with them all:

devoted wives and mothers who found themselves in the fight of their lives to not only survive their insane marriages but also to keep their children from being taken away by manipulative and unconscionable men who once vowed to love, honor, and protect them!

This woman was in a marriage situation akin to my own. Her narcissist husband used, abused, and manipulated her by playing serious mind games not long into their marriage. Although I recognized many of the patterns from my own dysfunctional union, it would be years before I had a name for this shared insanity. Over time, as the abuse intensified, she began to medicate her pain with a temporary "numbing agent"; this would only escalate into more trouble for her. This desire to numb our pain—to take the edge off of an aching broken heart and blur the daily reality of the endless cycle of hopelessness, loneliness, and emptiness—is a universal problem escalating as quickly as the world's other epidemics! (The only truly safe *addictive* "Agent" is Jesus; this healthy choice for relieving heart "burn" will keep us from incurring additional negative, costly, and long-term consequences!)

This couple had one child together, who was unfortunately used as yet another manipulation "tool," especially after their bitter divorce. As I began to get glimpses of her downward slide into deep depression, anxiety, and insomnia, coupled with the numbing agent, I became concerned with her overall well-being. I repeatedly encouraged her to seek professional help like counseling and prescription medication to stabilize her declining physical and emotional state, as well as offered wisdom on how to navigate through the rocky relationships emerging with her confused child and ex-spouse. I was very compassionate about her plight, as I was living my own private and silent "hell." As the remedies of the world became inadequate, I steadily turned more toward my faith for strength, peace, wisdom, and direction along this pathway of shifting sands. I regularly offered her the same anchor, which was keeping me from being swept away in the ever-increasing storms. I extended to her the only true hope I had found in Jesus Christ. By this time, I had already surrendered much of my own striving and pride, and was entering into blessed peace in the wake of forgiveness.[82]

This hurting, dejected, and despairing woman decided to take the road widely traveled but that lends itself to prideful and negative choices. This ultimately can lead to destruction and loss, instead of taking the narrow, though initially often difficult, road that leads to life, peace, and freedom.

> **"Enter by the narrow gate. For the gate is wide and the way is easy that leads to destruction, and those who enter by it are many. For the gate is narrow and the way is hard that leads to life, and those who find it are few."** (Matt. 7:13-14)

I was on that wide road for a time. By God's grace and the conviction of the Spirit, I saw what I was becoming while withholding forgiveness and didn't want to end up being that kind of negative and bitter person; hadn't I already lost enough of myself? I saw the look in our daughters' eyes when I was angry, impatient, and frustrated to tears because of an abuse they could not see. I began to understand that if I did not change the course of direction I was going in, I would lose them to the enemy's side. This realization made my mother's heart faint—to lose my children too? I couldn't bear the thought. Because narcissism is often silent yet deadly, especially children cannot discern the victim from the abuser, and they often choose "sides" based on their understandable confusion. They often sympathize with the parent who *outwardly* "appears" to be more easygoing, happy, stable, and safe—trying to avoid the bitterness oozing from the victim who is often filled with confusion, pain, fear, frustration, anger, grief, and withheld forgiveness.

---

[82] Author and speaker Joyce Meyers has a wonderful book out entitled *Do Yourself a Favor...Forgive*. I found it very insightful and empowering. Joyce reiterates the benefits of surrendering our desire to fight our own battles and seek justice or vengeance on our own terms, and allowing God to take control of the situation.
Joyce Meyer, *Do Yourself a Favor ... Forgive* (Brentwood, TN: FaithWords, 2012).

I see now how close I could have come to this other woman's story being my own story. As I sit with tears in my eyes and ponder the grace and blessings the Lord has showered upon these past years of drastic change and separation, and the fractures that have touched our beautiful family, I see that one thing has not been lost: my relationship with our daughters. For me, that is all that really matters!

A Finale of Peace

Eventually, in my own situation, the Lord said that it was time for me to go. He saw my tears, heard my prayers, knew my plight, and in His great love and mercy made a way and was rescuing me. When the appointed day came, I was strangely calm. It was time. The children were raised, teaching was done, their roots of faith were deep, and they were all starting their next seasons of life. To stay at that point would only prolong the pain of not being wanted and the continued slow death of my already withered heart and soul. I wasn't exactly sure how my spouse would react when I told him. I expected either great anger at losing control over his "object" or great happiness and relief that he had finally succeeded in pushing me to the point where I would just go quietly without any more fight—the wife who abandoned him. It proved to be the latter.

I sat outside on a beautiful summer day waiting for him to come home. I had already spoken to the girls beforehand. We said our tearful, temporary good-byes among tight hugs, with a courage that only comes from the Lord. Despite their sadness, they all supported me because they knew I had fought the good fight with every ounce I had in me; their Momma was not a quitter. Even though they couldn't know the full depth of it, they understood how bad it had to be for this drastic move to have become my only remaining option. They could have a measure of peace as they knew I was walking in the will of God.

They had watched me live out my faith while answering the calls to serve inside and outside our home, with obedience and perseverance, even in the face of great sorrow, trials, and tragedy. They had graciously toiled beside me, and together we saw miracle after miracle unfold as God used us "jars of clay" to love, nurture, heal, encourage, grieve with, and invest in many who blessed our home and shared our lives. At a young age, they learned many lessons about selfless love, empathy, tolerance, and grace way beyond their years. They also had seen their mother change, ever so slowly, despite my desire to hide my physical and emotional pain from them. They are certainly my love-lights, my joy, and the apples of my eye—so brave and compassionate. I would do it all again and wouldn't trade a single tear if it meant keeping them in my life—my daughters and now my dear friends!

I sat at the picnic table and waited. I asked the Spirit to tell me what to say that would create peace and not anger or harm. He did not tarry with His answer. He said, "Ask him to forgive you." When he arrived, he sat down across from me. My eyes began to tear up as I spoke my first words:

I need to ask for your forgiveness. To forgive me for all of the times I was not a good and respectful wife. All of the times I spoke in anger because of frustration and was unloving. I have come to understand that all of the tears and pain and struggle come down to this—I cannot be the wife that you want me to be, and you cannot be the husband that I need you to be.

That was it...a simple yet deeply profound truth. I could no longer be the inanimate object that he wanted me to be; I was dying inside. He couldn't be the husband I needed, for many reasons, and didn't want to pretend to fit that mold anymore. We were both tired of the game. A few more words of exchange, and then I left. I drove away from my husband of almost 25 years without even a fight; my "knight in shining armor" had long ago faded into a distant memory of a dream I once had. I felt strangely calm but realized later that I was numb—which was a loving, protective covering from my Father in heaven who knew I couldn't feel everything I had just left and lost all at once. The road to where I was going was a short one compared

308

to the one I would walk next, as I began the process of healing and recovery.

But—it was a road that led away from silent desperation and onto this new path of freedom leading to quiet strength, and I accepted it with a deeply humble and grateful heart!

22

From Silent Desperation
to Quiet Strength

"Behold, I am making all things new."
(Rev. 21:5)

REVELATION, THE LAST book of the Bible, is often considered the most complex and mysterious of all the Scriptures. Even pastors and theologians often hesitate to delve into these pages of mystery, intrigue, unearthly creatures, and word pictures, which fascinate and perplex. But one passage in this book's final chapter is familiar to most believers: Revelation 21:1-5. If your life has seemed to be a chain of pain (in all its diverse forms) and a trail of tears, sorrow, abandonment, loneliness, poverty, etc., the promises in these few easy-to-understand verses will be a refreshing oasis in the midst of your desert experience. God promises those who believe in His beloved Son that He will bring forth **"...a new heaven and a new earth, for the first heaven and the first earth had passed away...and God Himself will be with them as their God"** (Rev. 21:1, 3). Our Father God will dwell among His children. No more abandonment, orphans, homelessness, or loneliness, for He will be among us forever! And as if this were not enough, the Bible promises that

> **He will wipe away every tear from their eyes, and death shall be no more, neither shall there be mourning, nor crying, nor pain anymore, for the former things have passed away.**
> (Rev. 21:4)

Bible scholars who study the original meanings of the Hebrew and Greek languages used in the Scriptures have concluded that the word "new" earth means a renovated earth—like renovating an old house or a classic car. In other words, it means that God is not scrapping the whole first creation but, rather, is restoring it to its original, perfect, unblemished beauty. Our "new" home will be familiar, yet profoundly more wonderful than we could ever imagine!

Our heavenly Father is a God of restoration, of making things new. When an individual accepts Jesus as their personal Lord and Savior, the Bible says that they are "born again" and a "new" creation in Christ. **"Therefore, if anyone is in Christ, he is a new creation. The old has passed away; behold, the new has come"** (Rev. 5:17). This doesn't mean that God scraps the old "you" and starts with new raw material so that you are a completely different person. He just cleans you up and removes what has fallen into disrepair and decay (that which corrupted your body, heart, mind, and soul). He restores what has been lost or stolen from you. If you allow Him to, through the regenerating and transforming power of the Holy Spirit (as written about in Chapter 19), God will get you as close to the original design as He created you in (before the Fall) this side of heaven.

Why have I written about these beautiful promises? So that anyone reading this who has experienced an identity crisis and been stripped of their sense of self (by a narcissist or through some other form of abuse, neglect, or forced isolation) can know within the depth of their broken, bleeding, victimized heart that they will be restored and made new. All of you who have been robbed, abandoned, given away, or thrown away will be made whole in ways you can't even imagine! Unfulfilled promises from people, especially those we love and trust, are often the weapons that cut us the deepest. But I am here to tell you and bear witness to this truth, that God's promises are true and will never fail you!

* When He says, "I will never leave you nor forsake you" (Heb. 13:5), He means it; this I know.
* When He says, "I will love you with an everlasting love" (Jer. 31:3), He means it; this I know.

* When He says, "I will surround you with songs of deliverance" (Ps. 32:7), He means it; this I know.
* When He says, "I will fight for you against your enemies and win" (Deut. 20:4), He means it; this I know.
* When He says, "You will not be put to shame" (Isa. 54:4), He means it; this I know.

When you earnestly repent, He will forgive all your sins, bad choices, decisions, and mistakes—remembering them no more (even though others will not let you forget them). He will be with you always, and He will bear *all* of your burdens.

My life was a beautiful picture transposed onto a puzzle, or so I thought. Then, as the years unfolded and the craziness increased, my puzzle began to be torn apart and scattered, piece by painful piece. I frantically tried to gather up all of the scrambled and lost pieces and put them back together with every form of "glue" I could think of, but they would never stay in place for very long. The picture of my life was falling apart, and I lived in fear, anxiety, perplexity, insecurity, and pain of every kind because I couldn't salvage and restore what was being trampled on, tarnished, and now missing. As the puzzle of my life fell apart, I started to feel more and more fragmented and confused, and almost lost myself in the midst of all of the pieces that lay around me. The whole process was both excruciating and exhausting. All I can say to you now is that I praise God, and am in awe still to this very day, of how He carried me and our family in the midst of the broken mess. He empowered me to press on each day, to persevere and complete the tasks He had set my hands upon. This is a full testimony in itself!

JOURNAL ENTRY – May 8, 2014

Dear Heavenly Father, It is so hard to be both the father and the mother. How difficult it is to cultivate a gentle spirit and yet have to be the administrator of discipline and giver of "tough love." How hard it is to be submissive when you have to be the leader. To be quiet when you are the only one who really speaks. To desire to live in Your truth yet dwell in dark deception—and be still.

I admit that I am often a slow learner and have repeated many grade levels while in God's school of discipleship training. One plus is that I have a teachable spirit, so I didn't drop out of the "school of hard knocks"! What I *finally* learned through my years of tears and prayers is that our loving and devoted God is also a determined Father who has to break apart and scatter most of our puzzles because we have imagined and drawn our own version of the picture on the pieces, which often does not reflect God's original design for our lives. Oh, He might sort through and keep many of the individual pieces—maybe even whole sections—but He has to break apart most of them piece by painful piece because our finite interpretation doesn't even begin to depict the great masterpiece He has designed for our days here on earth.

We are looking at our lives (our puzzles) at an angle that is nearsighted and from a position that is blurred by self-will, seen through the eyes of fallen humanity, as well as the lens of selfish desires and often unrealistic dreams. We cannot fully envision how the pieces all fit together because we are putting in one piece at a time as we live out our days. God sees our life in its entirety while looking down from above at what appears to us to be random pieces. But because He envisioned our life and drew up the blueprint, then creating all of the pieces to fit into it perfectly, only He knows the order and direction that they need to be placed, one into another, to create the final masterpiece. This is why it is so essential for us to relinquish our lives, loves, dreams, and even losses into His capable hands and let Him work a miracle of wholeness and beauty.

> "You'll never have the healing your heart cries for until you've walked through what it's going to take to get you there."
> —The Reverend Charlie Guest[83]

---

[83] Linda Huffman, "The Silent Battle," "We" Magazine: Online Magazine for Women, http://www.womenencouraged.org/p/women.html.

Words given to me during the middle of the night in the wake of prayers for my husband:

Why he shed tears?— "because some deep part of him knew he had let the best part of himself, the sane part of himself, just walk away for one reason alone...he loves himself more than God or any other man or woman. He lives by no moral code or guiding force other than his own desires fueled by the invisible power of self-will and fantasy; a place where there is no moral compass, integrity, or guilt for sin."

JOURNAL ENTRY — August 27, 2013

Lord, I am not asking You to remove or lessen my trials; just for the power to overcome them, the strength to rise above them, and the grace to be merciful to those who cause them. Amen.

* As I did in previous chapters, I am sharing the raw words in my journal entries so that you know that you do not walk this road alone and that there is abundant light, hope, healing, freedom, and renewed strength at the end of the tunnel.

JOURNAL ENTRY —No date recorded

Help me, dear Lord, through my written words to open the eyes of the blind that long for truth and understanding, the ears and mouth of those who have lived in silence, and the heart that longs to be known. Amen.

JOURNAL ENTRY — July 18, 2014

Spirit of Truth, You are hovering near. I feel as if a breakthrough is near. I am nearing something big; I am both ready and fearful at the same time because when truth is fully known, you can never turn back without complete deception. "The truth will set you free." What does that look like? What will it mean for me? Our marriage? Our family? "The project you are working on you need to abort." The full revelation of those spoken words to me from a stranger are near. I have wrestled with them often. I have felt strongly since that first night that they were regarding our marriage, but in what way? Stop trying to work on your marriage did not seem biblical. Stop trying to work on your husband seemed closer to the truth, yet allowing deceit and sin to reign freely within a marriage and family unit didn't feel biblical either. Whether of the faith or not, we need to be kept accountable for our actions.

You revealed the Narcissistic Personality Disorder, but I still didn't know how to fully engage it. Freed by knowledge yet still imprisoned by a vow has only left me more confused. I have trusted in Your strength and wisdom to see me through and help me to be still (when I really desired to fly away) and wait upon Your leading. I do not wish to step out from beneath the shadow of Your wings. But I felt a twinge of possible revelation this morning while reading Dietrich Bonhoeffer's Life Together in regard to confession. Could the Spirit be telling me to openly—before our daughters, close family members, friends, and even the Church—bring into the light that which has been cloaked in deception? For years I left truth hidden because of both fear and pride; fear of unsettling our family and pride in the reputation our family has had in the circles we move in. But more and more the sham has pricked at my conscience.

I have recently confessed to some dear Christian sisters. It has helped, but I still do not feel free from the ties that bind; still feel too much deceit and unspoken tension. But, I may have a new piece of the puzzle to work with. The question: Am I enabling my spouse to stay embedded and cloaked in his sin by covering up and masking over his narcissism? By carrying his load and presenting him as someone he is not to his children, family, friends, and church members; am I being a part of his game and allowing it to continue to play? Even though I have exposed his nature to himself, he has not acknowledged it nor repented of his sin and feels no remorse or shame. I believe he is trusting in me to keep playing the game to "save face" for our family and/or trusting in the knowledge that he has already deceived his daughters and family enough so they will not believe nor accept the truth revealed by me. Could this be the project I need to abort; working on building up the deceitful tower and instead tear it down? This could only be accomplished with the decisive and delicate work and leading of Your Holy Spirit as loving and truthful guide. I leave it all in Your trustworthy hands! Amen.

JOURNAL ENTRY — March 17, 2015 (my 49th birthday)

...I saw that in the last entry I acknowledged my need to completely empty myself and surrender to God. At the same time I realized that this past year was the most emotionally and spiritually trying of all; I never felt so empty, numb, and willing to give up on my marriage. I couldn't seem to be able to reconcile and renew what I (not we) had desired to have; it had died. I felt so humbled by the thoughts that I had failed; failed myself, my husband, our daughters, our family and friends. I grieved deeply. You met me there in my deep sorrow and offered Your peace, support of friends, and comfort for my tears. My heart and mind, body and spirit were in conflict; I couldn't go back and felt stuck to move forward. I felt that my identity had been stolen and my desire crushed.

But in this deep place of loneliness, rejection, confusion, and brokenness, I saw a light—a flicker of hope. These women's conferences put a spark to my extinguished wick and started to fan a flame. I started to see a new woman arising; empowered by the Spirit of grace, mercy, and love. A new identity emerging; still myself and yet somehow changed. A confidence that had long been stripped away. Purpose renewed rising out of the ashes; beauty from pain. And as I gave the Spirit of Jesus freedom to align my confused heart, mind, and will with His own; peace and clarity have overtaken the fog and scattered pieces. I feel renewed passion in every sense and a sharpness of purpose not felt for many years. A new boldness to love openly and deeply; an acute sense of my created womanhood.

The revelation was that not only did my old nature and dreams and pain have to die, but my "old" marriage as well. The pain, suffering, and ugliness of the past had to die—it couldn't be resurrected or restored; too much damage was done and the foundation and structure—it had to be demolished. We cannot rebuild it again; it can only be restored and raised up again in Christ. I finally see a hope of renewal and reconciliation only if based on a foundation of truth, trust, and mutual love and respect. The difference is that I know if it doesn't happen, I will be okay. Jesus holds me in His hands, and I will not fear the future. I am yielded to His perfect love and will; whatever it is and whatever the cost. Satan hates me for this vow, but I will persevere in the strength of the Lord my God and the tireless Holy Spirit. Guide my every step, Jesus; I will follow You. Amen.

*I would be called out to embark on my personal exodus almost exactly one year and three months from the date this was written.

JOURNAL ENTRY — November 10, 2015

So, Father, I rejoice in You! Your faithful holiness which brings peace to my shattered dreams and saddened heart. You have taken me through some kind of obstacle these last few weeks, and I have experienced some clearer thinking; both a calm and an excitement I can't quite understand yet. The bitter and the sweet seem not to be so far apart and a steadiness of mind, body, and spirit seem to have surfaced. Strange in the wake of unveiling truth; maybe that is the key—truth! The pieces to the truth of the insanity are settling into place, and I am finally seeing a picture emerging. Although disturbing in nature, I feel somewhat lighter in knowing that is the reason I am rejected. Forgiveness seems to be flowing with more and more ease. Just knowing how to proceed now is what lies before me. Please, Holy Spirit, guide me in all truth and direct my path. I trust not myself or my will, but only that of God. Keep me safe from evil and snares, I pray, in Jesus' name. Amen!

JOURNAL ENTRY — November 17, 2015

I feel so scattered, foggy, and weak. I can't hold back the truth much longer; it is literally killing my soul and my spirit—all hope is gone. I have no vision of a future together; it has dried up and blown away on the breeze. I do not seek vengeance, just truth and freedom. It will come at a huge cost, I know—this grieves me deeper than anyone can know. Denial is a hard swallow. I know, I tried to push back the truth for so many years that the dam is ready to burst. Only Your Spirit keeps it at bay. I tried, I failed. I can't do it. Where do I go from here? I haven't any more ideas! I could end up all alone in a shack somewhere, but it is better than this prison. If he would give me just one ounce of thought that he feels he needs to give to those he needs for his purposes, I would be happy. 24 years of nothing. A scrap of anything sounds like a treasure to this empty and sad heart. I grieve alone. I want to lay down and sleep for a year and wake up to a new place of peace. Peace—that is all I ever wanted. He wouldn't even let me have that without daily torture. The tears come again. I cry almost every day but no one sees or hears. What difference does it make? You hear and see, but still I sit on the dung heap in pain and anguish. I hold out my empty hand to You anyway; it is all I have to give...

Doing wrong is like a joke to a fool, but wisdom is pleasure to a man of understanding. (Prov. 10:23)

JOURNAL ENTRY — November 20, 2015

Father, I am so weary again today. Lack of sleep, head pain, heart pain. I feel sick and want to climb into a deep hole and cover my head and lay in silence; no voices outside or inside my head. Today's devotion says, "I am pleased with you, My child." But I feel like a failure in the flesh and in the spirit. Sounds like self-pity, right? I know You hate self-pity so; therefore, I feel like a failure. But I was doomed to failure when I married a narcissist who also has other secrets—wow, a double-failure!

Any shred of sweet innocence I had left within me has been torn from my grasp. It doesn't matter how far I go down, the games never stop or change. Why am I still hurt by them? Hope? Does it still exist somewhere in me? I feel so sad for our girls. I had hoped for so much more to give them. I laugh (or cry) when I think of how I wanted to create here a special place of peace, joy, comfort, hope for them and others; a real "old-fashioned" home. It has been for many...but for me it is a house of pain, lies, deception, lacking peace and comfort...no rest, no happiness. Prison.

I wanted to be like Joseph was in prison; trusting in the Lord for release. I did for years, praying that He would change the "N" heart or release me—rescue me—but the bars remain. I sang with Paul and Silas for years; even if it was weak, I sang, but the chains never fell off my feet nor did the doors burst wide open.

Yes, dear sweet Lord, You have healed me in so many wonderful ways—thank You! I have delighted in our wilderness days and my faith was strengthened. But I feel like I have sunk back in time, to the place I was before the desert sojourn, and I am parched. I cannot be in the desert again. I need to get to an oasis and be refreshed in the water so I can grow and bloom again. I need new life. This old record plays a song I have come to despise; it makes me sick to hear it all again—over and over—the manipulative lies. I cannot bear it. Your Word says that "hope will not disappoint nor put to shame"—I have had both. Jesus, the burden is too heavy—carry me.

*The emotional roller coaster ride one takes at the "Insanity Fair"; once the bars come down over you...you can't get off.

JOURNAL ENTRY — November 29, 2015

The girls prepared a special anniversary celebration for us. It was all so lovely. I wanted to cry because the truth—somehow and some way—will come soon. The "picture perfect" family will end soon; how will it affect them all? I can't live the lie anymore—not for them or anyone. I am dying and what good is a "dead" Mom. I have tried to create a special place of love and nurture, and it could be such a blessed place if not for the "N." He is kicking into high gear to "win" friends (I say that loosely) and bring others to his side in the "me versus her" game. I will not play. I am who I am, and if no one can see truth; then I will not force reality upon them. I am trusting in Your protection, truth, and justice—maybe not even on this side of heaven, but it will be done. Spirit, give me discernment; I need to be careful. Hedge me in; Your lowly yet faithful servant. I need You to show me the way of peace. Help me to be strong against my emotions to please everyone first and not care for myself. I need healing. I pray I am not too far gone and can live the rest of my days in joyful service, peace, comfort for others, and love in You. I am ready—Let's roll!

> Turn to me and be gracious to me; give Your strength to Your servant...Show me a sign of Your favor; that those who hate me may see and be put to shame because You, **LORD**, have helped me and comforted me. (Ps. 86:16-17)

JOURNAL ENTRY — February 8, 2016

This Scripture continues to speak deeply to my heart and path: "I will go before you and make the crooked places straight, I will break in pieces the doors of bronze and cut through the bars of iron" (Isaiah 45:2). It is a constant reminder to me that no gates or doors or bars can hold in the faithful forever; God will have His way and make every wrong right. That neither gold rings, nor walls, nor titles can keep those who trust in the name and power and justice of the Lord in bondage forever. That only the wicked and those who reject the life-changing gift found in Jesus remain in bondage, while those who call upon and trust in His name are made free indeed! Such peace; the heart cry for freedom to fly and soar with the Master!

JOURNAL ENTRY — February 11, 2016

As Your Holy Spirit opens my eyes and ears to hear His voice, as again I read Isaiah 40 and thought about how we need to wait upon You in patience and loving trust, I saw myself not only soaring with You like an eagle above the storms but also needing to run the race set before me with patient and steady endurance. And even when I become too tired and weary to run and soar, that You will lovingly walk beside me and help me each weary step I take or just carry me across the finish line. I will achieve victory in and with You! Amen.

JOURNAL ENTRY — February 15, 2016

Yesterday was the celebration of "love"—Valentine's Day—which can be a day of great joy or great pain depending on where you are stationed presently. Isn't that just like earthly love, constantly shifting and swinging from mountain top to the valley floor? Yesterday was awkward for me. I had the mountain top experience by spending time with our girls and son-in-law; then the valley, always near, making me aware of the painful echo of empty words and promises of "happily ever after" and the words of bondage " until death do us part." God hates divorce. I hate the word myself; so dark and troubling. Separation—that is what my soul needs—a chance to step out of the painful silence and emptiness and find peace and light and fresh air. To fill the lungs with expanded hope and let the muscles, tight with carrying the heavy burden of pretense, finally release and relax. As always, he was as absent as usual; opting to be alone. Holy God, the One who made a way for reconciliation through Jesus Christ and the Spirit; only You can reconcile this growing silence and gaping hole—only You can mend what is beyond repair in the flesh. I cling to Your words that if I continue forward, all will be well. I feel very sad today, and he is home on holiday; strengthen me I pray.

JOURNAL ENTRY — February 2016

May desire for reconciliation, compassion, and love always override my anger, frustration, and my own pain.

JOURNAL ENTRY — February 27, 2016

Dear Lord, You are showing me that in this situation I find myself, I have very little control over it—only how I react and what I allow to take place in my heart, soul, mind, and spirit. Will I let it overtake me, or will I allow You to use this time of great trial to refine me completely to the woman You created me to be? I already have the victory in Jesus; will I take it? You have already done a huge work in me, for which I am grateful.

As You dig now into the deeper recesses of my frail heart, give me courage and strength to endure what is being unearthed there. One important insight that has been solidified for me was how I need to not allow the narcissist to manipulate me into doing/saying things that encourage his ego to feel justified to continue his sinful actions and thoughts; to fuel his secret life. He needs to have no excuses for his ungodly behavior. I surely need Your wisdom here! When I react the way he wants me to, he considers (in his sick mind) it is an invitation to indulge himself in the secret rooms of the mind of fantasy. Please continue to reveal the changes needed in me to be right before You, while continuing to pray for him.

P.S. Thank You for the joy of our daughters who help bring peace and added joy to my life which is in great need of "sparkle"!

JOURNAL ENTRY — March 1, 2016

Holy God of my Lord and Spirit: I sit before You. I have "heard" Your words through the Scriptures and readings, but I mostly hear the deafening silence. Today is the first day toward something, but I do not know what. The full weight of truth is sinking into my mind and overwhelmed heart which is filled with pain, emptiness, and my bowels twist within me. I am seeking Your voice but can't be still too long, my mind crawling toward the truth and then hurrying away as it is confronted with its stench, ugliness, and evil. I told the girls to pray for their father, that he is in a bad place. That is all I can say.

Change is coming and we all need to recalculate. The Holy Spirit needs to sort and imprint truth in me so I can speak with clarity and wisdom. Am I safe here? I cover myself with You and trust that You have my back. I do not want any false security though; I lived the deadly tragedy of that! His mind is truly in bondage; deeper than I could have guessed. He has totally "checked out" on us all. My heart can't bear the pain I know is coming.

Take this whole burden from me, I beg You. Be the righteous Judge. I did forgive him last night—the last words I spoke to him—by Your grace. I meant it. What gain is there for me if I hold it back? Only separation from You (he has already left me long ago), and I can't bear that. I am so weary. I still go through the motions, taking care of the children and home. Always kept some normalcy in the midst of the abnormal.

Keep my mind focused and clear. I can't see the way in the dark; be my guiding light. I trust that You will not put the girls through any unnecessary pain. Take good care of them—that is really all that I care about! Be near, O God. Amen.

Because he (she) holds fast to Me in love, I will deliver him (her); I will protect him (her) because he (she) knows My name. (Ps. 91:14, parentheses added)

JOURNAL ENTRY – March 26, 2016

I was thinking about why the Lord waited so long to reveal the truth of the NPD, and I was reminded again of His grace and perfect timing. He allowed me to live with hope in my heart—however faint—to keep me moving forward as I completed the divine tasks He called me to. He used those hard seasons to stretch my faith muscles so that when He finally revealed the truth, I was strong enough to continue walking forward in His strength and not be consumed by the hopelessness of the situation. Such amazing wisdom, power, and grace!

> "Are you bound by your immediate present condition? Are you interpreting your life by the things which just now touch you? The present is only passing. Make the current circumstances serve you; get out of them everything you possibly can; even the tragic experiences that touch your life."
> —John Wright Follette, *Breaking Bread* [84]

JOURNAL ENTRY – April 7, 2016

I feel such peace! I laid awake last night and just felt Your perfect peace and protection. I am secure in Your love, and behind Your shield, I am learning to be an over-comer; to be confident in who I am in You with the power to face all circumstances in Your perfect peace and joy! How humbled I am by Your grace and love for me; Your care of me! Amen.

JOURNAL ENTRY – April 18, 2016

I praise You alone for setting my feet on solid ground when I was slipping, falling, and wandering. You have given me this inner strength, peace, and joy that I can't explain but know they are more real than the present circumstances, sorrow, and pain of this world. I was just thinking about all of the support and encouragement from my sisters in Christ and feel quite unworthy of their words of how strong I am trusting in You and being faithful at this difficult time, as my heart is struggling so. If I look too far ahead or too long at the day, I feel I will get swallowed up sometimes or panic and either run back and stay despite the emptiness and evil, or run ahead too quickly and get caught in something worse. Thank You, dear Adonai, for Your hand upon me which keeps me anchored at Your sure feet and the Holy Spirit's voice behind me saying, "This is the way, walk in it with Me; continue forward and all will be well."

The wise heart will know the proper time and the just way.
(Eccles. 8:5)

---

[84] John Wright Follette, *Broken Bread* (Chicago, IL: Word & Witness, 1960).

JOURNAL ENTRY – December 9, 2015

Lord, I pray that I have served You well here. I pray that I have been a faithful wife and mother, wholly committed and diligent in raising our family as well as caring for and supporting my husband—encouraging him to be a good spouse, father, son, friend, and worker (not to much avail). I pray I have been faithful to Your calls on my life and loved and cared for others here—and elsewhere—with passion and love. I can still love my enemy, yet be a servant elsewhere. It is my heart's desire that our daughters be Your servants wherever You send them. Now I ask that You send me. As my confidence has been crushed by the "N," I will need You to lovingly lift me back to my feet and set me in forward motion again. I have been climbing uphill so long, I have lost steam. I need to be refreshed and filled so I can build up my momentum and get back on track. The servant of the Lord is awakening, devil; you can only keep this gal down for so long! I will not only survive, but I will thrive in the hands of my King! I will not live my life in captivity and fear—I am an over-comer. I will not feel responsible for the choices made anymore. I have no regrets. Although I have made many mistakes, I poured in every last drop of myself into building up and now everyone needs to stand on their own. Amen.

JOURNAL ENTRY – 2017

This verse in Psalm 18:19 speaks of where my heart is now: "He brought me out into a spacious place; He rescued me because He delighted in me." The writer asks, "What is this spacious place?" What can it be but God himself—the infinite Being! I love this verse in Exodus 19:4, "I carried you on eagles' wings and brought you to Myself." You, dear Lord, have most certainly brought me unto Yourself. Delight in me as I delight in You!

A friend and I were talking recently about many of our shared experiences. Although some of the details were different, both of our stories were very difficult and life-changing. We also talked about our ability to now speak openly and truthfully regarding our painful experiences with others in shared fellowship. It is a healthy and important part of healing, as it opens the portal to more abundant resources of understanding, encouragement, strength, and freedom— knowledge is power. Many people are uncomfortable when it comes to sharing their personal pain, as well as uncomfortable when hearing that of others. But to be free and honest in our pain and broken places is the door of freedom opened and offered, allowing others to feel safe to walk through it knowing that they walk not alone but with a fellow sufferer who understands and is traveling the same road. This is my calling, my new path and purpose: to be a *heard* voice. A voice once so thoroughly silenced by the narcissist's muzzle of manipulative abuse and deception...now made free to speak into the darkness with the light of wisdom, truth, and understanding rooted in the power of knowledge gleaned through 25 years of pain and heartache. I am excited for both of us, as I see much healing, renewed joy, deep peace, direction, focus, and inner strength emerging from our broken and damaged pasts and subsequent injuries. As I wrote previously, I do not seek vengeance but only justice in the light of truth. For our daughters alone, I wouldn't trade the pain and suffering of it all if it meant not having them. How could I not forgive the unforgivable in light of the forgiveness bestowed upon me, a sinner? How could I not show mercy when my Father has gone to such great lengths to rescue me and give me this new life and freedom? How could I not extend grace in light of God's extravagant love poured out upon this simple woman of no repute? I do not even have an alabaster bottle of expensive perfumed oil to pour out upon my Savior, only my tears of gratitude to wash His holy feet (Luke 7:37-38).

So, what have I learned from my silent desperation?

I have learned that the God I have worshiped is truly my "Abba, Father" (my Papa), and I am His beloved child. The pages of this book couldn't contain all of the ways He has shown me this truth. I have learned that apart from my Lord and Savior, Jesus Christ, I truly can do nothing of significance as I am—but there is *nothing* I cannot do, be, or accomplish when He empowers me. That He *is* truth and peace, hope and joy, and that until the day I die, I want to shine His love to a world longing to be seen, heard, and known, as He desires to be seen, heard, and known by all who will receive Him.

I have learned to love my enemies and do good to those who hate me, to bless those who curse me, and to pray for those who spitefully use me. I also acknowledge that this is impossible in my fallen flesh but contingent upon the power of the Holy Spirit, who enables me to extend love

324

and compassion while the wounds are still bleeding and the heart still aches. That forgiveness is not a feeling but, rather, a supernatural act of obedience granted by the yielded will covered in mercy and grace.

I have learned that the Holy Spirit is everywhere and available 24/7 with His comfort, strength, wisdom, healing, interceding, speaking, guiding, teaching, and correcting. He leads all surrendered souls into humility and repentance, yet with the assurance that we are loved and forgiven—without shame—and emboldened to approach God as sons and daughters. He reminds me to buy bread as timely as meeting a crucial deadline, or when to duck on the battlefield. From the mundane and simple to the very important or even life-saving, He is ever-present as our Helper and power source. I thank Him countless times a day!

I have learned that there is a time to be still and a time for action, a time to be silent and a time for words. There truly is a time for all things but that only God knows the time and the way. He holds the keys to success and blessing as well as failure and unnecessary pain.

I have learned to embrace the silence and listen as God often speaks in a whisper.

I have learned that following Jesus truly comes at a great price—your very life—but that it is also the most fulfilling and freeing life you could ever hope for or dream of this side of heaven. Being a believer is certainly not boring, and when you jump on board, you better hold on tight because it is one wild ride—yet exhilarating and ever-changing...*life-changing!*

I have learned that, although the Father desires for me to have an abundant, meaningful, and joyous life this side of the veil, that my life is not my own and my purpose here (all of our purposes) are for something so much bigger than ourselves. This is bad news for a narcissist but beautiful words to those asking, "Does my life really matter? Is there purpose and meaning to my existence? Should I still have hope for more? Does anyone really see me, hear me, know me, love me?" Yes, a thousand times yes! Even if the Lord was the only one, I promise you, that is more than enough. But He isn't. I see you. Many desire to see, hear, know, and love you—you just haven't met them yet!

I have learned that when we are hurting, suffering, and grieving a loss of any kind or wrestling with disappointments and failed/broken dreams, we need to guard our hearts and minds from closing in on us. It is important to our health and well-being to not get so introspective that we become consumed by our own pain and problems, thereby pulling inward—often projecting our negative energy and feelings onto others. We need to exchange them for avenues of positive and creative expression as well as in service toward others. We should not neglect our own self-care, but find a healthy balance so we don't withdraw and harden into self-contained vessels who begin to fear the power of love. Mankind's deepest need is to receive love as much as to give it away!

I have learned that, although society would teach and direct us otherwise, the place where we all truly need to get is at the end of ourselves. We need to look at our brokenness, wounds, and raw places and not be afraid to reach out for help and seek wholeness. We also need to look our sins and destructive behavior patterns in the eye and acknowledge how they are hurting us and those closest to us. How they are destroying the very fabric of our own lives, families, communities, churches, nation, and world. How by not facing *our own truth*, we are losing the ability to connect with ourselves and with one another. When we avoid reality, we extinguish our motivation and passion to strive for personal excellence and greatly diminish our full potential in creativity and productivity in both our toil and rest.

I have learned that the measuring rod for our lives and our identities is not rooted in the world's standards. We are truly seen through the eyes of Jesus, who looks upon the broken as beautiful and only sees our potential. He sees us not as a human mass but as a unique and individual creation. There will always be someone who is smarter, thinner, stronger, faster, richer, and more successful than us; this measuring rod will always keep us bound in a state of perpetual striving. In this sad state, the words "peace, joy, and freedom" will never become our reality because there will always be jealousy, bitterness, resentment, self-pity, self-loathing, self-condemnation, insecurities, pride, and even hatred when we are in constant competition mode. Christ's matchless love is our matchless ability—we can find rest and wholeness in knowing that we are a "one-of-a-kind" jewel of great worth.

I have learned that because I was not accepted by my husband, I was in a constant state of recreating myself into someone I wasn't in an attempt to become the woman he would finally want. I felt that I had to meet a model standard to measure up as someone worthy of belonging to him and his conditional love. I never made the mark—not for lack of effort but because it doesn't really exist. I know I am certainly not alone when it comes to this unhealthy mindset for both men and women alike. It is an elusive bar that constantly sways with the winds of time, culture change, popular opinion, and our shallow estimation of God's amazing creative energy, which we cannot even begin to fathom. The ways in which we try to alter and disguise our true "selves"—the endless hoops we jump through to belong and feel important—keep us frantic, conflicted, confused, depressed, oppressed, and constantly striving. This robs us of precious time that can never be recovered. When I finally stopped trying to be what my spouse and society pressured me to be, I truly began living fully—fully living! I was silently desperate once, ardently and heroically saved twice; I now know who I am, Whose I am—nothing more, yet certainly nothing less!

> Christ's matchless love is our matchless ability—we can find rest and wholeness in knowing that we are a "one-of-a-kind" jewel of great worth.

I have learned from my own depth of silent desperation that there is so much suffering and sorrow endured in silence throughout the world. My heart aches for every man, woman, and child who lives within the prison of silence and abuse in all of its forms—feeling isolated and alone without love, comfort, or someone to be their advocate (a voice that offers the hope of freedom).

*I have learned that there can **always be purpose** in our pain.* If we are willing to surrender both ourselves and our suffering to God, He will use it in powerful ways beyond our imagination, bringing beauty from our ashes for the sake of others and for His glory. He will restore the years that the locusts have eaten and give you double for your trouble (Joel 2:22-26). I have developed both a yielded heart of compassion and a spirit for justice. With God's help and grace, may He use my personal experience to not only speak into the growing epidemic of narcissism in all of its dark and destructive forms, but to also shine light into the greater abyss of silent desperation. This untamed force is spreading across lines of gender, race, language, economic classes, and religion into every nation. Through my hands, may the Father's words speak loud and clear that He *sees* His beloved children, *hears* your cries for help, *knows* your hearts and pain, and *loves* you without measure. He alone is the One who can truly rescue and set us free.

Quiet Strength

Hillsdale College's motto:
"Virtus tentamine gaudet—strength rejoices in the challenge."

I recall the day so clearly, yet it was just an ordinary day in the late summer of 2016. Several months had passed since that fateful day I made my exodus into a drastic life change I couldn't fully picture at the time; I just knew it was a change that would save my life and sanity. I had been at our old home—now just a house to me—several times since I left to pick up a few items that were left behind. I usually came when my spouse was not there, but an interesting encounter would happen this day, profound in its simplicity.

I was exiting the bathroom and entering the short hallway to the kitchen. My husband, who had just arrived, was simultaneously entering the hallway from the direction of the kitchen as well. He stopped short and stood there a moment as I slowly made my way toward him. I was wearing a simple yet pretty royal blue sundress, and he said, "You look nice in that dress." The unexpected compliment took me aback as it sounded like something that a husband would say to a wife he desired and wanted to feel good about herself; neither of which had he felt in a very long time—perhaps never. I just said, "Thank you." I was so used to hearing him say things that he didn't mean, and he was so used to saying things that he didn't mean; therefore, neither of us will ever know what he was really thinking. We stood in the kitchen for a short while and exchanged surface conversation. I asked about his parents and work. He asked a few things as well. Then we went our separate ways. But I was very aware of a significant change: an ease between us that hadn't previously existed amid the constant underlying tension that had been the norm for so long.

On the long ride back to the city, I pondered what it all had meant. What had made the usually negative atmosphere now feel semi-peaceful and almost strangely pleasant? Nothing had changed within him as if some magic spell of kindness, empathy, or love had broken through the hardened heart. But the Spirit gave me insight into my question; there had been a silent yet tangible ceasefire on the battlefield. I realized that, in the wake of our separation, I no longer had to be the ardent warrior fighting the adversary's constant attacks while also trying to save our marriage and family from toppling into ruins. He didn't have to pretend that he wanted me or our marriage for the sake of saving face, and could live in what he falsely perceived as freedom with selfish abandon. The invisible white flag had been waved, and there was finally surrender in the midst of truth...sad truth. No longer did I have to do battle with him to be the husband and father I needed him to be, or hold onto the false dream that he would finally realize what he was losing and be the gallant knight in shining armor who would stop at nothing to rescue me, us, and our family. He was so relieved that he didn't have to pretend anymore to be someone he wasn't; he didn't have to preserve the lie that he wanted me in any way.

So, what was the exchange in the hallway about that was so significant to me personally? The Spirit of the Lord showed me that, too. It was the understanding that I was *truly* off the battlefield and could finally let my guard down and relinquish all of the heavy protective armor. The often hard-shell I had to encompass myself in, to protect my wounded heart and battle-worn soul, had been fully removed. This shell was like the protective scab over a deep cut or a blister that forms over the rawness of a place irritated by constant, unnatural rubbing against tender flesh but now no longer necessary. The thick cloud of gunpowder smoke had dissipated with the winds of change, and to my delight, I discovered that I had come off the field still intact. I had incurred numerous injuries and bore the scars of many battles, but they were not remnants or symbols of shame and failure, nor were they badges of pride; they were merely reminders that it didn't matter who had won or lost, but only that—in the end— I had fought the good fight and achieved a *personal* victory!

The woman he had married was the same, yet different. The fire of youth had been softened to an ember, and the hard edges were smoothed over by steady and painful sanding at the hands of suffering, loss, and grief. Pride was worn away and replaced by humility and surrender, as I yielded to and accepted "the loss" as well as the needful stripping away of self-effort and human reasoning. I was pleasantly surprised to discover that the soft and trusting woman that had said, "I do," still remained, yet she was matured by time and painful growth. I like these words of wisdom from author Maya Angelou in her book, *Wouldn't Take Nothing For My Journey Now*:

> The woman who survives intact and happy must be at once tender and tough. She will need to prize her tenderness and be able to display it at appropriate times in order to prevent toughness from gaining total authority and to avoid becoming a mirror image of those men who value power above life, and control over love. It is imperative that a woman keep her sense of humor intact and at the ready. Women should be tough, tender, laugh as much as possible and live long lives. The struggle for equality continues unabated,

and the woman warrior who is armed with wit and courage will be among the first to celebrate victory.[85]

I arose stronger and wiser; not filled with girlhood dreams but living fully in reality and truth, yet with the courage to look it in the face and still love: love others, love my enemies, and maybe for the first time, truly love myself. I had looked to my husband to make me feel complete, whole, and worthy of love, and to feel needed—yet more importantly—*wanted*. I have come to believe that this is a crucial element that needs to be fulfilled in a woman; I would think it is for a man as well. Although I like to "feel needed," my deepest personal longing is to "know" that I am *wanted*. I always felt that I was "needed" by my husband, as he needed me to do just about everything necessary to keep life moving forward and productively until our family was raised up and mostly self-sufficient. But I never really felt that I was truly wanted for who I was as a person of self-identity; a woman of worth; a wife of value; a faithful friend; a confidante of private thoughts, dreams, desires, fears; or a helpmate in mutual goals and plans for our marriage, family, and daily living. I longed to be with someone who wanted me enough that he would come looking for me—seeking after me and would not stop until he found me— whether I was in the next room or on the other side of the country! Wanted for who I am, in all my brokenness or wholeness, whether empty or full.

I looked to my spouse and our life together for validation of my self-worth and was always disappointed and left wanting. I truly felt fulfilled as a mother, homemaker, teacher, friend, server, caregiver, etc., but what a wife really needs to know is that she is beloved by her husband, her soulmate, her confidant, her lover, and her closest companion. I have also come to understand and accept the truth that, although my spouse didn't desire me or want to fill those places in my life, he really *couldn't* satisfy all of my needs fully, nor should he have. No matter how ardent we are in loving one another, because we are

[85] Angelou, *Wouldn't Take Nothing For My Journey Now,* pp. 61-66.

human, we will always come up short and disappoint each other. Of course, my case is a bit extreme in this regard because of dealing with a narcissist, where little to no effort—or even initial intent—is ever made to fuel and maintain love and care in the relationship; this is wrong on so many levels.

To enter into a marriage vow with deceptive intent is both unjust and cruel. But in reality, even with the highest of intentions, we cannot attain a height of perfection in love within our fallen natures. We need to be mindful of this so that we don't unfairly place too great an expectation on other people; this would alleviate many instances of disappointment in each other. Both partners must cultivate and be intentional about finding other avenues of fulfillment and validation of self-identity and worth through healthy outlets in order to maintain balance and harmony, whether together or apart. Unfortunately, the "bar" of expectations in my marriage had been lowered so many times over 25 years that it lay on the ground. Even at that, he would not step over it.

> JOURNAL ENTRY — June 24, 2017
>
> I don't know how I am feeling right now even writing this...nervous and excited at the same time! Ready yet not ready all at once. Feeling very much like the day just over a year ago when You called me out of the midst of all I had known and loved to be rescued from the pit of "hell" that was killing me and given a chance at freedom, new life, and purpose. But even in the rescue there was still much struggle, sorrow, trials, testing, tears, and fervent prayers...still days of silence, yet not the silence of abuse. I heard the Spirit counsel me, "Listen to the silence; it will teach you." Yes, silence does "talk" and teach us much; it is both a messenger of peace and a companion of loneliness. Silence is a great teacher of painful truths as well as glorious revelations. You know I covet the solitude but hate the loneliness; my cross—bitter with the sweet. I write out the ending of this chapter of my life as the Spirit leads..."As You wish, Lord!"

So, how did I emerge from the ashes of my charred dreams and smoldering pain of grief and loss? Well, I emerged with a new and deeper understanding that our dreams are usually too small and often unrealistic in nature. I believe that we are really here on earth to fulfill God's dream for our lives, which was designed to give us a remarkably abundant life overflowing with great purpose and personal fulfillment. Our life, in turn, gives Him honor and glory. I came out of the wreckage with a personal testimony of our Father's deep love for His children, and with the incredible knowledge that He can still bring forth much inner beauty from us despite our fallen natures; this is nothing short of a miracle of grace wrought in tender love. I arose in a new kind of strength steeped in a higher love that isn't tainted by the selfish and finite limitations of human love...finding true love, wholeness, and self-worth in the only One who could extend such a gift: my Papa and my Lord.

God is love: perfect, selfless, unlimited love. This heavenly gift of love is available to all who ask to receive it in faith. This perfect love casts out fear: the fear of being rejected, abandoned, shamed, disappointed, and left empty and wanting. This is what I felt that ordinary yet revealing day, and this is what my husband saw that day: the woman who had left exhausted, beaten down, dejected, scorned, and grieved to the core was now walking upright, face lifted and smiling, peaceful, rested, and with renewed youth—an inner beauty that is deeper than the flesh. A woman gentle yet with an inner strength that speaks of wholeness, self-possession, renewed freedom, and personal victory. This is the story of my spoken and unspoken transformation during a wilderness journey that took me from silent desperation to quiet strength. Now, I rise up daily and soar with wings like the eagle—flying to new and greater heights than I could have ever dreamed of!

Your beauty should not come from outward adornment... Rather, it should be that of your inner self, the unfading beauty of a gentle and quiet spirit, which is of great worth in God's sight. (1 Pet. 3:3-4)

> "Rest your heart in Me.
> For in quietness and in returning shall be your peace and your strength."
> —Frances J. Roberts, *Come Away My Beloved* [86]

JOURNAL ENTRY – November 29, 2016
(Tomorrow is our 25th wedding anniversary spent miles apart in distance and in heart.)

Dear Father God, I am so overwhelmed by Your grace. Not that I am anyone special, but I am so personally touched by Your desire to make me feel like I am! I know there are so many women out there silently suffering too, and my heart goes out to their pain. They need to know they are not alone or crazy or just "no good" because people they love have rejected and hurt them unjustly. If You deem me worthy of relaying such a needful message of Your great love and desire to deliver those who will believe You are able, needing only to wait for Your perfect timing while knowing that there is new life waiting for their silently desperate hearts, I will. Amen.

But he (she) who is noble plans noble things,
and on noble things he (she) stands.
(Isa. 32:8, parentheses added)

---

[86] Frances J. Roberts, *Come Away, My Beloved: A Six Part Compilation of the Writings of Frances J. Roberts* (Palos Verdes Estates, CA: King's Press, 1973).

APPENDIX:
Symbolism of the Cover

**Those who wait upon the LORD shall renew their strength,
they will mount up (soar) on wings like eagles.**
(Isa. 40:31, parentheses added)

T HE POWER AND majesty of an eagle, I believe, is not matched by many other creatures in the animal kingdom. Unlike most birds, which live and move in flocks and tend to be social, the eagle spends most of its life flying solo, except during mating season. The often-lonesome life of an eagle parallels my own life in greater ways than I had ever anticipated, yet I have come to recognize that it is sometimes necessary and even desirous on many levels. I am a social person by nature and love to meet fellow travelers from all walks of life with a heart to see, hear, and know them as unique individuals. I also relish time spent with my beautiful daughters, son-in-law, precious granddaughters, extended family, and dear friends; I cherish these moments as some of my greatest joys. But the many years in which I was forced into loneliness, isolation, and silence have established within me an ability to be alone and still, and to appreciate the quiet life of solitude.

My spirit embraces these words written by John Wright Follette in his book *Broken Bread*; they come from a man who had spent much time in this place of solitude and reflected on how it changes a person from the inside out:

> In this isolation experience we develop an independence of faith and life so that the soul needs no longer the constant help, prayer, faith, and attention of her neighbor. They have their place, but there comes a time when they act as a direct hindrance to an individual's faith and welfare. God knows how to shape the circumstances in order to give us an isolation experience. We yield

to God and He takes us through something and when it is over, those about us, who are no less loved than before, are no longer depended upon. He has wrought some change in us and in that the wings of our soul have learned to sweep the upper air. This isolation produces the characteristic of quietness. The soul acquires a new grip upon her life and is now moved by God rather than by things seen. She can trust God to control her spirit in the most vexing circumstances. One's silence and self-possession is mightier than words.[87]

I consider his insights both profound and beautiful. As I have already mentioned, this did not happen overnight but, rather, over the course of many difficult and painful years of deep and almost consuming loneliness. Developing the peace within that would give me the ability to be alone, and not be overcome with the loneliness, was itself an arduous part of my desert experience. I will admit that I still struggle at times when a wave of loneliness hits me unexpectedly, but I find it more of a *desire* to share my life with someone than a *desperate need* to be filled by another. Since my release from the confined space of the "gilded" cage, my once-clipped wings have been preened, strengthened, and tested to the point where I can now soar unfettered above the circumstances that once kept me in silent bondage.

But the woman was given the two wings of the great eagle so that she might fly from the serpent into the wilderness, to the place where she is to be nourished for a time. (Rev. 12:14)

Another unique feature of eagles is that they are not daunted by nor do they fly away from storms. To the contrary, they fly into the force of it and then, at the precise moment, rise above what is coming against them and soar on its power. They take advantage of the air pressure that could otherwise deter them or force them backward, and instead utilize the force of nature to glide upward at higher altitudes. *What wisdom can be found in their instinct to employ the very thing that could be used against them to hinder their progress as a means of propelling them forward, gaining greater distance with less self-effort!* We could surely benefit from the example of these majestic creatures! How

---

[87] Follette, *Broken Bread.*

often do we fight the storms that are constantly affronting us, wasting precious time and energy? If we could be still long enough and wait upon the Father's great wisdom to show us how we can use life's stormy circumstances to our advantage, then we would be able to persevere while preserving our precious resources for a higher purpose.

The eagle is often considered the king of birds, as it can soar above the highest heights and is also said to fly directly toward the sun. Because I have come to love eagles for both their natural strength and the spiritual symbolism relating to my personal journey, I have spent time getting to know them better and have come to admire their amazing qualities even more. I have found that many of their traits either mirror my story already or are worth incorporating into my life. If you would like to learn more about these amazing birds, please visit the website included at the bottom of this page.[88]

An eagle's desire is never to just "exist" but to truly "live" and fly as whole, strong, and free creatures in all of their magnificent loftiness! During the course of my journey from silent desperation to quiet strength I, too, have developed this deep and resilient desire to live and "fly" as a whole, strong, and free person...never to be bound by anyone or anything again! Sometimes we are taught the most basic, yet life-changing lessons from the least likely of places. May these few important lessons on living well enhance and empower your own journey. By imitating these marvelous birds, may you discover a zest and freedom in your life that could never be taught in a classroom.

JOURNAL ENTRY – October 10, 2014

Thank You for continuing to teach me, Lord, even when I am a poor student. Amen.

---

[88] Prince George's County, ed., "Prince George's County Parents, Maryland Blog," *Prince George's County Parents, Maryland Blog* (blog) (February 27, 2014), https://pgcpsmess.wordpress.com/2014/02/27/7-highly-effective-habits-of-eagles/.

From the onset of this book, I just knew in my heart that an eagle would grace its cover. When a friend of mine learned of my growing intrigue with the desert lands of the West as well as my love of the eagle (both becoming symbolic to my natural and spiritual journey), she loaned me an enlarged photograph of a soaring eagle...it's outstretched wings spanning the breadth of my vision for the book's cover. During my months with this photograph of a "captured" eagle in flight, it became an inspiring presence. Perched near a second-story window, I slowly began to see beyond the eagle's majestic form—taking special note of the barren limbs it soared above as well as the background shades of blue and gray that constantly shifted in unison with the daily changes in weather. These varying hues brought to remembrance a mood ring I once had—a continual reminder of how quickly our human feelings can shift based on what is happening within us and around us. Each separate element of the photo began to tell its own story, holding unexpected significance that granted visual substance to my often-invisible emotional pain. I will take some time to break down their intimate connections to my life; perhaps they will also bear meaning to yours.

The Story of the Background

So often the backdrop of a picture is overshadowed by the more prominent features in the foreground, but I would like to draw your attention to the vista of the sky as depicted on the book's cover. As mentioned previously, because this photograph was displayed near a window I often wrote by, I noticed that the background color looked quite different depending on the day and weather. When the sun was hitting it, the beautiful shades of blue would noticeably stand out and made the whole scene appear more happy and uplifting to the soul. But if it was a cloudy day, often accompanied by snow or rain, the background was muted with shades of gray, which made the whole scene feel more sad and forlorn. After several months of observing these fluctuating hues, I could see how closely they depicted the range of shades that often colored my world for too many years. And even though I was aware of the changing colors of the background depending on the weather outside—the majesty, power, and beauty of the eagle never changed.

The symbolism for me in all of this is that changes in the weather, seasons, my mood, my circumstances, or my surroundings should never alter my set course, focus, or passion within or without. Likewise, an eagle is not continually looking down or behind where it has already been, but is keenly focused ahead at some specific destination. It knows in what direction it is headed and is unwavering as it sets its sights on that target. Its wings are locked into position, undisturbed and undaunted by the winds of change and fluctuations in atmospheric pressure. It is not detoured, whether flying in peaceful sunshine or a raging storm. It is no matter to the eagle if it is flying over the barren desert or the lushness of the rainy season. It has no want, as its needs are met by the Creator who supplies all sustenance for life.

So, I ask you the same questions I have had to ask myself many times during years of trials, sorrow, and hard lessons:

* What "locks" your heart and mind into place so that you can stay the course *despite* ever-changing circumstances, surroundings, moods, attitudes, people who share your space, seasons of joy and sorrow, etc.?
* Who or what is the source of your motivation to keep you on track and persevering through the valleys, up the mountains, and everywhere in between? Is it an internal force or external pressures from yourself, others, and society?
* Is the motivational force within you rooted in your character as part of the essence of who you are, or is it navigated by a fluctuating temperament, often producing frustration, insecurity, fear, and the need to control?
* Are you firmly anchored to concrete beliefs, ideals, values, virtues, and life goals, or do you get thrown off-course based on elements in and around you? This may include things such as changing atmospheres and circumstances in your life, your singleness or marriage, family or friends, your home, your workplace, your community, your church, your nation, your leaders, times of war, catastrophes, and world events?

* Does your focus and course of direction constantly change with the background of your life, or are your eyes keenly focused ahead at your destination point—mind sharp with clarity and vision beyond your present physical, emotional, mental, and/or spiritual conditions that may throw shadows over your blue skies?

* Can your eyes be aware of your surroundings, alert for danger and predators, yet also remain sensitive and keen to see the needs of others?

I believe these are important questions that are at least deserving of consideration. They may help to pinpoint the source of your confusion, anxiety, disharmony, loss of direction and creativity as well as feelings of unfulfilled voids, dreams, passions, and freedom in your life.

The strength of an eagle is not renewed by a daily dose of worry, anxiety, and fear of the unknown future, which would only drain precious energy—but, rather, by its deep passion to live and be free in the present moment. **"So teach us to number our days that we may get a heart of wisdom"** (Ps. 90:12). Likewise, your strength of youth will be restored like the eagle's because the Father desires to fill your life with good things. **"Bless the Lord, O my soul...who satisfies you with good so that your youth (your strength and vitality) is renewed like the eagle's"** (Ps. 103:1,5, parentheses added). This is not something you can restore or preserve through your own self-sufficiency, self-knowledge, or efforts at self-preservation; this is a wonderful gift from our Creator and Father to His beloved children!

JOURNAL ENTRY – January 30, 2016

In prayer, I saw our daughters as my eaglets. The oldest has already flown away and, with her desired mate, built their own nest. Though independent, she is still close enough to receive my love and gentle guidance. She is where she needs to be.

My middle eaglet is flying out and testing her wings for greater distance. She still returns to the nest for brief visits of rest, refreshment, spiritual nourishment, and encouragement; then she flies off again—gaining new strength and freedom each time. She is where she needs to be.

My youngest eaglet is walking on the edge of the nest, timidly flapping her wings to build strength and hopping about to get her balance. She flies off for short spans of time usually accompanied by an older eaglet. She is in that tender yet exciting stage of getting ready to leave the nest but still enjoys the comfort it offers. I am doing what the mama eagle does, nudging and encouraging; making her step out in faith that I will still catch her if she falls. She is where she needs to be.

The nest is slowly getting empty, and I have longer periods of quiet and time alone. My mate has equipped me for being in silence and flying solo. I, too, am being prepared for the next season of my life. Once my eaglets are gone, I have no reason to stay connected to the nest. My mate has abandoned the nest; often physically but always in heart and soul. God is training me to be an eagle-woman (eaglemen–Follette); one who soars alone on wings of faith. One who is asked to fly into the storms of life and then swiftly soar above them and glide upon their strength wherever God takes me. He is training me on how to use my afflictions to my advantage and to employ the power in them to rise to a higher level of life in the Spirit with my Master Teacher. I am where I need to be!

Amen.

> "No man ever comes into realization of the best things of God, who does not, upon the Godward side of his life, learn to walk *alone* with God."
> —John Wright Follette, *Broken Bread* [89]

"…I bore you on eagles' wings and brought you to Myself."
(Exod. 19:4)

Barrenness

He found him (her) in a desert (barren) land, and in the howling waste of the wilderness; He encircled him (her) and cared for him (her) and kept him (her) as the apple (pupil) of His eye. (Deut. 32:10, parentheses added)

The first time I saw the photograph, the raw power and soaring beauty of the eagle taking center stage took my breath away! Initially, I really didn't give much heed to the barren tree it soared over. But once I took note of it, I pondered whether or not I should incorporate into the cover design something that appeared so lifeless,

---

[89] Follette, *Broken Bread.*

even if it was a natural element in the desert. Didn't I desire to depict a positive image and hopeful message of new beginnings, fresh starts, second chances, and renewed life? My original thoughts were of an eagle hovering over peaceful waters or the desert floor all abloom after the spring rains, or perhaps mounting up toward the heights of a mountain range. The gray, motionless, and barren limbs of the tree seemed depressing and sad in contrast to the vastness of the sky and strength of this gliding eagle. But something in my soul said to not just dismiss the option—to give it time and more consideration. I believe it was the same day that I felt inspired to write about my journey from loneliness to solitude while looking at that dormant tree outside the window on that cold, dreary late winter morn, when I realized how closely that barren tree reflected so many years of my life. How it was reflecting my soul in that very moment. Shifting my eyes from the "hibernating" tree outside to the barren tree depicted in this photograph was a perfect match to what I was feeling in my still-healing heart. I instantly knew that the individual elements, just waiting to be discovered, symbolized the scope of my desert wilderness journey from the barrenness experienced in my silent desperation to the fullness of new life slowly emerging with the quiet strength of the eagle!

Recently, as I was reading an *Our Daily Bread* devotional message for Monday, August 7, 2017, it spoke about another woman of faith named Hannah whose story has been preserved in the Bible. She endured a rough season of barrenness as well. This sterile time was literal, as she could not conceive a child. But our barren seasons, no matter how long or short and for whatever the reasons, bring deep distress and sorrow to our hearts that long for something. Her grief was for a child; mine was a longing I once had for our marriage to be restored and made whole for the benefit of my entire family. Ironically, she had the loving and devoted husband that I had longed for, and I had the blessing of children that she longed for—the joy and the sadness that often walk side-by-side in this life. Many of her feelings and silent prayers mirrored my own; two silently desperate women who knew Whom to turn to in our deep sorrow.

> **She was deeply distressed and prayed to the LORD and wept bitterly.** (1 Sam. 1:10)

> **"If You will indeed look upon the affliction of Your servant and remember me and not forget Your servant."** (1 Sam. 1:11)

> **"I am a woman troubled in my spirit...but I have been pouring out my soul before the LORD."** (1 Sam. 1:15-16)

> **Eli, the priest, then told her to "Go in peace, and the God of Israel grant your petition that you have made of Him." Then the woman went her way and ate, and her face was no longer sad.** (1 Sam. 1:17-18)

> For Hannah, in time, **"the LORD remembered her. And in due time she conceived and bore a son...for she said, 'I have asked for him from the LORD.'"** (1 Sam. 1:19-20)

As I write this book, I have seen countless answers to my own prayers because I have asked of the Lord while pouring out my soul in affliction, distress, and silent desperation to a Father God who I trusted saw, heard, knew, and loved me.

Previously, I have written about how I began to pray Scripture in earnest during the last few years before being separated from the one who afflicted me. I would often pray the following verse throughout the really rough days:

> **I will be glad and rejoice in Your mercy, for You have considered my trouble; You have known my soul in adversities, and You have not shut me up into the hand of the enemy; but have set my feet in a wide place.** (Ps. 31:7-8)

I have learned many lessons during the long, barren seasons of my life. One is that when we pour out our desperate hearts to God, no matter the reason or source of our despair, we must do so with a heart that *trusts* and *believes* that He hears our prayers and will answer them *before we see or receive the manifestation of our petition(s)*. If you reread the above Scripture, I did not speak it as a prayer for some time in the distant future, but, trusting that it was actively—in the present moment—being heard and answered for me *before* I had any visible indication that it would be.

In the same way, Hannah left the temple—where she had entered burdened and afflicted in her soul—with a face that was no longer sad. Why? She couldn't possibly be pregnant yet. Didn't physically feel any different in her body. Yet she was no longer sad because she trusted and believed that the Lord had heard her prayers, considered her trouble, and would act according to His faithfulness and the prophetically spoken promise of the priest. When we offer up prayers in faith and hope (*in accordance with God's Word, will, and promises*), and believe that we will receive our request sight-unseen, this is the whole essence of faith—for who needs faith *after* they receive a blessed answer? **"Now faith is the assurance of things hoped for, the conviction of things not seen"** (Heb. 11:1).

I really like this quote from preacher and author, Charles Haddon Spurgeon, which fits nicely here: "To trust God in the light is nothing, but to trust Him in the dark—that is faith." We need to shed our tears, cry forth our prayers (often with much sorrow, distress, and travailing), and then leave the throne room of grace with a face that is no longer sad. This is the central part of one of my favorite verses, which began this chapter: **"Those who wait upon the LORD shall renew their strength; they shall mount up with wings like eagles"** (Isa. 40:31). Some versions use the words "hope in" instead of "wait upon." The words are really interchangeable because we only feel empowered to wait upon something if we believe, or have hope, that it will come true, happen, or be fulfilled.

Hannah awaited the conception and birth of her child with hope and happiness in her heart while trusting in what she could not know for certain, see, or even feel yet. I waited with this same hope in my heart, even though a time frame was not made known. I have experienced the fulfillment of many silent yet very desperate prayers, but am still waiting in hope as the *fullness* of God's promises and purposes remain unseen, unknown, and unrevealed. I wait upon the Lord with joyful expectation of what is to come, in His timing and in

344

His precise and always perfect way. In the meantime, He prepares and quietly strengthens me to receive the promise of total freedom to fly with eagle's wings above the barrenness and into the wide-open places. In our barren seasons, let us wait with expectant hope—and watch God move mountains and cut the bars of iron (Isaiah 45:2)!

> "A waiting person is a patient person. The word patience means the willingness to stay where we are and live the situation out to the full in the belief that something hidden there will manifest itself to us."
> —Henri J. Nouwen, Dutch priest, author, professor[90]

And though the time would come when that "loaned" photograph would be returned to its owner, and another artist would take that initial vision under their "wings" to create the book's cover...I will always be grateful for its inspiration. I stand in awe at how God uses every experience and encounter we have to teach, preach, reach, and breach the limits of human reasoning as a means of revealing Himself to us—and all we can do and become in Him!

As my story continues to unfold beyond the pages of this book, may the "snapshots" I have shared continue to enhance my life as well as that of many others...wherever love and freedom calls us. To God be the glory! Amen.

"Come away, My beloved." (Song of Sol. 8:14)

The Gilded Cage

> **"The Spirit of the Lord God is upon Me, because the LORD has anointed Me to bring good news to the afflicted; He has sent Me to bind up the brokenhearted, to proclaim liberty to the captives, and the opening of the prison to those who are bound...."** (Isa. 61:1)

Just as wide-open places do not always mean freedom, neither do confining places always mean bondage or captivity. It can be a

---

[90] Henri J.M. Nouwen, *The Path of Waiting* (Pearl River, NY: Crossroad, 1995).

matter of a current situation, personal circumstances and choices, or life experiences—but it is ultimately a reflection of the state of the heart, soul, and mind. I once thought very differently about these things, as I lived most of my married life surrounded by hundreds of acres of woodland, water, and wildlife. My mind was deceived into a false reality because of how these peaceful sights, sounds, and space made me feel...free. But the vastness on the outside could not enter into the slowly encroaching darkness taking place on the inside: mentally and emotionally. Neither could it dispel the ever-growing loneliness and confinement that was encompassing every area of my life within the grip of a narcissist!

I fought desperately against the invisible bars closing in on me from every angle until I could barely move or breathe without some form of pain. Our earthly eyes and mind can so often deceive our heart's intuitions, which are often trying to tell us that something is terribly amiss. Only God's light, wisdom, and (sometimes hard) truth can dispel the spell we fall under in wanting to believe our life is "alright" when the truth is that something is indeed very wrong. Proverbs 3:7 counsels the reader to: **"Be not wise in your own eyes."** Many Scriptures lovingly warn us about deception. **"Do not be deceived"** (Gal. 6:7) and to **"...be wise (spiritually) as serpents and innocent (guiltless) as doves"** (Matt. 10:16, parentheses added). Gene Taylor writes,

> We can be deceived in many ways, but one of the major sources of deception is self. We find ways to avoid facing unpleasant truth and rationalize away personal guilt.[91]

The wide-open spaces gave me a false sense of security that I was alive, well, and free, but the *truth* was that I was slowly suffocating, unwell, and anything but free. I was entangled in cords I couldn't see, but over time I realized that they were strangling me, as they cut off my voice box and bound me into years of silent

---

[91] Gene Taylor, "Fooling God," The Church of Christ in Zion, Illinois, https://www.padfield.com/2000/foolgod.html.

desperation.

> **For wicked men are found among My people; they lurk like fowlers lying in wait. They set a trap; they catch men (women). Like a cage full of birds, their houses are full of deceit....** (Jer. 5:26-27, parentheses added)

So, why a gilded cage instead of just a plain, ordinary birdcage? Well, the definition of the word "gilded" actually explains a lot! It means: *"to coat with gold leaf or gold color; to make seem more attractive or valuable than it is."*[92] The human eye loves to look at and admire what it sees as beautiful, attractive, and worthy of our attention—that which is stimulating to the heart, soul, and imagination. We are drawn to things that exhibit and emulate something or someone we perceive to have great value and/or influence. So, the gold veneer on the cage would make it *appear* to be more valuable; therefore, the "bird" inside its bars must also be considered valuable and worthy of such a special place to live by its *owner*. I was placed inside the gilded cage by my narcissistic husband, to be on display, having the appearance that I was of great value to him as he began building his "house of deception" to the outside world looking in. I, of course, also thought I was loved, wanted, and valued, as I sat on my perch and sang the love songs of youth. Yet, all too soon, I would realize that in actuality, behind closed doors, I was made to feel most unworthy, unattractive, and of very little value other than what I could do for my spouse and to "look good" for the cameras when the "show" was playing.

Years of walking in my faith have taught me that once a person truly enters into life in the Spirit (Holy Spirit), the spiritual realm becomes much more alive and real to the soul than that of the physical world and all of its trappings. Walking with feet on the ground begins to feel foreign to the now-free spirit that desires to spend most of its time "flying" above the earth. Being earth-bound can lead to bondage and entrapment, as our earthly days are too often filled with endless finite pursuits that drain the soul of its needed

---

[92] Agnes, *Webster's New World Dictionary.*

strength to soar. One aspect of the work of the Spirit is to strip us down to more closely resemble the created beings we were meant to be *before* the world and all of its demands, restraints, boundaries, labels, responsibilities, self-striving, and self-preservation were placed on *or* taken upon our now weary and over-burdened shoulders.

Once you taste the freedom of living out from underneath that which steals your strength, peace, creativity, joy, and rest—I can tell you that you will *never* desire to go back into the gilded cage no matter how safe or enticing it may appear to your newly opened spiritual eyes, which have taken in the view from unearthly heights! So many people are living out their days in a gilded cage yet do not realize they are surrounded by bars that bind. We have been lulled and deceived into thinking that because we can see beyond the bars and some light is filtering through the hinged doors we can open and close by our own volition, that this indicates true freedom. We think we are free, but our wings are really clipped and our claws are bound to the perch we swing and sing upon.

These words make me swallow hard, but I can't stop proclaiming freedom for both the prisoner who knows they are imprisoned, and those deceived by the father of lies (the devil) who came only to steal, kill, and destroy—the one who entraps people in beautiful and comfortable places and convinces them they are safe, happy, content, and free. The pernicious lie!

It is one thing to know that you are in captivity because you can see the bars, feel the shackles around your wrists and ankles, and hear the rattle of the chains and the voice of the one who restrains you. Yet, it is quite another to blissfully believe you are free because you live in your beautiful "gilded cage" and see life through its lovely stained-glass windows, only to find out in the end that you were never truly free, nor did you ever learn to fly. I do not know which is more tragic, as my heart aches equally for both.

One of the greatest revelations I received during my barred and barren wilderness journey was that:

if I trusted God during the dark storms in my life,

if I didn't run away in fear,

if I didn't turn my back but faced the truth, and

if I didn't settle for the confining yet familiar gilded cage of bondage,

but was willing to follow Him into the great unknown,

only then could He teach and train me—

to fly with quiet strength on wings like eagles

to places and at heights I never dreamed I could go!

Love deeply but loosely—fly freely wherever the Lord's wind blows!

**She is clothed with strength and dignity
and laughs without fear of the future.**
(Prov. 31)

BELIEVE TO RECEIVE

A Sinner's Prayer, Two Versions[93]

Dear God,

I know that I am a sinner and there is nothing that I can do to save myself. I confess my complete helplessness to forgive my own sin or to work my way to heaven. At this moment, I trust Jesus Christ alone as the One who bore my sin when He died on the cross. I believe that He did all that was necessary for me to stand in Your holy presence. I thank You that Christ was raised from the dead as a guarantee of my own resurrection. As best I can, I now transfer my trust in Him. I am grateful that He has promised to receive me despite my many sins and failures. Father, I take You at Your word. I thank You that I can face death now that You are my Savior. Thank You for the assurance that You will walk with me through the deep valley. Thank You for hearing this prayer.

In Jesus's name. Amen.

*****

Lord God,

Please forgive me for my sins. I believe that You sent Your Son, Jesus, to die on the cross for my sins. I believe that You love me. I believe in my heart who You are. You are the Son of God. I confess with my mouth that I am a sinner. I accept you, Lord Jesus, as my Savior. Please cleanse me from my sin and create a new and clean heart in me. I do believe that You are my Savior, and I now want to live for You as my Lord and my God. I know that I have eternal life in You because of the work You did on Calvary's cross for me. Thank You, God.

In Jesus's name I pray. Amen.

---

[93] These are just sample prayers. You can speak your own prayer as you are led, or speak one or both written above. The important thing is that you truly believe what you are saying and make it very personal, as it should spring forth from your heart and not your head.

ABOUT THE AUTHOR

DEBORAH JAYNE is the proud mother of three beautiful daughters and blessed grandmother of two precious granddaughters. She is often told that she has just the right words at the right time.

With Jesus at the epicenter of finding her way through decades of pain to freedom and quiet strength, her personal mission is to take all that she has learned through her suffering and come alongside other victims—not with the mindset to remain one, but with the purpose and vision to help them attain victory!

She loves to make heart-connections with fellow travelers and offer purpose in the pain.

**"...and you will know the truth,
and the truth will set you free."**
(John 8:32)

ABOUT THIS BOOK
(A Word From Deborah Jayne)

From SILENT DESPERATION *to* QUIET STRENGTH is so much more than just my story. I believe it mirrors multitudes of other people's stories. Suffering people need others to not only listen to their stories—but to also understand them.

While flying out West in 2019, I discovered that the man sitting next to me also journaled about his life, travels, and work experiences. He openly shared how they impacted him and the way he saw both the world and himself. I told him that he should consider sharing his writing as I felt he had gleaned noteworthy insights that could benefit others. He couldn't envision their worth and said, "A memoir is only worth writing if you have something important to say." I pray that by God's grace, love, and infinite wisdom, He has taken my life story and experiences...and granted me something "important to say."

But even above these earthly treasures, it was my Lord and Savior, Jesus Christ, Who held me up when I was drowning in my silent suffering full of pain, grief, heartache, and turmoil of the soul. He alone rescued me, healed me, redeemed my lost years of health and life, and gave it a purpose beyond what I could have ever dreamed or imagined. Jesus has been at the epicenter of finding my way to freedom and quiet strength—needing to be rescued when at the very end of myself. He was the only way out of my fake, dysfunctional, and abusive marriage.

Now I am fully free in body, soul, mind, and spirit!

I pray that you will be too!

**Proceeds from the sale of this book will go toward organizations that offer refuge, restoration, and freedom for victims of abuse in all of its many forms.

Made in USA - Kendallville, IN
58610_9781735930794
08.03.2022 1255